Stalled

"INVENTIVE, IRREVERENT AND RELENTLESSLY FUNNY...
IF JOHN HUGHES WROTE A NOVEL SET IN A HIGH SCHOOL
BOY'S BATHROOM, THIS WOULD BE IT."
— WARREN P. SONODA, DIRECTOR, *SWEARNET*,
TRAILER PARK BOYS, TOTAL FRAT MOVIE

C.R. Bruce

By C.R. Bruce
Copyright © Christopher R. Bruce, 2015
All rights reserved.

Praise for *Stalled*

"Equal parts nostalgic nightmare and narrative roller coaster . . . Bruce has banded together a hilarious ensemble of old high school friends that are both iconic and original. If John Hughes wrote a novel set in a high school boy's bathroom, this would be it."

- Warren P. Sonoda, Director,
Swearnet, Trailer Park Boys, Total Frat Movie

"Stalled, with its raw and authentic dialogue, credible characters and their compelling interwoven stories, is definitely worth a look."

- IndieReader

About the Author

C.R. Bruce wrote dozens of screenplays before writing this novel. Some of those were made into obscure low-budget movies you've never heard of. He also taught film production and screenwriting at The University of New Brunswick. But that was then. Now he writes big books with lots of words. He lives and works in New Brunswick by way of Alberta, Manitoba, and Germany.

crbrucewrites.com

To my mother.

May she one day remember how much she loved books.

Contents

Praise for *Stalled* . . . . *iii*
About the Author . . . . *v*
Chapter 1: Everybody Have Fun Tonight 1
Chapter 2: The Warrior. 5
Chapter 3: Always Something There to Remind Me 10
Chapter 4: You Might Think. 15
Chapter 5: King of Pain 22
Chapter 6: Crazy for You 28
Chapter 7: Voices Carry 34
Chapter 8: Too Shy. 41
Chapter 9: The Wild Boys. 48
Chapter 10: Strange Animal 55
Chapter 11: Tell Her About It. 62
Chapter 12: That's What Friends Are For 66
Chapter 13: Photograph 70
Chapter 14: Tainted Love 76
Chapter 15: Fame. 80
Chapter 16: Pop Goes the World 85
Chapter 17: Touch of Gray. 94

Chapter 18: Against All Odds 102
Chapter 19: It's the End of the World As We Know It 106
Chapter 20: Pour Some Sugar on Me 119
Chapter 21: Walk This Way 125
Chapter 22: Burning Heart 129
Chapter 23: Need You Tonight 136
Chapter 24: Kiss You When It's Dangerous 145
Chapter 25: Our Lips Are Sealed 151
Chapter 26: Only in My Dreams 159
Chapter 27: Beat It 163
Chapter 28: Moment of Truth 169
Chapter 29: Down Under 175
Chapter 30: Like a Virgin 190
Chapter 31: Bad Medicine 202
Chapter 32: Centerfold 210
Chapter 33: A View to a Kill 221
Chapter 34: The Kid Is Hot Tonight 226
Chapter 35: The Never Ending Story 239
Chapter 36: Mad About You 245
Chapter 37: Broken Wings 248
Chapter 38: Mickey 253
Chapter 39: Every Rose Has Its Thorn 268
Chapter 40: If I Could Turn Back Time 273
Chapter 41: Don't Stop Believin' 281
Epilogue: Condition Critical 292
Thank you 295
Acknowledgments 297

Life is not a matter of holding good cards, but of playing a poor hand well.

Robert Louis Stevenson

Chapter 1

Rory
Everybody Have Fun Tonight

Rory swaggered through the gym, cool as he could be, bobbing his head to the ironic rhythms of "Relax" by Frankie Goes to Hollywood. Pockets of formerly pretty people dancing in tight circles tried to reel him in, but he was a porcelain-seeking missile, veering around human pylons, oblivious even to Emily Neeman's impressive new boob job. As soon as he spotted the door marked *Boys*, with the little stick man on the front, he got a running start, as if he were on a basketball court taking three big steps for his lay-up, slammed his shoulder into it, and bowled inside.

He was in. He was safe.

He inhaled the sweet lemon scent of fresh urinal cakes and disinfectant. The familiar smell calmed him. The place sparkled. The janitorial squad had done an outstanding job for the evening. Rory hated to ruin it.

With the exception of some modern amenities, it was just as he remembered. On one wall stood a row of urinals and three stalls, each scarred with high school graffiti. On the other wall, a line of mirrors and sinks. The middle faucet dripped steadily. Above the mirrors dangled a purple and green banner: *Class of '89. You Pissed Away 10 Years!* Behind the door squatted a garbage can, and halfway up the wall perched a shiny chrome hand-dryer. At the back was a condom machine. The chrome and condoms were new. There were no escape windows, which sucked. But at least the place was empty.

Rory burrowed into a stall, locked the deadbolt, and took a seat on the toilet. Then he opened his palm and stared at it.

It was a piece of paper folded into a square, but it was more complex than any ordinary paper square. It had a square's four sides, but it also had tucks, triangles, and pockets. Once he unraveled the puzzle, Rory could never put it back together the same way. He could build a kick-ass paper airplane, but these had always been beyond him. It was an anomaly, an antique, a precious time capsule, a harbinger of doom.

It was a handwritten note.

A note folded in that expert origami way that only high school girls could master. She wrote his name in purple ink. The *R* was a giant bubble towering over a small *o* and *r*, and the *y* had a tail that swung across like an ornate vine, cradling the other letters artfully. It was magnificent.

But Rory couldn't open it. Not yet. First he had to fight his crawling stomach, inching its way upwards like a zombie rising from the pit, its half-digested beef-tortellini corpse seeking the plate from whence it came.

It had been ten years since he'd seen her. He was standing by the bar, smiling, fresh drink in hand—

Rory suddenly remembered he carried a rum and pineapple and took a drink. The cool, soothing sip pushed the beef tortellini down a couple ribs.

She had sidled up to him, pretty as you please, and held out her hand for a shake. Was it a peace offering? Were they friends now? Rory hated that word, but liked it better than fuck nutz. So Rory shook—her hand; he did not suffer a convulsive fit and slide vibrating to the floor as he thought he might. He was shocked when the rough paper passed from her skin to his. For an instant, the covert and wondrous event had him feeling like the grade 10 version of James Bond, until the secret note fell from his sweaty palm, smacking the gymnasium floor like sheet metal.

Bonjour, Inspector Clouseau.

Rory was proud he didn't ralph on her shoes as he picked the note up, and was further surprised she didn't seize the opportunity to stab him in the back of the head with her stiletto heel. But somehow he managed to sift it off the floor, not say anything stupid (not say anything at all actually), and outrace his gurgling stomach to the bathroom.

Rory admonished himself. Open the note. It won't be that bad, he told himself, just do it.

One more sip. A deep breath.

He unraveled the intricate layers of paper, moving fast so his stomach didn't realize what he was doing. He read like a computer. His eyes scanned letters, words, and sentences. His legs bounced with each syllable, the rhythm helping him get through before it happened.

Rory fell to his knees, heaving and gasping. But nothing came.

He tore off a square of toilet paper and dabbed the sweat from his forehead. The thin paper drenched and stuck. Rory peeled it off strip by strip, but knew with a certainty bred from experience that he'd not gotten all of it. He imagined if he connected the dots of toilet paper leavings they'd make the *L* for *Loo-zer*. He rubbed his head angrily and watched the remaining tufts float into the bowl.

Spitting made him feel better, as if he'd accomplished something, like he'd been teasing the water and fulfilled his end of the bargain for once. The note was not what he expected. It was impossible.

Another heave.

Another zombie false start.

Don't think about it, he told himself. It's only a note. He took a drink instead. Ahhh, that was better. A note from *her*.

Rory threw up.

In the aftermath, he watched the pasta chunks float around the bowl and fantasized they were tiny life preservers that he could latch onto and flush himself to safety. It didn't matter where he wound up, so long as he made good his escape.

Before a second kamikaze butterfly could dive-bomb his intestines, Rory clumsily refolded the note and jammed it down the inside pocket of his suit jacket.

He didn't want to do this, but he had to. It was survival. He pulled out a bottle of green pills, twisted off the cap and—

The sound of the bathroom door opening froze him. Rory listened as footsteps approached his stall and stopped. He imagined a person looking in the mirror, oblivious to his presence. He would leave soon. Just have to wait him out.

"Rory?"

BAM!

The kick on Rory's stall door jarred him. His body jerked, and like a pile of cartoon Mexican jumping beans, his pills leaped from their container and plunged into the puke water.

Chapter 2

Todd
The Warrior

Todd smiled. It was déjà vu. Ten years later and here was Rory back in his stall. "You okay, man? Do we have a prom situation?"

"Funny," Rory said.

Todd was double fisting, a beer in each hand, and happy to have an excuse to slink back into the bathroom. It was his second trip in fifteen minutes, and no bladder was small enough to explain that.

He'd left his wife Stacy in her element, surrounded by laughing nincompoops, luxuriating in gobs of gossip. Todd hoped she'd stick to their deal, but his confidence was not high on that issue. Loitering in the bathroom seemed the sensible way to make sure he didn't get into a fight with her, *him*, or some other asshole.

"Why? Did somebody say something?" Rory asked.

Todd was about to torture him when he spotted it. How did he miss that the first time? "There's a condom machine in here."

A machine. Full of condoms. In the high school boy's bathroom.

He'd bought his first one from ninth-grader Jay Timmons for two dollars. Crisp plastic edges, watery center, the rim pushing through like a nipple hard-on. Having all of that potential in his back pocket had given him an all-day woody.

Todd raised his voice so Rory could hear. "Remember those embarrassing runs to a convenience store for a three-pack? Imagine the sex I could have had with this around. Damn."

The "in-convenience" store dash gave her time to change her mind, which happened more than once to Todd.

Back in the late '80s, high school sex was a big secret. You couldn't advertise it with a large metal machine in the guy's can. Nobody could know. Not the teachers and certainly not parents. The plan was to let them think what they wanted to think, that Todd's Mr. Winky never touched Ms. Honorable's hoo-ha. It was a gift for all parents, the blessing of ignorant bliss. If you didn't see Little Johnny buying condoms, then Little Johnny must be in his room doing geometry homework and not feverishly plotting to stick it to Little Betty. But here they were, a year's supply of condoms stuck to the wall of the guy's can like a Pez dispenser. What's next? Arranged conjugal visits for teens? Have Little Johnny and his sweetheart tested for bugs and crawlies, and then lend them the teacher's lounge for lunch hour supervised sex? Where's the glory, the chase, the cloak-and-dagger spy hunter maneuvers Todd pulled off to get laid?

"Are people watching me? I can't go to the can now?" Rory's voice invaded Todd's memories of old conquests.

Sauntering over to Rory's stall with a devilish grin, Todd picked up where he left off, beginning his torture. "I saw you talking to *The Panther*."

No reply from Rory. Todd's grin grew little horns and steamed. His words were a verbal cattle prod. He knew they left a mark.

"Did you hear me?" Todd said.

"Yeah? And?"

"And? Did you talk prom?"

Rory cleared his throat. "Sure, we laughed about it. No big deal."

Todd squeezed the thumbscrews. "Let me tell you something. Besides her wedding, the prom is the most important event in a woman's life. She may not say it to your face, but she's praying your prick grows little arms in the night and strangles you in your sleep."

Silence.

The leaky faucet went drip, drip, drip.

And then a gruesome sound, like a cat coughing up the fur ball of the decade.

Grimacing, but loving it at the same time, Todd knocked on Rory's door. "How many did you have?"

Between gasps, Rory managed a response. "Just two and a shot."

"A shot of what?"

"Tequila."

"Tequila?" Todd checked his watch. It was 9:42 p.m. "It's a little early to invite tequila to the party."

Rory retched again. Todd heard each chunky piece hit water like coins in a fountain.

"A few more of those, amigo," Todd warned, feeling a little sympathy for his friend, "and you'll blow any chance you've got with the seniorittas."

Todd peeked through the crack in the door. Rory knelt before the bowl, head bowed, sucking air. "Is that big-dicked Jamaican here?"

"Would you stop with the prom shit!" Rory snapped. "New rule. Nobody brings up the prom, deal?"

"This is a time for reminiscing," Todd said.

"I mean it. Give me a couple minutes. Go."

"See ya out there." Todd headed to the door with a smile, happy to have had some entertainment to shake his mood. This is why he loved hanging out with Rory in high school. He was entertaining!

Of course, Rory was also a teenage darling who always got stuff handed to him. That could piss Todd off. But Rory usually managed to blow it all in grandiose fashion, leaving Todd and Brent to pick up the pieces while laughing their asses off. Many were the stories, with prom being the granddaddy of them all. But that was a long time ago. When Rory and Brent moved away a few years after high school, Rory to the next town over and Brent to the big city hours away, that was the end of it all.

KNOCK, KNOCK. "Todd?"

Todd halted in his tracks. He withdrew his hand from the doorknob and rubbed his bald head. It was Stacy. She'd come looking for him, which meant something bad. Todd guessed she'd chatted with friends about their "thing" and wanted to change the agreement, find a loophole, or tell him again how wrong he was.

"What?" he barked.

"Are you alone?" she asked from behind the door.

"No, there's a guy in here. You can't come in. What do you want?"

"What are you doing?"

"I'm in the bathroom, so I'm playing Yahtzee."

"You've been gone, like, fifteen minutes."

"I had to hold Rory's hand."

"Shut up, asshole!" Rory hissed.

"I forgot the pictures in the car and you've got the keys."

Todd had not taken one step since Stacy's knock. He was bracing himself, readying for the inevitable switcheroo discussion, despite the ground rules they'd agreed upon earlier. Instead, he released a sigh, able to breathe again.

Pictures. All she wanted were pictures.

"Would you just get out there?" Rory said.

Todd opened the bathroom door and got "the look" from his wife. He tossed her the keys. She missed them, rolled her eyes, scooped them up, and didn't look back.

Todd followed five steps behind like a bad puppy.

Chapter 3

Brent
Always Something There to Remind Me

Brent opened the bathroom door and caught Rory gargling in front of a mirror. Rory was pale, and the sides of his wispy blonde hair were a slick brown and matted to his head. His gray suit, the kind with that slight sheen to it, was speckled with water. He reminded Brent of a preening bird fresh from the birdbath. One that just blew chunks.

"Heard you were sick?" Brent said.

Rory scoffed. "Todd tell you that?"

"Nope, Stacy." Brent lounged against the sinks watching his friend.

Rory popped a stick of gum in his mouth and stroked his hair. "Prick. I bet he tells her everything. I'm worried about that, considering what he knows."

"I think it was someone else. Did you puke?"

"What?" Rory paused, fumbling with his thoughts. "Todd didn't tell Stacy? Nobody else knew."

"Alice."

"My Alice? As in *The Panther* Alice?"

Brent couldn't immediately judge Rory's reaction, but his psychologically intuitive brain registered some ominous clues.

"Did you talk to her? Did she say something about prom?" Rory asked.

Yes, Brent thought, but should he share it with Rory?

Brent had arrived at the reunion in a mood; he'd been in a mood all day after his boss summoned him to his plush, new-car-smelling office and said, "Brent, we like you here at Lahrson Tech, but we've established certain systems and protocols over the years, and I needed you to adhere strictly to our procedures. We've had this discussion before, so getting right to the point, we have to let you go." Another crap job in the books.

"She mentioned something," Brent said, with an involuntary smirk.

"It was funny? What she said was funny? What'd she say?"

"She said . . . ." Impressions weren't Brent's thing, so he opted for the stereotypical female falsetto with valley girl slang: "*Oh my God, like, what is this? Potty Party II? This time he actually dies?*"

Rory looked nauseous.

So, Brent thought, this again? Ten years later? Shit, he shouldn't have told him.

"What. The. Fuck," Rory said, drawing out each word, "does that mean?"

Brent took a drink, trying to stifle the giggles. "It's funny because—" He gestured around the bathroom, hoping Rory would see the irony.

While Brent's eyes flitted around the room, they locked, and briefly lingered on the second stall from the right. That was enough to squash Brent's mirth. Patience, he lectured himself. He'd deal with that tonight. That's why he was here.

"What? I'm a little queasy after a shot of tequila and suddenly it's prom night again?" Rory said.

Tequila? Brent checked his watch. Not even 10:00. The reunion dance had barely started and Rory was into tequila?

"She doesn't know the truth, right?"

Brent reassured him. "She knows what everybody knows. What we told them."

"So only you, me, and Todd know the truth?"

"It's been ten years. Who cares?"

Rory took three steps to stand in front of him. His finger jabbed Brent in the chest. "I care. It doesn't matter how long it's been. Who'd you tell? Don't lie to me, Brent!"

"Nobody. Shit, calm down. Is that a condom machine?" Brent asked, trying to distract him.

Rory sighed and leaned against a sink. "Yes, that's what it is." He bowed his head and rubbed the ridge of his nose.

"Does it work?" Brent dug in his pockets for change.

"Brent," Rory said in exasperation, as if he'd been talking about this condom machine for days. "Just leave them for generation X, Y, Z, ABC, whatever."

Brent ignored him, dropped money into the slot, pulled the lever, and seconds later stared at a shiny red condom in a transparent wrapper. He held it up for Rory. "Check it out!"

"Amazing," Rory said, not bothering to look.

"Come on. There's a do-it machine in our old can. That's crazy."

"You and Todd should write a book."

The bathroom door opened for Gary Bean. He wore an expensive tailored suit that compensated for various physical imperfections, but couldn't mask his rolling midsection. Pinned to his chest was a special nametag that read "Reunion Coordinator." He spotted Brent and hesitated, but his eyes latched onto Rory and he smiled. Gary pointed two fingers at him like pistols.

"You! I heard about you. Should I call an ambulance?"

Rory glared and opened his mouth for a retort, but Brent interrupted. "Everything's cool, Gary. Just a nasty shot of tequila."

Rory managed a strained, "I'm fine."

Gary cleared his throat and straightened his pear-shaped body. In a very officious tone, he said, "You guys know there isn't supposed to be any liquor in here, right?"

Rory and Brent exchanged a confused glance.

"Why not?" Brent asked.

"We call it the Rory rule." Gary laughed at his joke. Brent smiled and nodded, all the while watching the fuse on top of Rory's head get shorter and shorter.

"But seriously, there isn't supposed to be any liquor in here. Only in the designated gym area. There's a sign out front. You probably didn't see it."

This time Gary meant it, or tried to mean it. He talked fast and backed away as he spoke, grinning feebly.

Brent felt sorry for him. Gary was a one-flippered, lazy-eyed baby seal put in charge of watching the sharks. As long as the sharks were kept fed and happy, the seal would survive. So why get in the shark's face about his martini?

"Right," Brent said, moving forward to shake Gary's hand, his other firmly holding his martini. "Great job with everything. Super time so far. Absolutely. Good to see you again."

Rory nodded his agreement. Gary pointed two fingers at them

like pistols again, and then wandered over to the urinals, passing the second stall from the right.

Again, Brent's eyes were drawn to it. This time they focused past its open door, at the blurry scratches and scrawlings beyond. Brent was not a vengeful man, but he'd had enough of bygones-be-bygones and trying to "let it go." Someone had to pay for the debacle his life had become. He'd start his hunt soon, but where? Who? It'd been ten years and still he only had one clue:

I am the rat
The one who told
On that presidential prick
Brent, the lying asshole

Chapter 4

Todd
You Might Think

Todd returned to the bathroom with another beer and a bottle of water. Rory raised his arms in greeting, happy to see the water he knew must be for him. As the door closed behind him, Todd felt relief. Outside were landmines, snipers, backstabbing ninjas, and hellfire. Inside meant safety. It was only him and his best friends from high school, and Gary Bean taking a piss.

He knew he couldn't stay in the bathroom for the whole reunion, but for now he could relax his vigil, avoid trouble, drink, laugh, and hope his gut was wrong.

Todd passed Rory the water. He expected a big thank you and a pat on the back.

"You told Alice?" Rory spat the question at him.

"Told her what?" Todd asked, surprised.

"That I was sick in the can."

"She asked where you were."

"And you had to add the 'sick' part?"

"Was I supposed to lie? What the hell's the matter with you?"

Rory grabbed him. "Brent told me that Alice told Stacy that this was Potty Party II."

"Potty Party II?" Todd laughed. "What the hell is Potty Party II?"

Rory shoved Todd. "Me! In here? Again? Duh. And it was Alice that told Stacy? Come, on Todd!"

Todd had to repeat it in his head before he understood the train of who told who what. If not for the precarious mood his wife had him in, he might have laughed more, but Rory's shove triggered a different response, one Todd had been repressing all night.

"What are you, six?" Todd shoved Rory back. He looked to Brent, wondering if the professor was in cahoots with his spazzing friend. "What's he talking about?"

Brent certainly dressed the part of the smarty pants, with his fake no-prescription glasses, fancy bow tie, white shoes, and that stubble above his upper lip. "The prom," Brent said, "was Potty Party I. You told Alice that Rory's in here sick. She's calling it the sequel."

"Ah." Ding. The bell went off in Todd's head. Brent nodded at him like an approving teacher.

"What'd I say before you left?" Rory said, scolding him. "I don't want anybody talking about prom. And then I hear this? What gives?"

"Hey, she made it about prom," Todd said. "I didn't bring up prom." He was about to throw a "screw you" at Rory and demand an apology, but amongst the blame and his admittedly poor judgment, he saw an opportunity.

When Todd arrived at the reunion, arm-in-arm with Stacy, fancied up in his sport coat, dressy jeans, and shiny shoes, he was sure the night would be full of napalm. The hope was that Stacy would do her thing and he'd do his—separately. She'd also curb her alcohol intake and not do what she's done in the past, and he'd be more sociable and less moody as a result of her not doing what she's done in the past. Avoiding her was the only way; otherwise, he'd hover beside her like a paranoid secret agent guarding the President, ready to pop a cap in the ass of any meathead who approached—one meathead in particular.

Within moments of arriving, they located a group of Stacy's old friends. Todd dropped her off on the fringes of the pack, and then was off to the bar, or so he thought. The lock that was her hand wouldn't release. Its lethal combination required hugs, shakes, introductions, lame jokes, remember whens, and painful smiles. Then she "ordered" a drink from him. Was this the plan? Was he the bartender? Hell, no. But at least the bar was a taste of freedom. After lingering at the oasis where the bartender was a twenty-year-old semi-hotty, Todd returned with Stacy's sunshine sparkle beach orgasm, and then stole away into the night.

If avoidance was the goal then an oasis was the solution. The bar was good, but short term. The bathroom is better, but also short term, *unless* Rory was having another incident. If so, then Rory, Mr. Entertainment, could be his savior.

Earlier, Todd had been joking with Rory about prom, never thinking that this might be Potty Party II. He'd need to arrange spies to watch Stacy, but that was easy. This way, he'd survive the night and learn the truth after the reunion, which would increase his chances of avoiding assault charges during the reunion.

Todd's mood changed from defensive to apologetic.

"I'm sorry, man," he told Rory. "I wasn't thinking. Are you seriously pissed?"

But Rory was no longer paying attention to Todd. "Problem?" he asked Gary Bean.

Gary Bean stood at the urinals gawking at them, one hand on his penis, midstream. Jolted by Rory's challenge, Gary whipped up his hand (the one he was peeing with) to point at himself. "Me?" he said, before drops of pee-pee sprinkled his face.

It was funny, disgusting, and embarrassing, which to Todd was the trifecta of funny. He laughed. Brent and Rory were more subdued, just groans and snickers from them.

"Nothing like a dab of eau-de-urine to attract the ladies," Todd said.

Head bowed, Gary zipped up and hobbled out the door. That was beautiful, Todd thought. *Gary Bean, ha!* Rich now, sure, but a little piss in the face was a nice reminder of his nerd roots.

"Okay," Brent said. "Let's keep that to ourselves. That's the kind of story that can ruin a person's high school reunion."

"What?" Todd was not on board this plan. "That was the Haley's Comet of bathroom mishaps. And it happened to Gary Bean! Remember Spring Carnival senior year? Hello? Keep it under wraps? No way."

"Spring Carnival? No. Whatever. We keep it under wraps for the same reason we keep Rory's prom story under wraps."

"Is Gary our friend? No. Gary is an El Dorko Grandé. But he thinks he's really something, doesn't he? Mr. Reunion Coordinator. We have to spread this story so he never forgets who he was."

Brent had an annoying mercy streak. In high school, Brent's policy as school president was to rule through wisdom and kindness. Todd preferred fear and punches. Everybody knew where Brent's method had gotten him; therefore, Todd's method was better, and it relied on regularly squashing the legion of dipshits that thought themselves smarter.

High school was short. You stayed on top however you could.

Nowadays it was Todd being stepped on by Gary and the rich assholes he represented, so he didn't feel bad reminding hoity-toity Gary of the time when Todd was King. The new world order was in Todd's face whenever he visited the bank. Gary kept his office door open so Todd could see him lounging inside. Sometimes Gary made the rounds when the bank lineup was long, chatting with customers, rubbing it in. He tried that with Todd once, just once. Nope, there was no comparing Gary's mishap with Rory's sad tale. Rory was a friend. Gary looked down on Todd and anyone like him.

"Have you ever told Stacy about prom?" Rory asked.

What the hell? Todd thought. Weren't we past this? "Stacy? No."

"You're married," Brent said.

"So?" Todd snorted. "What does that mean?"

"As a husband you're expected to share everything with your wife and vice versa."

"Not everything." Todd smiled and took a swig of beer.

Rory stared hard. "Todd?"

"No! Screw off with this," he said, getting agitated.

"She never pulled the 'tell me something I don't know about you' right before sex?"

"They all do that."

"Ah hah!" Rory said, pointing at him. "And you spilled everything, didn't you? All your little secrets including those about your friends."

"I told you. I never said anything about prom."

Todd flexed, gripping his beer and water bottle like eighty-pound free weights, biceps mashing against pecks. It was his sign, like a cobra flaring its hood. Back off.

"What did you say?" Brent asked.

"None of your business," Todd hissed.

He had a few secrets that he kept from Stacy, and prom was one. It had been a pact among brothers never to tell. It was too damn embarrassing, the kind of thing that could color Rory's reputation for life, give him a nickname like Blue Devil or Red Rover. But Rory still accused him of cracking. Todd bet he'd never say that to Brent. And once or twice a year, around Christmas or Thanksgiving, or any holiday where people talk about the old days, Stacy would ask him, *what happened in the bathroom again? At prom?* Each time Todd would tell her the same exact story, never flinching, always loyal. He didn't know if she sensed the lie, but once they brought up the past the conversation went deep into the abyss. Recently they'd become shouting matches. And he had questions of his own too. Why was she on the phone so much with her old boyfriend, Lewis Tinker? What was the point of being married if they don't have sex anymore? Why had she stopped baking cookies? And she had fired back with *Good question, why did we get married? Do you think you treat me as well as Lewis? Cookies? You want to talk about cookies? Define love for me, Todd?!*

"All right," Brent said, relenting. "If Todd never told and I never told, nobody knows."

Rory looked him and Brent in the eye one last time. "Fine," he conceded. "But what they think they know is that I got roaring drunk on prom night, right here in the bathroom—"

"Got alcohol poisoning and we took you to the hospital." Todd finished Rory's sentence.

"Right, so if I'm in here spewing tequila, I look like an alcoholic again, don't I? And that can't be good for meeting girls. Are you drinking that water?"

Rory licked his dry lips and eyed Todd's bottled water.

"I got it for you, dummy." Todd handed him the bottle.

Rory immediately downed half of it. He looked bad, thought Todd, which was perfect.

"So let's get out there!" Brent clapped his hands and pushed Rory ahead of him, towards the door.

Rory resisted. "Hold on. I'm still queasy."

Todd came to Rory's defense. "Yeah, ease up. Give the guy some time."

"You just need some fresh air." Brent pushed again.

"Brent." Rory held up a hand to warn him off. "You guys go. I'll be out in a minute."

Rory drank the rest of his water, and then walked to a sink to refill his bottle. While Rory rehydrated, Todd and Brent exchanged amused glances behind him. Todd wondered if Brent was thinking what he was thinking.

Chapter 5

Rory
King of Pain

Rory saw them in his mirror, grinning at each other like idiots behind him. *Leave,* he thought. *Leave!*

"I don't think any of us should leave," Todd said, further frustrating Rory. "It's too dangerous. What are we supposed to tell Alice this time?"

Rory answered without turning. "Nothing. Just ignore her."

"Ignore her? She's The Panther."

Rory turned and scowled. "You're married."

"So? Am I blind? I'm just saying—"

"You'd cheat on Stacy?" Brent said.

That soured Todd in a hurry. "No! What are you . . . ? That's not what I'm saying, asshole. Would you stop accusing me of shit?"

"Then tell her I'm primping, fixing my tie, bullshit like that," Rory suggested.

Brent agreed, ignoring Todd's protests. "Sounds good. See you in a few?"

"Save me a dance." Rory held his water bottle up. Brent knocked glasses with him, but Todd held back.

"This is stupid," Todd said. "If we go out there and Rory stays, what happens? More questions, more gossip. Let's just wait it out in here with him."

"I'm not hanging out in the bathroom all night," Brent said. "Besides, Rory's coming out in, what, five?"

Rory hated to let his friends down, but the only answer he could give was "Yes." Silently he finished the sentence in his mind. *There's a five percent chance of that happening.*

"Dude, you don't look good." Todd examined him like a doctor inspecting a boxer after a bruising, bloody round. He shook his head.

Brent eyed him critically too. It's not like Rory hadn't seen himself in the mirror. Fear plus anxiety plus puking does not achieve Sexiest Man Alive.

"Screw it. Let's go. Rory will catch up." Brent hauled Todd towards the door. Rory heard Todd mumble something about his wife, but they left.

He was alone again.

Rory leaned on the sink, pushing hard. He wondered if he could crash it out of the wall, burst the pipes, flood the bathroom, evacuate the gym, and cancel the whole reunion.

Pussy, he thought. He was a pussy. Can't talk to her.

Can't! He threw his water bottle at the garbage can. It bounced off the rim.

Talk! He kicked in a stall door.

To one girl! He retreated inside the stall and attacked the paper roll with both hands, rolling it like a water wheel, streaming paper onto the floor. When the roll was gone, Rory eased himself down onto the toilet seat. His eyes focused on a message etched into the back of the stall door, a wonderful bit of mockery perfectly positioned at eye level.

Carpé Diem Muthafucka!

Seize the day. That famous cliché. An English student's wet dream. The guy who wrote it probably went home and did the exact same thing he did every other day. If you don't apply the theory in practice, then practice writing it: English student credo. Rory had been an excellent English student. If there were a self-help group for Carpé-Diem-challenged individuals, Rory would be Grand Pooba High Chief Warlord.

But now was the time for hard questions. Here in the shitter where thoughts are the truest. Had he wasted ten years? All ten? Hadn't there been learning experiences? Hadn't he gained life skills? Or has it been all downhill since earning his driver's license? What useful skill had he picked up since? Unlike the muthafucka graffiti artist, he could at least spell motherfucker.

SQUEEAAKK. The bathroom door opened.

"Rory?" It was Brent, come to check up on him. Rory thought he might.

"Alice wants to come in and see you."

He leaped onto the toilet seat, suddenly nimble as a tree monkey and strong as a silverback gorilla. He stuck his head over the stall.

Brent held the door open, waiting for her.

"No!" Rory whispered.

"I couldn't stop her. She's coming."

"Now? She's coming now?" It was a scene from a horror film. Rory the whimpering cheerleader and Alice the unstoppable killer back for the sequel.

"Right now," Brent said.

The asshole smiled. If Rory had a gun, he didn't know who he'd shoot first, himself or Brent. Brent was always doing stuff like this in high school. Like a wise coach, Brent determined what was best for Rory. The problem was that either Rory never agreed with the solution, or the solution was a painful one, like now.

But in the eleventh hour, an epiphany.

"She can't! This is the guy's bathroom." Yes. Those were the rules. Where the hell was Gary Bean when you needed him?

"You want me to block the door?" Brent said, laughing.

"Yes, shit for brains." Rory wished he were close enough to punch air holes in Brent's head. Obviously his cerebral cortex needed oxygen. "Didn't you tell her I was fixing my tie?"

"Yeah, and you know what she said? She said tell him if he needs help, I can tie it with my tongue."

Rory lost his footing. He dangled from the stall partition. "Don't let her in," he pleaded. "C'mon, Brent. I mean it. Do this for me."

"This could be your lucky night, Rory. Ten years later."

"Wait!" Please don't let this happen, he thought. Please, God. "Brent, I'm sick. Swear on Mickey you won't do this!"

Brent turned and faced the unseen Alice. He greeted her with a deferential nod, lowering his gaze for the queen. "Alice."

Rory fell back into his stall, squatted on his throne, and waited for the headsman's axe.

A hush fell over the bathroom. There were no voices, no shuffles, no clearing of throats. Only the drip, drip of the leaky faucet. He imagined a soft, red carpet rolled out for her, ending at the entrance to his stall. In either a weird coincidence, or a manifestation of his own paranoid mind, the leaky faucet's cadence matched his heartbeat. Drip, drip; drip, drip; drip, drip.

"He's in the first one." Brent's voice.

The drip, drip of the faucet changed to the click, clack of high heels hitting linoleum, the tick-tock of his doomsday clock. She would see the truth of him, he would puke on her, and all hope would die in an unholy mess of yellows, greens, and browns.

The footsteps stopped outside his stall, and then nothing. The hush returned.

Rory waited ten torturous seconds, holding his breath . . . and a fart that threatened to break the silence in the least desirable way.

Slowly, he leaned down, willing his weight not to shift the seat and betray his presence with an errant squeak. Then he realized how stupid that was. Did it matter if he was quiet? Would silence trick her into thinking he wasn't in here? He was a pussy *and* insane. He peeked under the stall door and saw high heels.

Princess-white with gold bands.

Three to four inches.

Smoothly shaven legs.

Tiny ankles.

Heaven.

Hell.

Both places made him nervous.

KNOCK KNOCK.

His stomach lurched. She knocked on his stall door and it moved.

The door.

Moved.

The latch was open. The deadbolt preventing her from entering his cave, his only defense, had been, in his complete panic, overlooked.

Rory reached out slow, maintaining his insane policy of silence. His fingers squeezed the bolt and he pulled. It moved an inch.

The door flew open!

He fell back, raising his arms to block his face. It was an instinctive response to keep the door from slamming him in the head, but to onlookers it was a Hunchback of Notre Dame/Quasimodo gesture: *Look away, I'm hideous.*

The end had come.

Chapter 6

Rory
Crazy for You

One week before the high school reunion.

Why not a sofa? That's Rory's first thought when she asks uncomfortable questions. True, he sat in the big velvet chair with the thick, polished wooden armrests, which was supposed to be comfortable, but didn't recline and the back was tipped too far forward, which forced him to sit soldier-straight, eyeball-to-eyeball with Janice, his long-time therapist.

"You should have a sofa in here," Rory said, peering around the room.

"You're deflecting again. I know you can do it, Rory. You can." Janice stared at him with her lopsided smile, nodding with encouragement.

In every movie Rory saw there was a sofa in the psychologist's office. Why not this one?

Janice's office was just like his other doctor's office minus the bed, parchment paper, and stirrups. The differences were the big chair and the two posters: kittens playing with yarn, and flying ducks over a lake at sunset.

"All right, if you don't feel you can go then you shouldn't. Nobody's going to force you," Janice said. A heavy sigh followed.

"I didn't say I wasn't going. I was just telling you about it."

"And I appreciate you sharing. Thank you. That's very helpful." She leaned away, her encouraging hands sliding off her desk and falling into her lap. "I know this kind of thing dredges up old feelings, but it's good to work through them."

Eight, nine years? Was that how long he'd been "working through" old feelings? Maybe if Janice had a damn sofa he'd be cured already.

Rory watched her eyes flick to the wall clock as she stroked her greasy black hair. Professional or not, he knew he was frustrating her today. Maybe it was his fault she'd put on so much weight. Rory guessed five to ten pounds per year. When he first started sessions with Janice she'd had a solidly average body mass index, and her hair was shiny. The years are unkind to most, Rory thought.

"Lots of people don't go to their high school reunion. There's nothing weird about that," Rory said, returning to the uncomfortable topic.

"You're right. And everyone has their own reasons for not going. But we have to ask ourselves, are those reasons healthy?"

"Is avoiding pain healthy?"

"Okay." Janice planted her hands back on her desk, smiling but serious. "I think this is an important opportunity for you, so let's backtrack and review why you're here."

Why had he told her about the reunion? That was stupid,

thought Rory. Now she's going to harp and hammer until he has to lie and say he's going.

"You've had half a dozen relationships since high school, and ended them all because of anxiety and intimacy issues," Janice said. "You're not happy with that situation. You'd like to improve on that, reduce your anxiety, and form a healthy dating relationship. Is all of that correct?"

"Fine, I'll go," Rory said. "You talked me into it."

Janice frowned. "Rory, if we can't have honesty in this room then it's difficult for me to help you. Can you trust me when I say this is important?"

Trust you? Rory thought. If eight or nine years of "help" hadn't fixed him yet, it became more about hope than trust.

Rory first sought help with a visit to his family doctor, Dr. Turnbull. It was Dr. Turnbull who suggested seeing a therapist. Enter Janice, with her MA in Counseling, but not a doctor/psychiatrist with the power to prescribe drugs or attach electrodes to his head. They were Rory's team. He got his cocktail of anti-anxiety and depression meds from Dr. Turnbull, and helpful chats about the fairer sex from Janice. That combination was supposed to have him married to a Brazilian volleyball star by now.

Years back, both Turnbull and Janice suggested he see an actual psychiatrist, a behavior modification specialist. Too heavy for Rory. Anything beyond a G.P. and a run-of-the-mill therapist might imply he had a serious problem. Rory's stance was that anxiety wasn't cause for a frontal lobotomy, so he declined and kept faith in his team of quasi-experts.

"What's important?" Rory asked.

"This high school reunion is important!" Janice said, probably more emphatically than she wanted. "Your anxiety and failed adult relationships likely stem from your poor adolescent relationships. In particular your last high school relationship, which you've told me was an absolute disaster and one that you still think about."

"Therefore," Rory said, pointing at Janice, "I should move on rather than relive that moment by returning to the scene of the crime." Rory had seen a popular life guru on TV yapping about the importance of leaving the past behind. It was convenient to hide the truth behind that infomercial logic.

Janice took a deep breath. She leaned back and crossed her legs, pausing to gather her thoughts.

Ah hah! Rory thought. Point for him. Thank you, life guru.

"Yes and no," Janice said. "Avoidance is one way of tackling the issue. If you avoid dating then you avoid feelings of rejection and anxiety. But you also miss out on the good things: companionship, intimacy, sex."

Rory winced at the last one. It was a sore spot. But if he didn't involve a professional psychiatrist in his problem, then hookers weren't in the mix either.

"You're avoiding, Rory. And where has that got you these past eight years?"

So it was eight, not nine years. That provided some relief, like winning a bonus year; Rory could avoid making any drastic moves for another twelve months and not feel bad about it.

"Internet dating. You know anything about that? I think that's something I could try," Rory said.

"Okay. That's taking initiative. Good for you, Rory, but let's table that for now and stay on topic. I want to talk about your high school reunion and Alice."

He knew it wasn't there, but Rory looked around again for his missing sofa, wishing for a large sectional along with a cool cloth for his forehead, and a stiff drink. He'd talked to Janice about Alice before. Mostly general stuff. She was his high school girlfriend, first love, the one that got away, blah, blah, blah, and she dumped him at prom for another guy, but that's it. Oh, and she made him so nervous that his worst fear was puking on her.

Alice was Rory's alpha; the first woman to induce Rory's flu-like symptoms and irrational thoughts. Usually he was fine discussing her, but that was before seeing Alice became a real possibility. It was fine to talk about Alice hypothetically, in terms of the past, or as a lesson learned, but Brent had confirmed that Alice was returning home for the reunion. She'd be real again in one week.

"I have a theory. Well, two theories," Janice said, smiling her crooked smile. "Either your anxiety and intimacy issues manifested *during* your relationship with Alice, or your anxiety and intimacy issues were *caused* by your relationship with Alice. Either way, one of those theories is likely correct. To see her again as an adult, this woman that elicited such strong emotions during your adolescence, could be a profound and freeing experience. I think it's an avenue you should explore."

"Ha! You make it sound easy. What if she doesn't want to see me? What if she still hates me?"

"Now who's living in the past?" Janice asked, eyebrows raised. "She might be married. She might not care about her old high school flame. Would that bother you?"

Rory turned sullen and quiet. Bother him? A better phrasing would be destroy him, again. He hated the idea of Alice married or not caring about him. Along with puking on her, those were two more good reasons not to go to the reunion.

Heartbreak is an amazing thing. Break an arm and, for a short time, you experience pain. The cast might annoy you, but give it a few months, it comes off, et voila, you're healed. Have your heart broken and your rehabilitation can last a lifetime. You're a write-off. There is no ointment, salve, bandage, drug, or voodoo cure for what ails you.

Some claim the pain isn't physical, but they'd have a hard time convincing Rory. Over the past ten years, the soul-rending black hole that occupied his chest cavity—the one sucking all hope, joy, and reasons to practice good hygiene from his life—had been attacking him with stomach spasms and bouts of weakness so powerful that sometimes the strength to drag himself out of bed had been too much.

"If you want to move on and finally get a handle on your anxiety, it's possible you need to see Alice one more time."

Could he actually go, Rory wondered. Could he face Alice again? What would that be like?

"Do you have a friend you could go with?" Janice asked.

"Yeah, I got a couple," Rory said, weakly, his strength and confidence already waning.

Brent called him last week. It had been, what, three years since they last talked? And far longer since Brent moved to the big city. Brent was reunion-bound and wanted Rory to come with, and Todd too. Of course he talked about Mickey. Seeing Mick ten years from now was always the plan. Rory made his excuses, said he had to work, couldn't be helped, etc., etc., but Brent was having none of it. He poured on the guilt trip and the nostalgia, determined they had to go. Turns out Todd didn't want to go either, but since Stacy was going, he had to go too. Sure, they'd been best friends, the three of them, but everything changes after high school. And if that's true, then maybe he and Alice could be different too.

Chapter 7

Brent
Voices Carry

Brent peered inside the stall to check the experiment's results. Rory's face was a match for the toilet, porcelain white. If Rory had a pickaxe, he'd have chipped his way through the back wall into the parking lot.

"Am I done?" Emily Neeman and her impressive new boob job stood outside Rory's stall. "Is that it?"

"Yes," Todd said, slipping his arm around Emily and steering her toward the door. "You and your high heels did a masterful job. We owe you one."

Brent watched Rory closely. It took a moment for his shell-shocked friend to realize Emily was not Alice, and that this was all an elaborate prank. Rory peeked around the corner of his stall to be sure The Panther wasn't there. Only then did he smile.

"You guys are assholes," Rory said.

"You remember the deal, right?" Todd asked Emily. "Tell nobody."

"Uh-huh," said Emily, pausing at the door. "I don't blame him. After what she did to him, I wouldn't want to see her either. Stay away from her, Rory!"

As soon as Emily left, Brent turned on Rory. "You lied to me."

"About what?" Rory leaned back on the toilet seat, stretching cramped leg muscles. The color slowly returned to his cheeks.

"You're a mess. Did you do that?" Brent pointed at a carpet of toilet paper sprawled at Rory's feet. "Were you trying to wrap yourself up like a mummy and play dead?"

Rory ignored the question. "I told you I was sick."

"And would there be a correlation between your sensitive tummy and The Panther?"

Rory rose, swooped up the mounds of wasted toilet paper, and slammed them into the garbage can. "There's a correlation between my sensitive tummy and tequila."

"Tequila, huh?"

"Yup. And what if Emily talks? Hello?" Rory glared at Brent and Todd. "Anyone think of that? She could blab!"

"She won't blab," Todd said. "She promised."

"Oh, she promised?" Rory scoffed. "Nobody's ever broken a promise?"

"Fine," Brent said, "if you think she'll talk that's more reason to get off your toilet seat and get out there."

Rory ignored the logic and continued to complain. "What were you trying to prove?"

Brent would have answered Rory, would have, if he hadn't been standing outside the second stall from the right. Instead, his eyes tracked up the wall unerringly, right to the spot where the mystery person carved it.

I am the rat
The one who told
On that presidential prick
Brent, the lying asshole

Ten years had passed, but he reacted the same as he did the first time he saw it. Brent channeled Julius Caesar, Abraham Lincoln, and The Count of Monte Cristo.

Someone betrayed him.

Among the loyal subjects of Leelin High was a saboteur. But who? Brent eyed his two friends. Could they? Would they? Even for a joke?

Brent's life was an example of why human beings are inherently evil. Unprovoked, and with extreme malice, an unknown graffiti artist shattered Brent's senior year of high school and his entire future. Somewhere out there was a little green bug who'd been chewing on Brent's tree fort for ten years. And termites multiply, they spread, like rumors, like gossip. What else had the coward done to bring him down?

The question Brent came here tonight to answer, was who? Who was his John Wilkes Booth? Who was his Benedict Arnold? Who was the Brutus that knifed him in the back and stole his life? But before his hunt could begin in earnest, Brent felt compelled to get Rory out of the bathroom. To do that, he had to cure the nervy bastard. He peeled his eyes away from the graffiti and commenced psychological warfare.

"How come you hid in your stall? You didn't say anything when Alice knocked. Sick or not, that's rude."

"Well, gee, Brent, *she* never knocked."

"You know what I mean. You froze." Brent smacked Rory with a verbal left hook.

"Froze?" Rory straightened his shoulders.

"Just like prom." Brent finished with a right uppercut.

"Whoa, Brent, the guy puked," Todd said. "So what if he hasn't got the balls for Alice? Lots of guys don't have those balls. Give him a break. You want another water, Rory?"

"You're calling me a pussy too?" Rory turned on Todd.

"Dude, I'm on your side!" Todd said, surprised with Rory suddenly in his face.

The bathroom door opened and Mitchell Matthews took one step inside. In grade eleven, Mitchell was a first-hand recipient of a Todd pummeling, so witnessing the Todd-Rory stare-down may have triggered unpleasant memories.

"I'll come back," Mitchell said. The bathroom door shut quickly. Apparently, Mitchell did not need to pee that badly.

Brent slid between Todd and Rory. "Nobody's calling anybody a pussy, right?" Brent looked to Todd for support.

"Yeah, I wasn't saying that, but this is the second time you've been in my face tonight," Todd warned Rory.

They say one of the secrets to success is surrounding yourself with positive people. If that were true, Brent figured his life could be partly explained by his two old friends: the caveman and the cave dweller. First, the cave dweller.

He and Rory had lots in common. Brent was a problem solver and a thinker. Rory was a thinker, and often had problems. Their relationship worked great in high school, but had its frustrations. Rory could be as stubborn as a six-year-old at bedtime.

"Rory, I feel like we've had this conversation before," Brent said.

Blinking nervously, Rory stared at each of them. Brent knew

what he was thinking. Rory was debating whether to confess and confirm for the annals and records of Leelin High what Brent and Todd had already deduced. In his own head, Brent heard the sounds of Rory's thoughtful teeter-totter moving up and down. Screech, scronk, screech, scronk.

"That *was* bad tequila," Rory said, rubbing his stomach. "But, so what, maybe I am a little nervous tonight. Is there something wrong with that?"

A small victory. "No," Brent affirmed.

"Absolutely not." Even Todd was helpful. "I might be in here too. The Panther is still a 10+."

Rory acted confused. "What does Alice have to do with it?"

Brent groaned.

When Brent was a kid he used to play *Risk*, the board game of world domination. He and his friends marched their armies across the globe and attempted to take over the world with rolls of the dice. These were heated, competitive games, and there was always one jackass who couldn't handle the stress of losing his foothold in the Russian province of Kamchatka. He'd snap, flip the board, and send everyone's armies on a magic carpet ride, forcing them to start the game all over again.

Rory just flipped the board. Now they had to start the conversation all over again.

"Rory! Stop it. Would you just—"

Rory talked over him. "It's the reunion. It's intimidating. What?"

"You know I was joking when I said Alice would fix your tie with her tongue, right?"

"Sure," Rory said, deflated. "I knew that."

Yeah, he knew that *now*, Brent thought. But Rory believed it when he said it.

"He totally got you!" Todd laughed. "Alice. Tie it with her tongue? Are you gullible or what?"

Brent rolled his eyes. Ladies and gentlemen, Todd Bowman, tactless wonder boy. If it was obvious, if everybody knew, Todd would still point it out as if he'd spotted a UFO.

Next, Todd clubbed Rory with tough love. "No offense, buddy, and I know she was your prom date, but Alice is out of your league now. Times have changed. Move on."

Rory crossed his arms and didn't say a word.

"Rory?" Brent prodded.

Rory crossed his arms tighter and scowled. He began pacing, showing signs of life. "All right, so I get a little nervous around her."

"A little?"

"It doesn't matter! I'm not going to measure up. I've got ten years of pressure on me. How good is she expecting me to be now? Dreaming about her missed opportunity at the prom, fantasizing about how great I would have been. It's freaking me out!"

Rory was in turmoil. Brent knew this, but there was another, more immediate problem. When a male friend said something cocky, you were obligated to knock him back down, regardless of the circumstances. If Wyatt Earp and Doc Holiday were in the middle of the gunfight at the OK Corral, and Doc said to Wyatt, "Ya know, Wyatt, I'm about the best darn shot in this town," Wyatt would have said, "Good thing too. Because you're about the ugliest turd in this town." With best friends, first came the cut, then came the sympathy.

Todd cut first. "Who the hell are you?" he said, laughing. "Is your poster for sale at the mall? Do girls tape it up and diddle themselves to it? And why are you bothering with her anyway? She didn't miss her opportunity at the prom. Remember Jamaican Bob?"

Rory's face burned red. He didn't like that, so Brent took a softer angle. "You were a popular guy in high school, but you're putting too much pressure on yourself."

"You're delusional," Todd said. "And pukey. What'd you have for dinner? Might want to stick close to the stalls."

"Shut up." Rory was getting defensive again, which Brent knew wouldn't help them get out of this bathroom.

"Look, you're just uptight. You've always been that way. You hated road trips. You skipped classes that had oral presentations—"

"Until I finally did it!" Rory said. "I gave a damn good presentation once. And fear of public speaking happens to be the number one fear in Western society."

"I know, and there's a hell of a lot of people out there like you. It's a sign of intelligence, an active imagination. There's a famous quote from Hemingway you should know: *Cowardice, as distinguished from panic, is almost always simply a lack of ability to suspend functioning of the imagination.*"

"Hmm." That made Rory think.

"Haven't we proved this already?" asked Todd.

"Proved what?" Rory said, with a slice of venom.

"What do you think? How uptight you are."

"How?" Brent was curious too.

"Mitchell Matthew's house party? The test? Remember?"

"What test?" Rory looked at Brent as if to say, who invited the talking donkey dipshit to this party?

Brent smiled. He remembered. And he bet Rory remembered too. There was no way Rory could forget that party.

Chapter 8

Rory
Too Shy

10 years ago. High school house party.

The stereo blared "Welcome to the Jungle." Masses of laughing, sweaty, tipsy teenagers moved around him and beside him. He was a lizard in a pet store terrarium with fifty other lizards, each crawling over the other in the small space provided. But Rory had no complaints. He had his spot on the sofa and wasn't giving it up. His bladder pressured him an hour ago, but he would hold it until curfew. Once more he tabulated the evidence:

He had his arm around Alice.

His free hand stroked her leg.

She had not pushed arm or hand away.

She had kissed him at the party, i.e., in public.

He had kissed her at the party, i.e., ditto.

If she had to pee, she held it too.

Most importantly, when asked by a curious onlooker if they

were going out, Alice smiled and said, "Ask him." Rory's response had been, "Pretty much."

Alice looked like she stepped off the screen of a raunchy music video. Her blonde hair was wild, tossed, and teased. She wore bright red lipstick; tight, faded blue jeans; a cut-off white blouse showcasing ample cleavage; pink leg warmers; and little white socks with a pink pom pom on each heel.

Rory was no slouch himself. He had the perfect 80s hair: shoulder-length, straw-colored, blow-dried, and feathered back like an eagle's wings. He wore his favorite dress shirt, untucked, with a crisp white t-shirt underneath; white pants rolled up at the bottoms; and stylish brown loafers.

They were snuggled cheek to cheek like a pair of cute raccoons. Rory planted another kiss on her lips and took a swig of his wine cooler. Life was bliss.

Alice leaned in close and whispered, "You want to go upstairs?"

Ka-boom.

Rory's stomach lurched and his body tensed. Sweat oozed from his body. Before she could feel his suddenly clammy hands, he snatched them away. He stretched, trying to mask his panic.

"That'd be rude, wouldn't it? Leaving the party like that?" Rory stalled. He needed time to convince his stomach not to sabotage his dream.

"Going upstairs is not leaving the party," Alice said. "But whatever, if you don't want to go." She turned away, annoyed, embarrassed, or both.

Shit! Rory wanted to be someone else, but still be him, if that made any sense. He knew what "upstairs" meant.

It meant all things that a healthy, normal seventeen year-old male would trade his secret *Playboy* collection for. So why did it scare him more than the threat of nuclear war or *Nightmare on Elm Street*?

He sensed the widening gulf between them. They were still snuggled together, but it was more like two stone pillars leaning against each other. She'd offered to take their relationship to the next level, and he'd cited social etiquette as a bigger priority. He needed to regroup, man up, and salvage the moment.

"No, I want to go too. I, uh . . ." Rory linked words as he went along, not knowing how the sentence would end. "I'm just not, uh . . ."

"I didn't mean *that*, you know." Alice turned towards him, arms crossed and sour. "I meant a change of scenery, that's all."

"Well, yeah, I knew that." Relief flowed though Rory. "A change of scenery might be nice." He put his arm back around her and felt her muscles relax under his touch.

"But what would be so wrong if we did do that?" Alice said. "Lots of couples go to bedrooms. It's noisy down here and not very private. We could talk about anything upstairs. We could *do* anything." Alice stared at him.

Despite the three-hundred-pound butterfly careening through Rory's intestines, he steeled himself and smiled back. "Let's go."

As Rory moved up the stairs, hand-in-hand with Alice, each step brought a worse cramp. He hunched over in silent pain, a posture that thankfully didn't look too strange going up a staircase.

What if he wasn't great at it, whatever "it" wound up being? He didn't know what to do, not really. The one porn he'd watched at Todd's made it look easy, but those guys were professionals. Rory knew there was a knack to it, but he had no knack. He knew what he wanted to touch, but he didn't know how to touch. Should he push, pull, caress, rub, pat, squeeze, twist, lick, or slap? The porn guys did all those things! Oh my God, *what if he puked on her?*

Thinking about it made it worse, which was exactly what Rory couldn't stop doing. She was the center of his lustful dreams. He loved her! Give him Alice and nothing else mattered. But if she rejected him . . . Rory nearly buckled as a nasty cramp hit him at the top of the steps.

Deserted.

Alice was right. Not a soul in sight. Open bedroom doors beckoned on all sides, with nary a distraction to aid the escape Rory plotted. He hated himself for it, but his analysis came up with three possibilities: First, if his stars aligned, he'd have amazing sex with Alice. Second, and more likely, he'd fumble with her girl parts like a monkey at a typewriter, puke on her, and she'd never want to see his pathetic penis again. Third, he could cut his losses, concoct a good excuse to leave, keep Alice as his girlfriend, and live to fight another day. He swore to himself that on that future day he would be better prepared.

"Let's take this one." Alice dragged him to the furthest bedroom down the hallway.

Rory allowed himself to be led, bravely fighting cramps and nausea while his brain searched all avenues for the perfect excuse. It couldn't upset her, wouldn't raise suspicion, and had to make complete and logical sense. His desperate brain landed on the obvious excuse. Now he waited for the right opportunity to play his "get out of jail free" card.

Alice leaped onto the king-sized bed, laughing in surprise to discover it was a waterbed. In his seventeen years of life, Rory had never experienced a waterbed, but he'd heard they were designed specifically for sex. It was yet another sign that everything was falling in line for a once-in-a-lifetime virgin-busting night. The only hurdles were his Mothra-sized butterflies and a fear of embarrassment and failure so strong his body had a .00001 percent chance of spontaneously combusting.

Ignoring Alice's glorious body splayed out in all its perfection, Rory stalled. "Isn't this his parent's bedroom? We shouldn't be in here. We could get in trouble."

"Oh, who cares! Get over here and kiss me." Alice rose up to her knees, beckoning him.

"I should get us some drinks," Rory offered, his hand reaching back for the doorknob.

"Drinks after." Alice unbuttoned her shirt. Her long pink tongue snaked out and licked her lips. "Lock the door." She threw her shirt aside.

Rory's nausea threatened. He knew he only had seconds. Despite his nerves and fear of sexual ineptitude, a small part of his brain stood its ground. It knew one thing. He had to get a hand on those tits.

The Alamo of Rory's brain, strong enough to focus on breasts in the face of certain doom if he stayed one second too long, set its ballistic plan in motion. He played his "get out of jail free" card with a twist.

"I have to use the bathroom," Rory said, "but—"

He rushed to the bed. His internal stopwatch kept count as his lips met hers and his hands roamed free over her body. She moaned and pulled him down on top of her, but Rory kept one foot firmly planted on the ground. For ten seconds, desire washed over his fear, covering it like a band-aid over a blood-spurting bayonet wound. He was aggressive, he was passionate, and he was fast.

"Okay," he said, rising off the bed, out of breath. "I have to use the bathroom."

"Awww." Alice reluctantly released him. "Hurry back. I'm soooo horny."

The plan worked because he set a time limit. He knew he wouldn't last long, that he was seconds away from dry heaving or worse, but given a small window of time with a defined end-point, where the expectations on him were small, and with a confirmed escape route, he could smother his fear for short bursts. She accepted his reason. Who could deny someone the bathroom? She was happy and horny, not at all disappointed, and he'd got his hands on the goodies without puking on her. Win-win.

His eyes drank her in as he left, wishing he had the belly to stay longer. When he reached the door, his cramps and nausea were already subsiding.

"Rory! Look!"

Rory turned to see Alice pointing towards a door, a door that led to . . . an en-suite bathroom.

"There's a bathroom in here! Hurry up." Alice grinned and unbuttoned her pants, tugging them down her hips. She wriggled them down to her feet, and then kicked them off.

Panties. Alice's wondrous and forbidden panties. Striped, red and green, like a candy cane.

"Hurry," she moaned, sliding her hand down her panties and arching her back. Then she burst into a fit of giggles, crossing her legs, suddenly shy. "Go!" she said, smiling. "I'll get the bed ready." Alice pulled the sheets down, preparing the bed for sex.

Rory stared dumbfounded at the en-suite bathroom door, processing the loss of his escape route, what Alice was doing, and what it all implied.

Could he have ballistic ten-second sex?

Aw, fuck.

Rory hurled on the carpet.

"Rory! Oh my God!"

He rushed to the en-suite bathroom and slammed the door, locking it. He hurled again, loudly, followed by a few disgusting dry heaves.

"Rory? Are you all right?" Alice's voice echoed through the closed door. He could hear her wiggling the doorknob. Rory closed his eyes and concentrated, wishing hard for spontaneous combustion.

Chapter 9

Todd
The Wild Boys

10 years ago. Same high school house party.

It was a big en-suite bathroom. Alice wanted to come inside too, but Rory denied her entry. Todd leaned against the bathroom door. Rory slouched on the toilet seat, massaging his face. Brent sat on the bathroom counter, and took the first shot at lifting Rory's spirits.

"You can still salvage the night. The worst is over," Brent said. As usual, Brent sported his presidential wear. He liked to remind people of his important political status with sport coat and clip-on tie.

Todd liked to dress casual and show off his guns. He wore a UNLV Runnin' Rebels muscle shirt cut short with ripped sleeves, ultra-faded blue jeans, and high tops. He worked out and wanted people to notice, especially Stacy Davenport and her needle-dick boyfriend, Lewis Tinker. For different reasons, obviously.

Stacy had thrown major flirt-vibes his way tonight, and Todd had a score to settle with Tinker. How great would it be to steal her away and trounce Tinker at the same time?

Rory lifted his head. "Salvage the night? Really? You think she'll like my puke breath? It's over, man. Forget it."

"So brush your teeth." Brent shoved toothpaste at Rory. "Use your finger and scrub your tongue."

"I've got Juicy Fruit," Todd offered, digging into his pocket.

Rory accepted the gum and ignored the toothpaste. "Is there a back door out of here?"

"Oh, come on, for real?" Brent said. "Big deal, so you puked. It's a funny story. She'll think it's cute."

Todd didn't know about "cute." The Panther hadn't sounded cute when she'd scrambled down the stairs yelling, "Someone help! Rory's puking!" A stampede followed upstairs led by Mitchell Matthews, who freaked out over his parents' puke-stained carpet, which resulted in an upstairs ban and a general hate-on against Rory for ruining everyone else's make-out plans.

Rory had told them the story. He was on the bed with Alice making out when he took a bathroom break to check his wallet for a condom. At first, he didn't notice the en-suite bathroom, or he might have made it without puking. But before he'd taken five steps, he tasted booze in his throat and had to hurl.

Todd had laughed at his friend's amazing bad luck, but that turned to empathy after putting himself in his shoes.

"I could cause a distraction," Todd said. "You want out? I'll start a fight with Lewis Tinker."

Rory perked up. "And I could sneak out and not have to see Alice again."

"Let's do it!" Todd reached for the door, but Brent slid off the sink and grabbed his wrist.

"Neanderthals? Hello? That's not the plan."

"Doesn't have to be *your* plan," Todd said. "It's *our* plan."

Rory nodded his agreement. He stood and stretched, preparing for his mad dash.

"You're feeling better?" Brent asked.

"Some fresh air would be nice, but I feel better, yeah. Let's go."

"Tinker has it coming, Brent," Todd said. "He's getting his face smashed with or without a good excuse. I might as well help Rory at the same time."

"Grow up, Todd. You'll ruin it for everyone. And you." Brent examined Rory. "Were you a little nervous about this Alice thing tonight? Pretty big deal, right?"

"Nervous?" Rory laughed it off. "Were you watching me get busy? I think not. You would not have seen any nerves, my friend." Rory coughed and looked in the mirror. "Are we doing this or not, Todd?"

"How far did you get with her?" Brent asked. "You didn't give us many details."

Rory paused and leaned back on the counter. "It was quick, but we were all over each other, man. She had her top off. My hands were, like, everywhere. It was crazy. She took her pants off and I thought to myself, do I have a condom? I didn't want to check my wallet right in front of her, so—"

"Why not?" Todd asked. "She'd see the condom eventually. And you may have to pass latex inspection before she gives you the green light."

"I don't know," Rory said. "That's just what I did."

"Wait!" Brent hissed, waving everyone to be quiet. He changed his voice to a whisper. "She might be listening."

Rory wilted and eyed the door.

"Would she tell the same story you just told?" Brent asked.

Todd saw the hesitation and wide-eyed blip of fear in Rory's eyes. Rory was lying.

"Sure," Rory said. "But you can't ask her."

"Agh! Too late," Todd laughed. "You know who you are? You're Tommy Hobson, dude."

Brent cracked open the bathroom door and peeked outside.

"Anybody out there?" Rory asked.

"Nope. Although someone, likely Mitchell, left us cleaning supplies and paper towels. Guess that's on us."

"Yeah, right," Todd said. "You mean Tommy Hobson over here."

Tommy Hobson was the star center for the Leelin High Leopards, easily their best player. Before every game, Tommy puked, usually more than once. Getting the win meant so much to him, the thought of losing was so painful, that every game felt like life or death. Tommy's puking was a team ritual now. They didn't take to the ice until Tommy hurled.

"I'm not Tommy Hobson!" Rory said.

"This was your big game, wasn't it?" Todd said. "Sure it was. And you Tommy'd it. Don't lie."

"What's with the interrogation? How about a little sympathy?"

As much as Todd wanted to be Rory's distraction, make Lewis's nose bleed, and claim Stacy as his victory spoils, he didn't like being lied to. Whenever Rory asked Todd for the gory details about something that happened to him, Todd always obliged and told him everything, good and bad. He felt he deserved the same.

"You know what Tommy is?" Todd said. "He's a stall guy."

"A what guy?" Rory asked.

A stall guy is someone who can't piss at urinals. Tommy Hobson used to wander into the bathroom a dozen times to look in the mirror or wash his hands, waiting for that rare moment of privacy. Everyone caught on eventually, but because he was their star player, they gave him the privacy he needed. No big deal. But lying about it was. Todd never thought of Rory like Tommy before, but once you connected the dots it made sense.

"You want to prove you weren't nervous and your story's true? Fine. Then take a piss." Todd lifted the toilet seat for Rory.

"Are you for real?" Rory laughed. "I don't want to prove anything. Can you believe this?" Rory turned to Brent for sympathy, but only got a shrug.

"You won't do it?" Todd asked.

Before Rory could answer, Brent turned him around to face the toilet bowl. "It's just a little test," he said. "It's called urophobia. Very common in anxious people."

"We'll even turn our backs," Todd said. He turned around, but made sure to block the door. Brent joined him, shoulder to shoulder, his back to Rory.

"This is half gay. I'm not doing it."

"I understand," Todd said, looking back at Rory. "Because you can't." There was a dare in Todd's tone.

"This is so stupid." Rolling his eyes, Rory stepped up to the bowl and unzipped.

Todd turned back around. "Whenever you're ready." He and Brent exchanged smirks and then stared straight ahead at the door, as promised. And they waited.

And waited.

And waited.

And waited.

"What's the hold-up?" Todd asked. He and Brent stifled laughs.

"Give me a second, assholes!"

Todd stole a peek behind him. He watched Rory use his breathing to relax, taking a deep breath in through the nose, and then smoothly exhaling through the mouth. He appeared to be taking the test seriously.

Todd turned back around and began a whispered chant.

"Ror-y, Ror-y, Ror-y."

Brent picked up the chant. "Ror-y, Ror-y, Ror-y!"

And then the impossible. Todd heard a tinkle. And another tinkle. And then the sound of pee hitting water at full throttle. Todd and Brent looked at each other in disbelief. They turned around.

Rory poured beer into the toilet.

"That's cheating!" Todd laughed and grabbed the beer from Rory.

Rory quickly zipped up. "Warm beer tastes like piss. Same thing."

"You wasted a beer, dummy," Todd said. "Admit it, I win."

"How could I go with all the 'Rory, Rory, Rory' bullshit?"

As far as Todd was concerned, the test was over and Rory had failed. "Case closed, Rory. You're a stall guy."

"Fine," Rory said. "What does that mean? I know it doesn't mean I can play hockey like Tommy Hobson."

"It means tell us the truth, dude," Todd said. "What happened with you and The Panther? Full disclosure this time. I tell you every time I mess up. Now it's your turn. Talk."

Rory leaned against the counter and crossed his arms. "Look, whether it was nerves, booze, or E-coli, I puked before I got to third base. That's the fuckin' story. You can laugh if you want."

Todd did laugh. Rory's angry face was hilarious.

Rory including "nerves" as a potential reason for what happened to him was as much of a confession as Todd was likely to get. Regardless, he was satisfied. Todd felt better about himself. That's what he'd been pushing for.

Whenever his friends messed up, Todd felt normal. In Todd's mind, that was pretty much the most important function of a friend: to screw up in a bunch of ways that you haven't, so you forget about all the ways you *have* screwed up. It shows you that things could be worse, you're not a total screw-up, and that other people are as clueless about things as you are. That's what friends are for.

"Look," Todd said. "You know what this means?"

"I can hardly wait for you to tell me," Rory said.

"It means you should drink a lot more before you jump between the sheets with Alice. Tommy told me once that if he drank five beers he wasn't a stall guy anymore. It's the cure for—what'd you call it, Brent?"

"Urophobia."

"That's your test, buddy." Todd slapped Rory on the back. "If you can piss outside a stall next time, if you ever get a next time with Alice, you'll be ready for your big game."

Chapter 10

Rory
Strange Animal

Yes, Rory remembered that party and the stupid test. He'd listened stoically while Todd talked, his own memory filling in the gaps that only he knew. Now, ten years later, history was repeating itself. Alice's affections had returned, and so had the three-hundred-pound butterfly that liked to visit Rory's stomach on special occasions.

"Watch me," Todd said, stepping up to the urinals. "I can piss anywhere anytime."

Brent intervened. "Todd? No," he laughed. "Keep it in your pants, please."

Todd relented and didn't haul out the rod. This was surprising. Give Todd an excuse to pull it out and it's like trying to stop a dog from sniffing poop.

"Okay, then. Your turn, Rory," Todd said. "Or you can default."

Rory was cursed with a shy bladder. When placed in a social situation, his bladder didn't take calls. It was incommunicado. Rory needed a bubble, which made him a peeing bubble boy. How could The Panther like a peeing bubble boy? But he wouldn't give his pee-easy, bladder-blessed pals the satisfaction of admitting his deficiency.

"Maybe I don't need to go?" Rory said.

"Maybe you piss in stalls because the close proximity of other dongs makes you nervous?" Brent leaned against a sink, grinning his secret smile.

"Maybe you read too many psychology journals?"

"Maybe you're uptight?"

"Maybe *I'm* the normal one?" It was that sort of BS, out-there, counter-intuitive thinking that could sidetrack Brent. It seemed to work. Brent laughed but made no further argument.

"Okay, listen. Wait here," Todd said. "I've got something that'll help."

"Hurry up. We've been stuck in here too long," Brent said.

"Two minutes," Todd assured him. He flashed a mischievous smile.

"Fine," Brent said. "Go."

Rory wasn't paying much attention. He'd drifted off into a depression. Being reminded of the house party, of his lost opportunity, drilled home the fact that once, maybe, if he'd played his cards differently, he coulda been a contender.

Love, success, recognition, respect, each one you earn is like winning a championship belt. Some people are perennial contenders for those belts, and some people are spit buckets.

Sadly, somewhere along the line, Rory's hands got slow, his chin turned to glass, abs became flab, and he was positive he had an irregular heartbeat. But before all that? Yeah, he coulda been a contender. Coulda.

Brent's piercing brain did its Vulcan mind trick. "What? You still pissed off?"

Rory debated what to do. With Todd gone, now was the time. It was a complex issue and Todd would have two answers: Get out there and fuck her; or fuck it, just leave. Todd's reckless bravado made Rory nervous, and jealous. Todd was the first to fight, the first to fuck, and usually the first to fail. Avoiding failure was Rory's skill and primary directive in life, so sharing this with Todd was pointless.

Brent liked to discuss and debate, roll the issue around the sandbox before making a decision. Rory liked that too. He just hated the decision part.

Screw it. It was his official induction letter into the High School Hall of Fame, stud category. Rory reached into his pocket and pulled it out, triumphant.

"What's that?" Brent asked.

Proof, Rory thought. "Do you think I have a chance with The Panther?"

"Is that a note?"

"Answer me. Todd said I haven't got a chance anymore. What do you think?"

"A chance tonight? To hook up?"

"Yup."

"After everything that happened at prom?" Brent whistled. "I don't know, buddy. She liked you ten years ago, but that was before prom."

"So what are you saying, do I or don't I?"

"If she's over it? Maybe. That *is* a note."

Brent reached for it, but Rory backed away. He didn't think Brent was ready yet.

"But you wouldn't expect it, right? Not now. I had my chance."

"You had two chances, maybe more, and look at the odds. Every guy in high school wanted her. One look at Alice doing her special thing and she had you. How many guys went to Leelin High?"

Brent tried another lunge and grab. Rory outmaneuvered him. They danced around the bathroom.

"If we split it fifty-fifty? All three grades? About two hundred."

Brent did the math. "Accounting for key variables like freshmen, ugly dudes, and . . . how many classes of hers were you in?"

"Two." Rory shoved the note behind his back and stiff-armed Brent.

"I'd say your chances were one in five back then. I don't think Vegas would give those odds again, post-prom. Are you going to show me that thing?" Brent gave up the chase and held out his hand.

"I'm still a good looking guy, right." He expected a yes, so Rory didn't make it a question.

"Sure you are."

Rory handed him the note.

"Relative to other rodents," Brent said.

Rory ignored the cut, intent on Brent as he examined the note.

"What is this? Did you get it tonight?"

Rory shrugged, letting the anticipation build.

Brent tugged at the note's corners, pulling it apart. As he read, Rory watched his face, savoring the moment.

Brent's eyes bulged. "Ho-ly shit. Is this for real?"

"She handed it to me herself." Rory stood tall and cocky, brimming with recognition and respect.

"When?"

"Right before I came in here."

"Right before?"

"Uh . . ." Rory made a show of thinking hard, "yeah, I think so."

Brent chuckled and shook his head. He read the note aloud.

"They say that anticipation is the seed of passion. Planted ten years ago, that seed has grown in me to a ripe fruit, ready to be plucked. Do you want to pluck me, Rory?"

"She underlined pluck," Rory said, wringing his hands.

"Do you want to *pluck* me?" Brent reread that part. "She's a poet."

"Keep reading."

"Ten years is a long time to wait," Brent read. "But now the wait is over. You owe me tonight. Alice."

Rory snatched the note back, wanting the security of holding it in his hands. "What do you think?"

"You had that and you asked me if you have a chance with her?"

That was the fun part for Rory. The "he coulda been a contender" part. Now came the part where Rory acknowledged he wouldn't be a contender, not tonight, not ever, but hopefully he could sit around years from now and talk about the coulda part.

"It's gotten worse," Rory said.

"What has?"

Say it.

"Well?"

Just say it.

"Rory?"

Say it!

"My nerves," Rory said. And it was out. "Doctor called it an anxiety thing. Gave me something."

Brent laughed. The prick actually laughed.

"Excuse me, asshole? Little support?"

"Rory! Hello? Like I didn't know that already?"

"You didn't know I was on meds."

Brent choked off his laughter. "Okay, well," he cleared his throat. "I didn't know that, but what's the big deal? If it's helping, great, right?"

"I think it's helping, I dunno, but stupid Todd knocked them into the toilet. I'm out."

"How'd he do that? Never mind. You have the bottle?"

Rory pulled it from his pocket and showed him.

"Huh. I don't recognize it." Brent turned the plastic bottle to read the pharmacy's label. "Could be a placebo."

"A what?"

"A placebo. A sugar pill. A fake. If you think it's working then it is, even if it isn't."

"My doctor lied to me?"

"It's not a lie, Rory. But it only works if you think it's real."

"How do I know if they're real?"

"You said they're working."

"Yeah, but—"

"Then who cares?"

"Is that what they teach you in college? All the ways the establishment is secretly screwing us over?"

"Exactly. And that it's pointless to resist. The establishment will tell you to just take the pill and shut up. Lovely system we've got, really."

Rory had one crutch, his pills. One friend dunked them in puke; the other friend told him they were fake.

Crutch broken.

Fear stronger.

Rory knew when he read her note he couldn't make the dream

happen. He'd swallowed that jagged pill. Now he wondered about life after the reunion. Could he make that work? He was chewing on that tasty nugget of hopelessness when the bathroom door swung open for Todd and his tray of drinks. The tray was a smorgasbord of beers, martinis, and Rory's favorite, rum and pineapple.

Chapter 11

Brent
Tell Her About It

Brent enjoyed hanging out with Todd in high school. Around Todd, you could undergo a process of de-evolution. Brent's morals, judgment, scruples, compassion, and logical decision skills could get tossed aside like so many banana peels, replaced by an urgent desire to mock, beat, or fornicate. Brent was usually drinking during these times. *An intelligent man is sometimes forced to be drunk to spend time with his fools.* Hemingway again.

Unfortunately, Todd was sometimes like a dog who loves you and has the best of intentions, but pisses in your bed. Case in point.

"Gentlemen!"

Todd balanced the tray with one meaty paw and made his announcement. "I have found the cure. Within these potions is the power to kill all things nervous. Side effects include stupidity, vomiting, headache, loss of friends, jobs, memory, and liver damage."

He reminded Brent of a snake oil salesman from the Old West peddling his rattlesnake/whiskey mixture as a medicinal cure-all.

But Whiskey Todd was about to get tarred and feathered for forgetting which towns he'd visited . . .

Todd held his tray out for Rory. "You got the rums."

Rory swallowed hard, trying to keep calm. He had to be struggling, Brent thought. Rory had a monkey on his back with four arms, eight legs, a beer gut, and a bad attitude.

"Weren't you here," Rory said, "when we talked about people perceiving me as a raging alcoholic?" He gestured wildly at the tray. Spit bubbled from his mouth, but no more words.

"Oh, yeah," Todd said. "Shit." To his credit, he frowned and looked apologetic.

But to be truly sorry you had to be sensitive, affected by the emotions and feelings of others. Sensitive was not a quality Brent associated with Todd. Todd cared about chicks, fights, and chicken wings.

True enough, Todd's apologetic frown didn't last long. "But you gotta be kidding me. We can't drink because some girl you have no chance with thinks you hit the sauce too much? Which, if you remember, was part of the story I helped come up with on prom night."

Rory wiped his mouth and found his voice. "You had a little something to do with prom night, remember? So forgive me if I don't kiss your hairy knuckles!"

Rory resented Todd for prom night, and got no argument from Brent, but Brent didn't want to waste another minute down that ugly rabbit hole. He could not stomach another episode of Planet of the Adolescent Apes.

"Relax you two," he said, lifting a martini from Todd's tray. "Prom night's history. Let it go. And, honestly, some women like a guy with a sensitive side. If Alice knew about Rory's anxiety it might have made him endearing."

"Bullshit," Todd said.

"You're saying," Rory paused to get this right, "that it might be good that I'm nervous around Alice?" Rory grabbed a rum and pineapple from Todd's tray.

"It could be. Displaying vulnerability *is* a form of strength. Maybe not as much in adolescence, but as adults honesty is important and valued. That's my hypothesis."

"Would you stop that?" Todd said. "You've been doing it all night."

"Doing what?" Brent said.

"Adolescence? Hypothesis? Endearing? You're talking professorish again. You're not a prof, so please."

"How many degrees do you have? And by the way, spell *adolescence*."

"They're bachelor degrees. Calm down."

"Right. Degrees. Plural. A little respect?"

Todd bowed to Brent. "Carry on, Mr. BA and BS."

This is why Brent didn't hang out with Todd after graduation. Todd was Fletcher Christian.

Fletcher Christian was the guy who mutinied against Captain Bligh on the HMS Bounty on 28 April 1789. Bligh obviously couldn't trust Christian, a guy he'd promoted on his own ship, and Brent couldn't trust Todd anymore, a guy he once counted on to have his back. Now Todd was the heckler at the corner table, trying to break you down and steal the stage. Pretty much ever since Todd got married he'd been a moody son of a bitch.

Brent ignored Todd, as he had for much of the ten years since high school, forced a smile, and spoke to Rory. "I'm suggesting, just putting it out there, that *mature women* could interpret shyness as a sign of sensitivity and be attracted to it. But it's just a guess."

Brent stared hard at Todd on the word *guess*.

"I like it. It's a good theory," Rory said.

Brent knew he would. That's why he said it. Mind you, Brent thought it was complete and total bullshit. Strength and confidence were the most attractive male qualities to women. But Brent had to do what he had to do to get his friend off his ass and out of the bathroom. And as it pertained to The Panther, Rory was a lost cause. Brent knew it, and he was sure Rory knew it too, so why not ease his friend's pain and give the dying patient some morphine?

"You should write a note back," Brent suggested. "Find something that rhymes with pluck."

Rory flashed Brent a warning glance. Not fast enough.

Chapter 12

Todd
That's What Friends Are For

"What note? What are you guys talking about?" Todd asked. Then he saw the look on Rory's face. He knew that look.

"Sorry." Brent apologized to Rory and sipped his martini.

Todd played it cool. They had a secret. He slapped on a fake smile and tried to coax the truth without drawing blood. "Come on, Rory. What is it?"

Rory confessed without a fight. "The Panther slipped me a note."

Todd didn't like it. He didn't like himself for not liking it, but all the same, he didn't like it. He didn't even know what the note said and he didn't like it. It was a struggle, but he kept his smile.

"No shit? What'd it say?" Todd sipped casually from his beer.

The room was quiet as Rory unfolded the note, except for the annoying leaky faucet. Drip, drip; drip, drip; drip, drip.

"It's wild," Brent said.

Shut up, Brent, thought Todd.

Rory handed him the note. Todd put his beer down and read.

He hated it. He so fucking hated it.

How could the universe reward Rory, a guy whose balls have shrunk every year since high school? Why give that guy another shot at glory? Why not Todd? Todd wanted to rip the note up and say, "you don't get this, you don't deserve this." Wasn't the world supposed to reward the fighters? Fortune favored the bold? Wasn't that the steaming pile of horseshit college professors always spouted? He wanted to ask Brent, but couldn't fake another smile. When was Todd's return to the podium? Where was his do-over? If he had a chance like this he'd, well, and Stacy, well, he'd, he didn't know right now! But if a wuss like Rory got his chance, then he wanted one too. And there was another thing about this that stank.

"That is wild. Wow. The Panther." He handed the note back to Rory and looked at Brent, trying not to show his fangs. "When did you read it?"

"A little while ago. You'd gone for drinks."

Brent cleared his throat and stared at his shoes. That was all the evidence Todd needed. He kept his composure as he asked Rory the key question. "Were you planning on showing me? I'm feeling a little left out here."

"Of course. You weren't here, like Brent said."

"And when I was here?" Composure cracking . . .

"We were talking about other stuff."

And . . . cracked.

"Bullshit! You two always have your own secret shit going on. Like that time you blew me off for Cindy Campbell and her friend Kyra."

"Cindy Campbell?"

"Graduated a year before us? Lived down the street?"

"I know who she is," Rory said. "What are you talking about?"

"The time she had that kinky sex party, the summer before grade nine? Huh? You remember?"

Todd always felt third in the friends' pecking order. Brent would call Rory first, and then call him. Rory would call Brent first, and then him, and sometimes not at all. It had been that way since forever. Todd first suspected his bronze podium status on the day of Brent and Rory's legendary *Sex 101: Does This Go With That?* Party.

Brent and Rory grinned at each other. The little peckers remembered now. Todd never forgot.

"I'd hardly call it a sex party," Brent said. "We were what, fourteen?"

"It was the first time I went up a girl's top!" Rory raised his glass in a toast to himself.

"You created peek-a-boo!" Brent said.

"Peek-a-boo! Holy shit. Yes!"

Brent and Rory stomped around the bathroom like contestants on *The Price is Right* after a loud, "How would you like to win a NEW CAR!" from the announcer. If Todd was a better man he'd have played the part of the supportive, clapping audience; instead, he lined up the sites on an imaginary M80 grenade launcher.

"Now that was a great game." Rory and Brent high-fived.

"This is exactly what I'm talking about!" Todd said. "That was a big deal back then and you bastards totally excluded me."

Mitchell Matthews opened the door and paused. Todd stopped yelling to look at him.

Mitchell smiled politely. "I'll come back." He left again. It seemed Mitchell was playing his own frustrated version of peek-a-boo.

"Look," Brent said, ignoring Mitchell's second appearance, "there were two guys and two girls. What could we do?"

"Yeah, I'm sorry about not showing you the note," Rory said, "but don't get all crazy about something we did in grade eight."

"I will if I want. Where was my invite? Or at least a sad look on your faces as you explained to me that the peek-a-boo rule book says girls may only show their tits to *two* fourteen-year-old dickheads!"

"Don't you think that would have been weird?" Brent said. "We suddenly show up with a third guy? Here, girls, he wants to see your tits too? It would have broken the spell. There was something magical happening. They were experimenting on us. We were like dummy-boyfriends. For one night only the rules about gettin' freaky with guys a grade lower didn't apply. Next year they were in high school. We were a year away. Once that happened we were dead to those girls."

Todd was sullen. He felt awkward, childish. "Yup, one of the best damn days of your *adolescent* lives and you didn't invite me because you thought I might ruin it for you."

"Todd, listen—"

"Didn't you think it was worth a shot? You could have asked Cindy, right? She knew me. But you didn't even try."

Neither Brent nor Rory could look him in the eye.

"I'm confused," Rory said, trying to wade through the awkwardness. "Weren't we talking about the note?"

"Aw, who gives a shit." Todd grabbed his beer. "It was a long time ago. You two like to leave me out and do things in secret and shit. That's fine. You want to be a pair of asshole spies, pass notes. Good. Fine. I'm used to it."

Brent sighed. "Todd, I think you're being a little irrational and paranoid."

"Oh fuck you, professor!"

Todd chucked his beer.

Chapter 13

Brent
Photograph

Brent saw the beer coming. His brain processed the threat and came up with three choices: Dodge left, dodge right, or . . .

Brent leaped backwards, thinking gravity was his ally. The further away he was, the more time gravity had to push the liquid to the ground.

He misjudged the aerodynamic properties of light beer.

It cut through the air like a missile.

Sploosh.

Bullseye.

Brent stood frozen, arms in the air, his brain informing him of the aftermath, of that cool, wet sensation below his belt. To the public at large, it now looked like he'd pissed himself.

"Asshole!" he screamed at Todd.

For a second, Brent entertained tossing a revenge martini, but even if it hit, its effect would never be as great as Todd's atomic beer bomb.

Brent's plans to root out the graffiti artist and solve his mystery had suffered another setback. Until his penis and the surrounding area dried, Brent was stuck in the bathroom.

In the silence of the room, the sound of a folded piece of paper sliding under the door was loud enough to grab everyone's attention. Brent's first thought was another note for Rory. Rory thought so too because he rushed over and swept it up.

Rory unfolded and scanned the note. He smiled. "Todd? It's for you."

"What?" Todd stomped over, angry and annoyed, like he was the victim in the room, and not the guy with the pee-pee pants.

Brent was curious too, so he waddled after him and instantly learned why babies cry when their diapers are wet. A wet crotch is an irritating sensation.

Brent leaned over his asshole friend's shoulder. It wasn't a note at all. It was a computer printout of an old and legendary photograph.

Brent first saw this picture near the end of senior year. The photo was different back then. This new computer version was zoomed in where the original was not, but there was no mistaking it. This was the infamous Frame-a-Friend photo that spurred Todd to swear eternal vengeance upon Lewis Tinker, the evil genius who took the picture, founder and creator of Frame-a-Friend, and the former long-time boyfriend of Todd's wife, Stacy.

Ten years ago, Todd was the enforcer for the Leelin High Leopards. He could skate, shoot, and score, but loved the rough stuff the most. The home crowd cheered his fights and punishing open-ice hip checks that sent opposing players head over skates. Inside the locker room he was cheered for something else.

For luck, Todd wore panties under his uniform, the underwear of whichever girl he was dating at the time. Todd went through lots of panties his senior year. He said they were comfortable, and maybe they were, but Brent figured he did it to brag about girls, impress the guys, and tell stories. It was easy gossip that leaked out. Everyone heard, but it was contained to the locker room. If you weren't a member of the Leelin High Leopards hockey team, you didn't get to see, so you never knew for sure.

Lewis Tinker changed that when he disguised himself as a hockey player, snuck into the locker room, and took the picture. Nobody saw him do it. Next week the picture appeared on the Frame-a-Friend bulletin board. It was full-frontal with Todd halfway out of his uniform, panties on. Unfortunate for Todd, but good for press, were the French cut, pink and frilly panties he'd worn that night.

And now the panties were back. Resurrected before their eyes were Todd and his lucky French-cut frillies in beautiful shades of cyan, magenta, yellow, and black. Brent read the caption under the photo.

"Todd Bowman's Secret Life."

For a second, Brent forgot his chafing crotch. He caught Rory's eye. "Top ten things you don't want circulating at your high school reunion?"

Rory played along in *Family Feud* style. "Number one answer?"

"Incriminating photograph!"

They peeled into fits of laughter. For Brent it felt good on two levels. It was one of those belly laughs with tears that gets rarer as one gets older, and of course, sweet, sweet revenge.

Todd's head snapped up. He glared at Brent as if he'd orchestrated the whole stunt.

"That's what they call karma, asshole," Brent said. "Do an evil deed," he pointed to his drenched crotch, "and bad things happen in return. You'd rather be a happy pig than an unhappy human, wouldn't you?"

Todd looked confused. "What?"

Regardless of his unmanly gait, Brent felt smug as he sauntered over to the hand-dryer and punched it on. Todd was the centerpiece of an embarrassing joke. Brent focused on that soothing thought as he positioned his crotch under the hot air.

The pig reference was something Brent picked up in moral philosophy class. The topic was hedonism. Professor Stapleton explained that pigs live a very satisfied life. They eat all day, root around in muck, and apparently a pig orgasm can last for thirty minutes. For the time they're on this earth, pigs live it up. In stark contrast, humans are cursed with self-awareness, hopes, dreams, and their always-close companion, disappointment. The question Professor Stapleton put to the class was this: Would you rather be a pig, happy all the time rolling around in your own filth, blissfully unaware of your own brief mortality, or a human, with all the fears and foibles therein? Most everyone picked human, but there was always one guy who picked pig. Todd would be that guy.

"Tinker. That son of a bitch," Todd said.

Brent added some historical perspective to the conversation. "Maybe he's still pissed that you stole his girlfriend?"

"She chose me!"

Brent ignored him. Rory filled the gap.

"You almost kicked his ass the first time this picture appeared."

"I planned to," Todd said. "Oh, man, I wanted to so bad. I should have at Mitchell Matthew's party, but I waited. When my opportunity finally came, Stacy stopped me. Said I was *picking on him*." Todd said the last in mocking baby talk.

"Looks like he's up to his old tricks," Rory said.

The hand-dryer stopped. After one cycle there was little effect on Brent's crotch. "He knows you and Stacy are married, right?" Brent asked.

"Yes. He calls the house some nights and they talk."

With that two-sentence exchange, Todd and Brent signed the amnesia treaty. As male friends, they could forgive a past indiscretion by acting as if it never happened. By engaging in a normal conversation, and by Todd making every effort not to stare at Brent's puddle pants, they signified acceptance of the amnesia treaty.

"Are you okay with him calling like that?" Rory asked Todd.

"No, it pisses me off. Then she calls me immature and possessive and we're in a fight."

"And you think he just likes her as a friend?" Brent laughed. "No guy spends his nights on the phone with a girl he doesn't want. Those are still 1-900 calls, only of the subtext variety."

"Subtext?"

Brent knew the Mr. Hyde in Todd wanted to say, "screw you, professor," and toss another beer at him. But Todd's more reasonable Dr. Jekyll was in control now, keeping his angry emotions in check.

"Subtext. Under the surface. Hidden. The dirty talk isn't obvious, but it's there."

"Like what?"

"Like when she says, 'I was out watering the garden today.' And he says, 'Did you get wet?' And she says, 'Anytime I handle a hose I get it alllllll over me.'"

Rory and Brent laughed. Neither one of them immediately noticed the transformation.

Todd crumpled the computer printout in his fist and stomped to the bathroom door.

"Where are you going?" Rory asked.

Todd ripped open the door.

"Todd?"

The bathroom door slammed shut. Brent's joke had inadvertently supplied Todd with the magical potion.

Jekyll had become Hyde.

Chapter 14

Rory
Tainted Love

Rory watched, confused, as Brent punched the hand-dryer on and started whistling. Did he not see the jealous madman with the crimson face and clenched fists charging out of the bathroom with murder in his eyes?

"I think he blew a circuit, Brent."

Brent shrugged and kept whistling. Rory figured he was still angry about the beer-in-the-pants. He didn't blame him, but for the greater good, Rory thought they might have to intervene on Todd's warpath.

"He had that look in his eye. That stare he got playing hockey right before he crushed some guy's face into the boards."

"Stacy can handle him," Brent said, as the hand-dryer once more petered out.

"Stacy? What about Tinker? That's whose ass he's going to kick."

"Why be mad at Tinker?"

The logic appeared obvious to Rory, but since Brent wasn't on the same page, he began doubting himself.

"Because of that picture, and because Lewis has been calling his wife and doing that sub-text thing, like you said."

"That picture's part of history. It's a reunion. Have a sense of humor. And those calls? That's her decision. She could shut the door on Tinker anytime she wants. But she won't. She likes Tinker."

"Yes, and that's why Todd is mad at Tinker, for hitting on his wife."

Brent sighed. "We've been in here too long."

Rory's first impulse was to defend the bathroom like a real estate agent pushing prime property. Why, this is a wonderful place, Mr. Fleetwood. You've got everything you could ever need. The plumbing is superb. Did I mention the plumbing?

If he were stuck in here alone, Rory would climb the ladder of loser-dom from antisocial drinker to weirdo bathroom guy. Rory didn't want that. He needed to fail with dignity. Brent had to stay.

"You can't go anywhere with those piss-stained pants."

"It's not piss. You were standing right here."

"Are you going to explain that to every person you meet?"

Brent glared, but a smile cracked through. He punched the hand-dryer on and stood under it. "I'm wearing black pants and it's dark in the gym, all working in my favor."

True, Rory thought. Black was the best color to wear if you pissed yourself. "Alright, so tell me why Todd shouldn't be mad at Tinker. Prove me wrong." Goading Brent into a debate bought Rory time to come up with a dignified exit strategy.

"It's like this," Brent said. "If we were still in high school, Todd should punch out Tinker. That would be the right move. But now, as a legal adult, what do you think happens if Todd pummels Tinker?"

"Tinker could sue for assault, sure, but would he?"

"Don't know, but the risk is there. So now, as adults, we're supposed to handle our relationship problems with a different tact. Assuming a problem like Todd's, wife flirting with another guy, the only way to solve it is through her. Kicking ass and taking names is no longer an option. And that is one thing I miss about high school."

"You never got into fights. That was Todd's lifestyle. You were too smart for that shit."

"But I liked the simplicity of it. A three-minute tussle outside the gym solved the problem in perpetuity. That kind of resolution doesn't exist for adults and, really, not even for kids these days. Back then we fought with honor, with rules. If the guy was down, we'd let him up. Nobody tried to kick a guy's head into the curb. One guy won, one guy lost. We shook hands. That was it."

"Yeah, amen to the good ol' days, but I still think Todd's going to kick Tinker's ass."

The hand-dryer slowed and stopped for the umpteenth cycle. Rory needed Brent in here, but that machine could get annoying.

"He might," Brent said. "But that won't solve his biggest problem."

"Which is?"

"Stacy likes Tinker, always has."

"She married Todd."

"Stacy likes Tinker, yes or no?"

"She married Todd."

"So? Does Stacy like Tinker or doesn't she?"

"Fine, okay, but she loves Todd."

"Let's not get into comparison concepts like love, lust, and like. Here's Todd's problem. How do you get your wife to stop liking a guy she's liked all her life? Do you *a*) beat him up? Or are there *b*, *c*, and *d* options? Or maybe the answer is *e*) you can't, she will always love, like, or lust after him?"

The more Rory thought about it, Brent was right. Option *a* had the stench of a backfire. "Then why'd she marry Todd?"

"Are you asking me why people get married? We could be in here all night with that one."

Perfect, thought Rory.

"Well, I'm asking, so you better—"

A knock on the door.

"Girl alert! Put your willies away! I'm coming in!"

The door opened and in walked Todd's wife, Stacy. Brent twisted away and pretended to primp in the mirror, hiding the dark patch around his crotch.

Stacy looked tipsy with a tottering blue cocktail stuffed with umbrellas sloshing around in her hand. She wore a low-cut, cleavage-alert, floor-length orange evening gown that set off her tight, red curls.

Wild, brazen and cute, Stacy was a spitfire pixie in high school, a 5'1 enchantress with freckled cheeks, a disarming smile, and a right knee that fearlessly targeted the crotch of disrespectful boys. Rory wondered if the years had mellowed her.

Chapter 15

Stacy
Fame

"**O**n second thought, show me yours and I'll show you mine. I won't tell Todd, promise," Stacy laughed.

Brent and Rory didn't laugh. Gawd, they're taking this so seriously, she thought.

Stacy did the 'Would You Now?' test. She and some of her friends had been doing it all night, just for fun. These boys were hunks in high school. Every girl wanted a snuggle, a cuddle, or a kiss from these two, but how did they stack up ten years later?

For a guy who'd been puking his rum supper, Rory looked good, although drink like Rory did and it was bound to take a toll. His hair was thinning. Stacy remembered his perfect 80s feathered blonde hair that was heaven to run your fingers through, unless he had that coat of superglue hairspray, which made it a blonde helmet. His tie matched his shirt, and his shoes were polished, so he was still a decent dresser, but that was never his allure. Rory was the mysterious one. There was something behind his cocky smile.

He was always doing something different, always had somewhere else to be, and that made him sexy. But spend an evening drunk in a urine-stained bathroom, up-chucking your din-din, and you're about as mysterious as a baby's suddenly full diaper. No panties would moisten with thoughts of Rory tonight.

Brent sported college professor chic complete with elbow patches on his sport coat. The white shoes were a bit much. She should tell him that hot professor becomes creepy professor sooner than he thinks. He wasn't the looker Rory was, but there was something sexy about an intelligent guy who wasn't a dork. Brent radiated confidence she could feel in her thighs, like she was in the blast radius of a warm and fuzzy nuclear bomb. He could also talk. And talk, and talk, and talk. Radiation sickness became a problem. Brent's annoying ability to always be right, or think he was right, could be a major turnoff.

Conclusion? Brent might warrant a make-out session. Rory just didn't have it tonight. Pass.

"Something wrong?" Stacy asked Brent, who was making love to the mirror.

"No."

He was stalling and Stacy knew why. "For Gawd sakes, Brent, if you have to go, go. Rory and I will talk loud so we don't hear. Don't you hate that?" Her question startled Rory.

"Huh? Hate what?"

"When it's all quiet and the sound of your pee hitting the water is like the roar of Niagara Falls? But people ignore it, right? Pretend they don't hear? Whatever. I run the tap water when I go. It covers the pee sound."

"I don't need to go," Brent said, and turned towards Stacy.

For a millisecond she thought, don't stare, but her eyes and mouth had minds of their own. They both grew instantly, ruining any chance of playing ignore-the-obvious. The obvious being the enormous pee-stain on Brent's pants.

"Didn't make it, Brent?" This would be a fantastic story for the girls.

"Why don't you ask your husband? He's training for the Olympics' newest event, the beer crotch toss. Judges determine scores based on accuracy and splash circumference. I'd give him a 9.5 on this one."

She wondered what Brent said to make Todd do that. But another thought quickly supplanted that one.

"Know what I miss most about being a teenager?" Stacy asked Rory. She didn't wait for his answer. "Teenage boys. It's the only time in a girl's life she can make a guy cum in his pants."

Rory laughed. Brent choked on his drink.

"When you guys get older the first thing you do is pull it out. You're like male cats. You like to spray. Is he in a stall?" Stacy asked about Todd. He must be, she thought. "Pinch it off and get out here, Todd!"

"He left a minute ago," Rory said.

She was too late. Stacy pulled the folded paper from her bra. She knew it gave them the excuse to stare, not that they needed it. She'd caught them both looking down her top already, them and every guy she stood within three feet of tonight. Her dress was doing its job. She liked it when guys looked, but also kinda wanted to slap them. Was that weird?

Stacy unraveled the paper for them. "Todd Bowman's Secret Life."

"Holy shit. How many of them are there?" Rory said.

"You've seen it?"

"Yes, and so has Todd," Brent said, flashing Stacy a look that screamed caution, slippery road ahead. "Lewis Tinker slid a copy under the door."

"Oh he did not!" She wanted to kick Brent for saying that. Why bring Lewis and her into this? "It could have been anybody. Maybe somebody was being helpful, warning Todd it was out there?"

"Don't be an idiot. It was Tinker."

Stacy rethought her 'Would You Now?' test and decided she would not make out with Brent, ever. Radiation sickness had set in.

"He wouldn't," she said. "Lewis isn't like that."

"Oh, no. Lewis is a saint," Brent scoffed. "If not Lewis, then who?"

"I don't know." Dammit, it probably was Lewis. "It's a fucking reunion. Anyone could have a copy of that picture."

Stacy forced herself to slow down. She pulled a smoke from her purse and lit it without spilling her drink, a trick that took years of practice she wished she didn't have.

"They're handing them out with the drinks like coasters," she said, trying to be as serious as these two party-poopers.

It was like they were discussing a virus spreading through the gym that in minutes would destroy the entire Class of '89.

"That's why I'm here. Like a good wife." She rolled her eyes and capped it off with a sarcastic smile. "Lending my support in this vulnerable time in my husband's life."

She finished her drink and immediately wished for another. "What have you guys been doing in here all night? Playing truth or dare?"

"Guys don't play that with other guys," Rory laughed.

"Why not?" Stacy asked. Of course she knew the answer. Guys only played truth or dare to learn sex secrets about girls, or get them naked. No girls, no truth or dare. And girls played truth or dare with guys because they were drunk, or wanted a guy they liked to see how terrific their breasts were.

The bathroom door burst open and Todd rushed inside. His hands were full of printouts, aka drink coasters, of the "Todd Bowman's Secret Life" photo. He came to an abrupt halt when he saw Stacy.

Chapter 16

Todd
Pop Goes the World

Todd was not happy.

"My poor baby." Stacy opened her arms for a hug.

"Does this convince you?" he barked at her, tossing the pictures into the air.

He was almost in a brawl. There were dickhead wieners out there, guys who used to scramble out of his way in high school hallways, yelling witty put-downs at him. At him! Todd 'The Rod' Bowman! If he hadn't been searching for Tinker, he'd have crushed a few noses, made a puddle of dork blood, and made them wipe it up with the drink coasters they found so funny.

"Baby? You okay?" Stacy was talking again.

Todd scooped the pictures up and dumped them in the garbage, but it wasn't enough. They were still there. They still existed. He could set fire to the garbage, he thought, raise the flaming barrel over his head and hurl it down the middle of the gym, roaring like a lion and sending the frightened wieners scattering.

Somebody touched Todd's shoulder. He whirled around.

Stacy.

Rory and Brent stood in the background, watching. Todd pictured them laughing inside.

"You want to talk about it?" Stacy asked, still playing nice.

"I want to kick his ass, Stacy! I want you to stop talking to that loser! I hate that prick, and I don't want him around you. He's a little weasel. Isn't this proof enough?" Todd grabbed a handful of pictures from the garbage and shook them at her.

"Calm down." Stacy looked back at Brent and Rory apologetically.

She's a great actress, Todd thought, but that mask won't stay on long.

"Do you even know Lewis did this?" she asked.

Brent groaned. "C'mon, Stacy."

Finally, a little help from his friends, thought Todd. It surprised him that it came from Brent. If anyone took Stacy's side he figured it'd be Brent.

"Well, do you?" Stacy asked, more animated. "Anyone see him do it?"

"Don't defend him," Todd fired back. "And don't play dumb. We have an agreement about tonight."

"Yes, we do, and have I broken it in the slightest?"

"Those pictures break our agreement! He's messing with our marriage. That's the problem."

"How do those pictures mess with our marriage? Are you drunk?"

"No, I'm not drunk! But this whole situation is fucked up. Do I hang around with my old girlfriends?"

"Go ahead. What do I care? Just don't sleep with them."

"Are you sleeping with him?"

Stacy's eyes widened and she turned bright red. Sparing a quick glance behind her at Rory and Brent, both of whom stared at the walls, Stacy leaned in and spoke quietly and intensely.

"What's our agreement, Todd? Did I do anything we said not to? No. I had nothing to do with him or that picture. But you lay one finger on Lewis and we're through, you hear me? Done."

Todd had no response. His wife opened the bathroom door and left. The room went quiet.

After a moment, Rory spoke. "You really think that?" he asked Todd. "About Lewis and Stacy?"

Todd took a deep breath and lifted his head, searching for a beer, slowly recovering from the familiar battle and outcome. She'd made him feel like a jackass again, like he was the one in the wrong. He'd been so sure of himself a minute ago, so righteous. What happened? Had he overreacted? Had the hot button topic made him see fire when there wasn't smoke? *Yes*, Stacy's voice screamed inside his head. *That's exactly what you did!* He felt embarrassed. He'd thrown a tantrum in front of his friends and then been berated, threatened, and put in his place by his apparently calm, reasonable wife. Stacy had always been better at keeping up appearances. Todd wasn't good at pretending.

"Have I caught them together? No," Todd said. "But the little shit mocks me, goes to dinner with her, flirts with her, and guess what Stacy and I argue about all the time?" Todd kicked at the scattered pictures remaining on the floor.

"Lewis," Rory said, answering the rhetorical question.

"And if that's the thorn in our marriage. If that's the elephant in the room all day every day, why does she keep the asshole around? What's the payoff?"

Brent cleared his throat. Todd knew what that meant. Brent was about to unload some professor shit on him, but that was good, he decided. This was part of his life he'd hidden from his friends. He'd barely spoken to Brent since high school, but he was desperate now. He needed a sounding board, and there was no better devil's advocate than Brent Fleetwood.

"Are we in the safe zone? You're not going to get angry if I put some tough theories on the table?" Brent asked.

"Safe zone," Todd agreed. "You're not going to say anything worse than what I've thought of already."

"Maybe," Brent said, unconvinced. "And these are just theories. I say it's one of two things. And, yes, there is a payoff. Stacy's getting something from her time with Lewis that she's not getting from you, and she's unwilling to give that up."

"What though? I'm a beast in bed, Brent. She cums multiple times, every time."

Brent and Rory laughed. Todd did too, which lightened the mood. Todd took a deep breath and felt his legs solidify under him.

"She's got no complaints in the bedroom? Not a one?" Rory asked. He sounded either skeptical or impressed.

"The bedroom is not our problem," Todd said. "She's not playing around because The Rod does not perform his marital duties. Period."

"But you don't screw when you're fighting, right?" Rory said. "And you said that's all day, every day?"

Todd shrugged. "Sometimes it takes a while to cool down, but we still do it once a week."

"Doesn't matter," Brent said. "Any sack issues you have are caused by something else. My first theory is that she has a resentment or control issue. She might be defying you for spite, or worse, she's enjoying her power to get away with doing the thing you hate the most."

"Yes!" Todd said. "Both of those."

"Okay," Brent continued. "You have to ask yourself, why? Why the resentment? Why the need for control? Is it just her, or are you partly to blame?"

Todd listened to Brent and did his best to examine the issue objectively. It wasn't easy. It was galling to admit he might not be innocent. "I might get jealous sometimes."

"Sure. All right," Brent said, nodding his approval. "She might resent that, right? Might want to throw it in your face, dare you to challenge her? Shit, maybe she likes to argue?"

"She loves to argue!"

"So here you are, faced with this problem," Brent said, "and if what I saw between you and Stacy is an accurate sampling of how you're both dealing with the problem, you're not doing a great job. Are you willing to try something else?"

Todd nodded. "Hit me."

"Call her bluff. Hang out with some of your exes and see how she likes it."

"Divorce," Todd said. "That's how that would end. I tried the tit-for-tat scheme years ago."

It was the first strategy he adopted when Stacy and Lewis heated up again. It caused a two-week separation and divorce discussions, which was counterproductive to Todd's end game of a happy marriage. He didn't get any enjoyment from it either. His exes were no longer hot.

"Ignore her then," Brent said. "Pretend her thing with Lewis doesn't exist, keep your jealousy in check, don't give her a reason to go, and maybe the high she gets from it will disappear?"

"Can't," Todd said.

He'd tried that too. It wasn't in his nature—too proud. Somewhere deep down he knew he was right and he needed Stacy to see it his way.

"You think she does it for spite?" Rory asked Brent. "What about the thing we talked about before? The thing about . . ." Rory trailed off as Todd's dangerous eyes latched onto him.

"Before? What'd you talk about before?" Todd felt heat rising in him again. It seemed like everywhere he turned tonight the people he trusted most kept stabbing him in the back.

Brent put his hands up. "We didn't leave you out of anything. After you stormed off to kill Tinker, Rory and I were concerned and we discussed theory number two."

"Which is?" Todd said. "Finish what you were about to say, Rory."

Rory seemed reluctant to continue. He looked to Brent for help.

"Say it," Brent prodded him. "If it's not control, spite, or resentment, it has to be the other thing. You know what it is already." Brent raised his eyebrows at Todd.

Brent was right. He did know. But he'd never heard anybody say it out loud.

"Go on, Rory. Tell me." Todd's bitter fire grew hotter. This time it was fueled by denial. It can't be this, he thought. No way she would.

"Well," Rory began, "before you, Lewis was Stacy's boyfriend. If he hadn't moved away to go to college, maybe they wouldn't have broken up. It makes sense, right?" Rory again looked to Brent for support.

"What makes sense?" Todd shouted, getting annoyed at Rory's coyness. "Spit it out!"

"She likes Lewis," Rory finished. "As in *likes him, likes him.* Maybe loves him."

Todd stared at Rory for a few seconds, feeling the steam coming out of his ears.

"That's theory two," Brent said. "That's a tough one. Before we get into that, did you and Stacy have an agreement about the reunion? Did I hear that when you guys were arguing?"

Todd turned away from Rory, trying to smother the flames in his belly. He preferred control and resentment issues to Stacy loving another man. Some part of him already recognized the possibility, but he never faced it, never heard it spoken as a real possibility. He was still trying to shake it off as he answered Brent.

"Yeah, we had a talk last night," Todd said. "Set down some ground rules. Worked out some stuff."

"Or maybe there's a third theory," Rory said. "It might not be Lewis at all. She batted her eyes at you when she was his girlfriend. Maybe she needs that extra attention?"

Todd's head snapped back to Rory, who grinned at him. Everything went gray and fuzzy in Todd's head.

Rory shrugged. "Maybe she's a bit, umm, you know, aggressively flirty to the point of crossing the line?"

Brent put a hand on Todd's shoulder. "I doubt that. Let's not go too—"

"You son of a bitch!"

Todd charged.

He slammed his shoulder into Rory's gut and speared him into the wall. Rory instinctively wrapped an arm around Todd's head, squeezing tight. They jabbered at each other as they wrestled around the room.

"Slut? You called my wife a slut?"

"You wanted to hear the theories, asshole! What happened to the safe zone?"

"Why don't you shut up and stay in your stall, pussy!"

"At least there's a woman out there who wants me. Nice job on the wife who hates you!"

Brent tried to break it up. "Guys! C'mon! Rory? Let go of him."

"I thought you liked this, Brent?" Rory said. "The simplicity of a fight? Wasn't that what you said?"

Todd took advantage of Rory's distraction, slipped his hands into a better position, twisted Rory around, and slammed him face first into the wall, pinning him there.

"She's not a slut!" Todd squished Rory's face into the wall. "Say you're sorry."

"No vay, ash-ol." It came out garbled due to Rory's mashed right cheek.

"Todd!" Brent said his name with a dose of authority. "Enough. Let him go."

Todd released Rory but kept one predatory eye on him. Brent slid himself between the combatants and put his mediator cap on. First, he addressed Todd.

"Safe zone, right? Isn't that what we agreed?"

"Did we agree on calling my wife a slut?"

"I never said slut!" Rory said. "What if there are other guys? What if Lewis isn't so special? This is what I'm saying."

Todd bowed his head. He felt hot tears coming and turned away from his friends. "Whatever. Sorry, Rory."

"Tell me about that agreement, Todd," Brent said. "Can we get back to that?"

Todd kept his back to his friends, watching them in the mirrors as he fought his tears. Brent gave Rory a disapproving shove, which made Todd feel better.

"Sorry too," Rory said. "Bad word choice."

Todd's mind wandered back to last night, to when he and Stacy talked about the reunion, their marriage, and if they could survive the night.

Chapter 17

Todd
Touch of Gray

The night before the reunion.

They did everything quick. Slept together on their first date, got married three months out of high school, and bought a condo before the end of year one. It was the only condo division near town, and Stacy attached a certain prestige to it. They both had full-time starter jobs but money is uber-tight for eighteen-year-old newly-weds, so Stacy's mom co-signed the mortgage. That made it feel more like Stacy's house than *their* home. Still, she was thrilled to be a condo owner and spent an entire year lovingly decorating it. Todd loved that someone else mowed his lawn, so he liked the condo too. Despite the cost-cutting to keep the home, the instant noodle suppers and all the video rental nights, he remembered her being happy for the first four years. Around that time, Lewis Tinker returned to town a college graduate and bought a condo unit in their building. The next six years weren't as good.

They sat on the balcony drinking cold beer and basking in the early evening sunshine. Todd had one thing on his mind, the reunion, but was unsure when to broach the topic. Things seemed to work out better when she started these types of conversations. Todd waited, drank, and got his opening.

"I love my dress," Stacy said. "Do you still have a problem with it?"

Her reunion dress. Yes, he had a problem with it. It covered a third of her breasts, and her nipples poked through the sheer fabric like nails covered by thin wallpaper. Pick your battles, Todd lectured himself, biting his tongue. There's a bigger problem.

"It's fine," he said. "I was just surprised. Haven't seen you dressed like that in a while. You think my shirt matches?"

"Hmm, close enough," Stacy said. "Although it might be nice if you wore a tie and dress pants. It's one night every ten years."

Todd sighed inwardly. He was happy to avoid the big issue for a moment, so long as the topic remained the reunion, but she was needling him, and if he took the bait they'd never solve anything. He played along.

"Dress pants never look good on me, but I'll take a look in my closet for a tie. I could even pick one up tomorrow."

Stacy didn't say anything. She may have nodded, but Todd wouldn't know. Through that whole exchange neither of them looked at each other. They watched the parking lot like an aquarium, using it as a distraction. Until Lewis drove in.

Now they *really* didn't look at each other. There's a silence and calm in good relationships where you can be with a person and not have to fill every moment with conversation; you're comfortable with the quiet and the other person's presence, and that's a very good thing. Todd and Stacy hadn't had that for years.

Then there's the silence that comes from not wanting to talk to the other person, from hoping just to be left alone to stew in your own thoughts and pray the other person either shuts up or, if you're forced to speak, agrees with everything you say. It's an uncomfortable silence that raises blood pressure. That's what Todd and Stacy had before Lewis showed up.

Then there's the silence that comes from a super-heated, stressful atmosphere. You don't want to talk; you want to scream! It's a struggle to hold back the frustration, the indignity, the injustice, the wrongness you feel inside you, around you, buzzing through the air like invisible bees, each of them whispering in unison, say it, say it, say it! But you can't. If you speak, it will spark the propane gas that surrounds you, igniting your world in a fiery mess of finger-pointing and righteous condemnation. So you endure the silence like you would a tarantula crawling up your arm. This was Todd and Stacy's experience as they watched Lewis park in their aquarium.

As soon as Lewis exited his car, his eyes tracked upwards to their balcony. He waved. Stacy waved back. Todd sneered. Lewis grabbed a suit from the back seat, draped it over his shoulder, and sashayed across the parking lot, looking up twice more.

Lewis was short, which Todd liked because he wasn't tall either, which made Lewis a runt, a gnome-like 5'5" or something. Girls called him stocky because he was in that middle ground of not quite chubby, but with extra weight that wasn't muscle. Stacy once called Lewis "proportionally heavy-set," which was PC for soon-to-be-fat guy.

Lewis still had all his hair. But he was one of those pricks that buzzed it short anyway, and left enough so everyone knew he could grow back every follicle. Todd hated him for that.

Lewis also had one of those baby faces, the kind that don't grow whiskers, only fuzzy, soft fur that chicks love. According to Stacy, the bastard only needed to shave twice a week. He wanted to crucify him for that. Todd could shave twice a day, and hated it.

Finally, the asshole was kinda good looking. Todd figured he could change that at the reunion, given the chance.

There was no holding back now. Tinker's appearance forced his hand. "We're going to have to talk about that," Todd said.

"What?" Stacy asked, playing dumb. "Oh. Lewis?" She sighed. "If you have to."

Todd noted that she said "you" instead of matching the polite "we" that he used.

"We've been fighting a lot about that guy lately," Todd said. "You know how I feel about it."

"And you know how I feel about it. We disagree. Big surprise."

Todd wanted to contain the discussion, keep it about the reunion, and not let it blossom into a general discussion about marriage, respect, fidelity, or adultery. That would lead straight to separate bedrooms.

"The reunion is tomorrow night. I just want to make sure we both have a good time."

"I know I'll have a good time. Why wouldn't you have a good time? You haven't seen Brent and Rory in how many years?"

Todd took an extra long sip of beer and waited as Stacy launched her countermeasures.

When faced with a missile attack, modern warplanes and warships have the ability to activate "electronic countermeasures." These countermeasures can disable or confuse a missile so that it detonates somewhere else besides in your lap. Stacy often used a similar delaying tactic, which forced Todd to fire missile after missile to get the desired results. It also gave her an out. In the middle of an argument full of countermeasures she'd suddenly scream, *how long have we been discussing this? We're not getting anywhere. Let's just forget it and go to sleep.*

Todd decided to ramp up the conversation, close in, and switch from missiles to guns. "I'll enjoy my time with the guys if you're not slow-dancing the night away with pretty boy down there."

Stacy turned to him, annoyed. "I'll be dancing with a lot of old friends. It's our ten-year reunion."

"You'll be slow dancing with a bunch of other guys? That's your plan? Will you fit me in on your dance card, or should I assume you'll be grinding other men all night?"

"Gawd, Todd. It won't be like that. They'll play, like, four slow songs at the most. If you're around, great; if not, then what's the big deal if I dance with a friend?"

"Is that friend Lewis Tinker?"

"Maybe. So what? Lewis and I hang out all the time. It'll be nothing out of the ordinary."

"Nothing out of the ordinary? You two slow dancing had better be out of the ordinary! What are you saying? You and Lewis go dancing together?"

"No!" Stacy paused. "Well, not usually. I think a couple times—"

"A couple times?" Todd set down his beer and twisted his chair around to face his wife. "Like when?"

"I don't know when. A while ago. It was just dancing at some pub. We weren't screwing. Geez."

"But you're dancing, going to dinner, chatting on the phone, having coffee in our living room, and flirting. That's all okay in your book?"

Stacy laughed. "Lewis and I don't flirt. We fight. We have different opinions on most things and we debate. I like debating with him."

"I caught him with his hand on your leg. I've seen you two hug.

In my book, back rubs and hair stroking are not part of friendly hugs. And you two aren't from France, so what's with all the kisses on the cheek?"

"Gawd! You are so jealous. This is crazy frustrating. How many times are we going to discuss this same topic?"

"We're discussing it now, so I don't wind up punching that loser all over the gym tomorrow night."

Stacy's sarcastic smile disappeared. "You start a fight with Lewis and I swear, Todd." She left the threat unspoken.

"Swear what? How about you swear that you'll stay away from that sleazeball for the good of our marriage?"

"If I have to do that for the good of our marriage then our marriage can't be too good to begin with."

"It's not ideal, that's for sure. How many husbands would put up with you and your ex-boyfriend messing around like this?"

"All of the normal ones. You're just a jealous freak."

Todd made a mental checkmark. That was the first name call of the discussion. It was a sign that the thin veil of respect and civility loosely draped over the conversation was falling away.

"If you had to choose our marriage or your friendship with Lewis, which would you pick?"

"That's not a decision I should ever have to make."

"What if I made you make it?"

"If you *made me* make it? Then I think you would make it an easy decision for me." Again, Stacy left the threat unspoken. Todd felt a sudden churn in his belly. He decided to back off that line of questioning.

"You make a good point," Todd said. "About how often we discuss this. But nothing ever changes, does it? You don't make the slightest concession or compromise."

"Because you're wrong, baby." Stacy put her hand on Todd's knee and looked him in the eye. "We're married, Todd. Married. We sleep together. I'm with you, not him. Isn't that enough to show you that I love you?"

Todd made another mental checkmark. That was the first "I love you" of the discussion. There were only ever two "I love you's" per conversation. That's as big as that list ever got. It was a weak spot for Todd. He wondered if Stacy used it on purpose, knowing it made him softer.

The feel of her hand on his knee was nice. She stroked it back and forth, waiting for his response. Todd had been here many times before. If the conversation was going to end nicely, if they were going to have sex tonight, he was supposed to say, "I love you too," kiss her, and drop the subject. If he didn't, more checkmarks would be needed for the name-calling section.

"I love you too," Todd said. Stacy smiled. Her hand slid up his thigh. "But what if I said you were cheating?"

Stacy snapped her hand back, her face livid. "Cheating? With Lewis? Is that what you think?"

"I'm only going by the list we both agree on. The coffees, the dinners, the phone calls, the dancing, the kisses, the flirting. Is that cheating?"

"No, that is not cheating, you idiot!"

Checkmark.

"You're such a dumbass. How could you think that?"

Checkmark.

"To say that means you're stupid. That's what that means."

Checkmark.

"Honestly, Todd. I can't keep having this discussion with you. Maybe this isn't working? Maybe you and I aren't compatible anymore?"

Todd took a long swig of his beer, finishing it. Whenever the conversation went to this place, the end-of-all-things place, a sudden fear gripped him. Why couldn't she just stop seeing that asshole? Or offer some sort of compromise, anything! She never gives an inch! Todd's eternal frustration mixed with his fear. His belly churned again.

"One night, Stacy. Really? You can't stay away from that creep for one night?"

Stacy leaned back in her chair, staring intently at Todd. "One night? Are you saying that if I stay away from Lewis at the reunion that we can drop this conversation forever?"

"No dances, no hugs, no kisses, no extended conversations. Nothing."

"For one night?"

Todd nodded. He knew this was a shit deal, but his fear of divorce coupled with his need for her to compromise had stewed his brain into desperation. Something had to change. They could not continue down this same path. And a small part of him still didn't think she could do it.

"And you," Stacy said, pointing at him. "No fights for any reason. Agreed?" Her tone had already softened.

"Agreed," Todd said, smiling.

"There," Stacy said, rising from her chair and settling herself onto Todd's lap. "Look at us compromising and agreeing." She peppered his cheek with kisses. "I love you," she said.

"I love you too."

Checkmark. Checkmark.

Todd turned his face to meet her lips. One way or another, this reunion was the battleground that would decide his marriage.

Chapter 18

Brent
Against All Odds

"What if Rory's right?" Todd said, wiping his nose. "What if Lewis is the one I know? What if she's cheating with other guys too?"

"That is not what Rory meant," Brent said. "Rory?"

"It came out wrong," Rory said. "I was remembering this." Rory walked to the second stall on the right and stabbed at a piece of graffiti. It read, *for a good time call 555-0790.*

"That's Stacy's old number," Todd said, surprised. "How did you know that?"

"How did I know that?" Rory looked at Brent, unsure what to say next, no doubt wanting to avoid any "sluttish" talk. Luckily, Todd carried on.

"This is how we hooked up."

"You're kidding," Brent said. "You mean writing a phone number inside a bathroom stall is a legitimate way to date?"

"For us," Todd said. "I was the only guy who ever called. Stacy said it was destiny." Todd laughed.

Brent wondered if he heard right. Todd thought he was the *only* guy who called? Was he in denial about his wife's checkered high school past? He—

> *I am the rat*
> *The one who told*
> *On that presidential prick*
> *Brent, the lying asshole*

Brent's thoughts were obliterated, Todd and Stacy forgotten. He downed the last drops of his martini and snatched another from Todd's buffet-of-booze tray. Stacy's old number wasn't the only controversial graffiti on that wall.

"I am the rat, the one who told, on that presidential prick, Brent, the lying asshole," Rory said, reading from the wall. "I wonder who, eh Brent?"

"Yeah, I wonder who," Brent said with calm, scientific disinterest.

"The son of a bitch," Todd said. "He's probably out there in the gym right now."

"Probably," Brent said, maintaining his cool.

Brent hoped the evil doer was here. That graffiti was his only clue to the man that tore the shingles off his future like an F5 tornado. His plan tonight, his only possible strategy, was to raise the topic with people. He'd watch for odd reactions, nervousness, drunken missteps, anything to inch him closer to the truth.

The day Brent Fleetwood's life ended he learned the sting of betrayal. Its effect on him was as powerful as discovering his parents didn't possess all life's answers, or learning his first love didn't have to love him back. There were days Brent marveled at how that single event reprogrammed his mind in one carpet-bombing neuron overload. Most days though, he yearned for answers, for revenge.

Brent heard Rory and Todd reading other graffiti. Wonderful rhymes like, *roses are red, my balls are blue, I think they'll explode, if I don't get screwed.* Or the insightful poem, Size Does Matter: *If she's small and tight, we're nice and big. If she's wide and loose, she calls it a twig!* But he didn't join in the fun. His thoughts were of fake smiles and shadowed enemies.

Before that day, Brent was a lucky recipient of high school's lottery—he was popular. And unlike most popular assholes, he lived his life under the physician's code: first, do no harm. He did not stomp on the acne-cursed masses, as Todd was prone to do, and he never ignored the wall-flowers, as Rory often would. Brent was the elected senior class president. He was a high school diplomat and beloved leader of teen angst. But someone shot him in the back. This was the way of the world, he learned, and Brent's post-high school experiences had borne that out. He lost scholarships to two Ivy-league schools, forcing him to attend his local college, and never lasted long at a job.

If one assumes humans are inherently bad, as Brent does, and that competition is ingrained in Western culture, then logic supports the notion of cutthroat behavior. Why would a superior promote a brilliant underling, like Brent, who might one day replace him? Why not take credit for the underling's insightful work; cite tough economic times, quotas, and outdated protocols; and keep the worker-bee in the nether regions of the hive? Trusting a superior was like trusting the witch in *Hansel and Gretel* to crack off pieces of her gingerbread house and send the children home with treat bags.

Because of that day, Brent did not do group projects. This

complicated his post-secondary career. If his professor wouldn't allow Brent to do the project himself, Brent dropped the course. Better to preserve his intellectual integrity than be made a fool by attaching his name to mediocre work. Group projects required trusting your assigned morons to do their work well. *Trust*, Brent no longer had.

Because of that day, Brent would fail in life. He could never stoop to the self-serving, knife-in-the-back, cockblocking, villainous tricks that successful people did; therefore, his failure was assured.

"Everybody liked me in high school," Brent said.

Rory and Todd stopped their reading to listen to the abrupt speech.

"Bangers, jocks, preps, geeks—everybody. So what was this guy's problem? Who was this guy? Tonight, I find out."

Brent marched to the hand-dryer and slammed it on. Rory and Todd's problems were theirs now. He was back on mission. Before this night was done, Brent would confront his attacker. In the back of his mind, he tickled himself with the idea of vigilante justice. It was still an accepted practice in many cultures of the world. Regardless, he had resigned himself to his fate. When it was all over, and if he wasn't in prison, he would slink off to observe the world's injustices through a fast-food delivery window before ultimately getting fired by his seventeen-year-old manager for revealing the carcinogenic in the secret sauce.

"Really?" Rory said. "How? He wrote it ten years ago."

Brent turned his back and ignored him. There was nothing except his mission, and the memory.

Chapter 19

Brent
It's the End of the World As We Know It

10 years ago. High school.

The crack.
As far as Brent knew, only he, Rory, and Todd were in on it. They discovered it on a dare.

Mr. Tally was their school janitor, and if movies had any truth to them, school janitors were either underemployed teenage mentors, or serial killers. Since Mr. Tally never offered a word of advice, by process of elimination, he could be a serial killer. With scraggly, unkempt hair; wide, spooky eyes; and a habit of muttering while working, he fit the profile.

Mr. Tally ruled two parts of the school: the janitor's closet and the old boiler room. Nobody but Mr. Tally ventured into the bowels of the old boiler room. Until one day, while Mr. Tally waxed the floors in a distant part of the school, Brent, Rory, and Todd dared to visit Tally's lair.

Down the rusty steel steps, they discovered a tidy desk and an endless supply of toilet paper and bleach. No bodies. No calls for help. The only sound, although faint . . . was girls laughing.

Following the laughter took them back to the steps, to a dim light shining though a crack in the wall. That crooked four-inch gash broke all the way through to the other side . . . to the girl's shower. For teenage boys, this was the pot of gold at the end of the testosterone rainbow.

It wasn't perfect. Looking through the crack was like learning how to peer through a riflescope. But the guys learned fast.

On the girls' side of the wall, the shower crack was at floor-level, which meant the spy hole only worked if a girl stood at the far end of the shower, under one particular shower nozzle. That was the only way you saw it all: bum, boobs, muff—the gold. When a girl showered against the wall crack, her feet blocked the view. Other days, boobs, bums, and muffs flitted in and out of sight like hummingbirds. If you were persistent, though, and visited the boiler room often, every once in awhile you saw what you wanted, what filled your dreams, what filled every teenage boy's fantasies.

Brent invented the method that ensured they'd never be caught. Girl's gym happened during the final two periods: 1:50-2:35 and 2:40-3:25. With that in mind, the guys monitored Mr. Tally's schedule, a regimen he stuck to with uncanny precision. He waxed the hallways at the other end of the school three times a week beginning at 2:40 p.m. To get his waxing machine there in time, he left the boiler room at 2:30. That was their window.

The guys dreamt up excuses to leave class early and ogle the girls showering between 2:30 and 2:35. The problem was the girls in period two gym, the 3:20-3:25 shower girls. The guys had their favorites and some were in period two. Brent had the solution.

The key was to be there when Mr. Tally *in* his boiler room office. His desk sat at the farthest end of the room, out of sight of the steps. If you were quick and quiet, you were uncatchable! And best of all, Mr. Tally was always at his desk during last period, which meant they could spy on the girls in period two gym.

That's what Brent was doing today. He stood at the bottom of the steps, face pushed against the crack, hoping for a glimpse of a special pair of boobs.

His luck and timing were brilliant. Wrapped in a sensuous pink towel, the girl he'd been wishing for, Patricia Mendelson, chose the correct shower nozzle. *Take it off,* Brent whispered. He was already grinning, imagining telling the guys. He projected his desire at her. *Take it off!*

And then the towel was off. Patricia's ass was divine.

"Ahem."

But Brent was a breast man. Turn around, he willed her. Show me boobs!

"Mr. Fleetwood!"

At the sound of his name, Brent tore his eye away from the crack. Mrs. Bobowski stood above him on the boiler room steps. It was a surreal moment, hard to process. His body, stuck in a pleasure zone, yearned for the crack. His mind, dulled by shock, slowly registered his danger.

"Come up here, young man," Mrs. Bobowski ordered, pointing to the top step.

Brent complied, crawling meekly up the steps to sit at her feet, careful to hide his boner.

"I thought you had to go to the bathroom?" she said. It was Mrs. Bobowski's English class that he'd made an excuse to leave.

"I did," he lied. "I do." But that's all he could think to say. He prayed that she wouldn't look through the crack.

"Wait right there," she commanded. Mrs. Bobowski carefully stepped down to the crack, her high heels clicking loudly on the steel steps.

"Eh! What's goin' on over there?" Mr. Tally hollered. Mrs. Bobowski stopped short of looking through the crack.

"It's all right, Mr. Tally. I found a student skipping class and hiding in your boiler room."

"Is that a fact?" Mr. Tally turned the corner and approached the steps. He chewed on a toothpick and his wide, spooky eyes focused on Brent. He whistled through his teeth. "Mr. Fleetwood. Class president. To what do I owe the pleasure?"

The shock began to recede along with his boner, and Brent's mind raced for a way out. "I wanted to be alone," he said. "I had stuff to think about and the bathroom was crowded."

"Mmm hmm," Mr. Tally nodded. "Well, that's fine. I don't mind an occasional visitor."

"What's this?" Mrs. Bobowski asked Mr. Tally, pointing to the glowing crack in the wall.

"Well, I don't know," Mr. Tally said. "Let me take a look."

Mr. Tally glanced at the crack, but made no effort to look through. "Crack in the foundation. Nothing to worry about. I could fill that in a jiffy. Shall I?" Mr. Tally took a step down, as if to go get his tools.

"Can you hear that?" Mrs. Bobowski said.

Brent could. The girls were loud today. He picked out Patricia Mendelson's muffled shrieks from the pack. "Yeah, I heard it too," Brent said. A plan formed in his head.

Mr. Tally cocked his ear. "My hearing ain't so good."

"What were you looking at?" Mrs. Bobowski asked Brent. She still hadn't peeked through the crack.

"Well, I—" Brent coughed nervously. "Don't know, really. I was sitting here thinking, umm, enjoying my privacy, when I heard sounds. I saw this faint light in the wall, started to look at it, and then you called my name."

Mr. Tally nodded approvingly and winked. Brent felt a surge of hope. Did he have an ally?

"You said 'take it off.'"

"Pardon?" Brent said. *Oh my God. Had he been talking out loud? How long had she been watching him?*

"You had your eye to that crack for quite a time before I got your attention, and you said 'take it off' twice." Mrs. Bobowski crouched down and peered through the crack.

Brent's pleading eyes found Mr. Tally. The old janitor frowned and shrugged, as if to say there was nothing he could do now.

"Well, then," Mrs. Bobowski stood and smoothed her dress. "I think I've seen enough. Move it, mister. You're going to the principal's office. Mr. Tally? Don't fill that crack yet. I'll want Mr. Kripps to see this for himself."

"Yes, Ma'am," Mr. Tally said. "I won't fix it until your say so."

"And don't look through it," she added as she took hold of Brent and hauled him out of the boiler room.

"It ain't drugs or stealing," Mr. Tally said, as the boiler room door closed behind them. "Just sayin'."

As Brent and Mrs. Bobowski walked briskly to the principal's office, the final bell rang and students poured from their classrooms. Most stopped to stare, easily interpreting the foreboding expressions on Brent and his captor. In the seconds remaining before they reached the principal's office, Brent tried to put a humorous spin on his predicament.

"Is this really a big deal?" Brent said. "Let's take a poll. How many male students would have looked? And think about raging hormones. My mind and body are not under my control. That's just biology. Put the pot roast in front of the puppy and who can blame the puppy, right?"

"You are not a puppy, Mr. Fleetwood. You are almost a grown man and the senior class president. You should be setting an example for your students, not victimizing them. Now shush!"

Victimizing? That's harsh, thought Brent. Was her extreme reaction gender-bias? Serial killer or not, Mr. Tally had a forgiving attitude about the whole thing. Principal Kripps was a man too. Surely he'd see it with more of a "human nature" slant, a little good-natured teenage hijinks? Brent was counting on that, and his good relationship with Mr. Kripps, to get him out of this jam.

Mrs. Bobowski ushered him directly into the principal's office while the secretary watched in confusion, wondering if she should stop them. There was a protocol to this. One couldn't interrupt Mr. Kripps without being announced.

Mr. Kripps lifted his head from a stack of papers, surprised to see them. "Brent, Mrs. Bobowski," he said, by way of greeting.

Brent slumped into the "I've been bad" chair while Mrs. Bobowski hovered over him, hands on hips, her lips a thin line of displeasure.

Mr. Kripps was a former football coach. He preached a doctrine of healthy hearts and minds through education, nutrition and exercise. As senior class president, Brent was almost de facto faculty. He'd had long talks with Mr. Kripps about school administration, special events, clubs, committees, budgets, colleges, his future, etc.

Mr. Kripps was "one of the guys." If anyone was going to stop the bleeding, it was Mr. Kripps.

Brent listened in pained silence as Mrs. Bobowski recounted what happened. She used words like *lewd* and *invasive* and *disgusting*. She reenacted Brent's whisperings of "take it off," making him sound perverted and desperate. By no means, did she sugarcoat anything for the senior class president. Mrs. Bobowski was the lawyer for the prosecution pushing for the death penalty.

When she finished, Mr. Kripps sighed and leaned back in his big leather chair. "Is this all true?" he asked Brent.

Clearly, Mrs. Bobowski was not Brent's friend. She had declared her intentions, raised the skull and crossbones, and fired a volley of cannon fire. He had no choice but to defend himself. His first tactic was the gender test: man vs. woman.

"I can't believe I'm in here," Brent said. "I looked through a hole in the wall and saw some girls. Big deal. What guy wouldn't take a quick peek? I obviously won't be doing it again. But isn't it a good thing that I accidentally discovered it? Now it can be covered up."

Brent stared hard at Mr. Kripps. *Join me, my brother*, Brent thought. *Don't let her defeat us.*

"It may not seem like it to you, Brent, but this is a serious matter," Mr. Kripps said, joining Mrs. Bobowski's side. "We can't take this lightly and say boys will be boys. You're our senior class president and a valedictorian candidate. More is expected from you, not less. How do you think those girls will feel after they learn you watched them in the shower?"

Tell the girls? The thought horrified Brent. "You're not going to use my name, are you?"

Mr. Kripps shook his head. "This is very disappointing. If everything Mrs. Bobowski said was true—"

"No, sir, it was not," Brent said. "Mrs. Bobowski is blowing things way out of proportion."

Brent wasn't happy about it, but the only way out of this mess was the refuge that all guilty criminals take, the time-honored he said/she said technique; in other words, prove it!

Brent leaned forward and adopted lawyer-speak. "Did I look through a crack in the wall? Yes, I did. As any curious student might. Was I surprised at what I saw? Absolutely. Mrs. Bobowski claims to have heard me say something, and maybe she did. But she certainly did not hear what she thinks she heard. I am offended by her accusations and portrayal of me. Would I have brought the crack to your attention immediately if given the opportunity? Yes, sir. But Mrs. Bobowski ambushed me and gave me no time to explain. You could not have learned about this hole-in-the-wall before now, and I'm the one who brought it to your attention. I should be rewarded, sir, not punished."

Mrs. Bobowski sucked in a mouthful of flabbergasted air. "Really, Mr. Fleetwood? First a peeping tom and now a liar? This is what you've become?"

"Are you lying, Brent?" Mr. Kripps asked. "Look me in the eye and tell me the truth."

Dammit, Brent thought. It was easy to lie about Mrs. Bobowski while she stood behind him advocating a firing squad and castration, but lying to Mr. Kripp's eyeballs was hard. The eye-to-eye truth test is difficult to beat, and this was a man Brent considered a mentor and a friend. He either had to lie straight to his face, or confess and hope for mercy.

Brent looked Mr. Kripps in the eye and said the only truth he could. "I peeked through the crack, sir. I did. But what does that make me guilty of? Is it proper for Mrs. Bobowski to say the things she has about me, to put a lewd spin on an innocent and natural inclination as curiosity?"

Mr. Kripps listened and weighed his response. He smiled. Brent smiled back. Had he won?

"You're the smartest student I know, Brent," Mr. Kripps said. "You would have written an excellent valedictorian speech. But if you expect me to believe that Mrs. Bobowski is railroading you, that the reason you were in the boiler room was for privacy, and that today was the first day you discovered that hole-in-the-wall, you're asking me to swallow an awful lot, young man. I thought our relationship was better than that. So here's what happens now." Mr. Kripp's tone became commanding and official. "First, I'm calling your parents to inform them of what happened and why you're being suspended."

"Suspended?" Brent reared up in his chair. "For this? That's crazy!"

"Five days," continued Mr. Kripps. "Second, you are removed as senior class president effective immediately. Your Vice, Mitchell Matthews, will assume your duties."

"You can't be serious?" In his fear and delirium, Brent turned to Mrs. Bobowski with pleading eyes, but there was no mercy from her. All Brent could do was sit quietly, fight back the tears, and listen to the terms of his court martial.

"Third, related to your suspension, you are no longer eligible to be the graduating class's valedictorian. Fourth, you are banned from participating in school athletics for the remainder of the school year. Fifth, you will issue a public apology in front of the entire school to each and every female student you violated. Have I been clear?"

Brent may have nodded. He wasn't sure. He saw his life disappearing through a crack in the wall.

"Then you're dismissed," said Mr. Kripps. "Go talk to your parents."

As Brent walked from the principal's office, a poisonous thought hissed in his ear. Did someone blab on him? Had there been a rat? Who knew? Just Rory and Todd. Did they tell someone? It was supposed to be their secret! Sullen and angry, Brent avoided his friends and made his way home to face his parents.

By the time he got home, Mr. Kripps had made good on his promise to call. The conversation with his parents went as Brent expected. Mom was livid and wondered where her parenting went wrong. Dad brushed it off as normal teenage behavior, but stressed that he had to suffer the consequences for getting caught. Brent was grounded for a month. They agreed on that, but it all led to an argument, which allowed Brent to beg off supper, hold all calls, crawl up to his room, fall on his bed, and drift into oblivion.

He woke to the sound of the doorbell and glanced at his alarm clock. 7:00 a.m. Brent sunk his face back into his pillow.

"Brent! Get down here now!" Mom hollered. There was something urgent in her voice. Usually it took three or four hollers to get him up, but considering yesterday's events, he figured it was prudent to be the good son this morning.

Stumbling sleepily down the stairs, Brent saw a police officer in his living room. His mom was crying. What the hell was this?

"Brent Fleetwood?" asked the police officer.

Brent looked to his father and mother, unsure what was going on. He stayed put on the stairs.

"Yes, officer, that's my son," Dad said.

"Brent, I'm Officer Hutch. I'm going to explain to you what I've told your mother and father. One of your fellow student's parents, a Mr—" He glanced at his notepad. "Mendelson, has filed invasion of privacy charges against you on behalf of his daughter, who is a minor."

"Don't you worry, honey! You're not going to jail." Mom rushed up the stairs and wrapped her arms around him, crushing him in a hug.

Jail? Brent's mind couldn't handle another catastrophic surprise. Embarrassed, suspended, impeached, banned, and now jailed? For peeking at Patricia Mendelson's ass? He didn't even see her tits!

"You are eighteen years old? Is that correct, young man?" Officer Hutch said.

Brent just turned eighteen, and in the eyes of the law he was now an adult, not a minor like seventeen-year-old Patricia Mendelson. That meant he was eligible for what? The electric chair? Brent remembered watching news about an eighteen-year-old kid who got ten years in prison because the cute girl sitting beside him in math class was still seventeen when she blew him at a house party. Flaw in the legal system? Ya-ha.

Again, his father answered for him. "Yes, officer, he is eighteen."

"Come down here, Brent," Officer Hutch said.

Mom released him so he could walk. But he couldn't. He was on stairs again, the same place he was yesterday. Brent's leg twitched, as if to take a step, but he didn't move. Mrs. Bobowski had commanded him to leave the boiler room stairs, which resulted in the worst day of his life. Officer Hutch was asking him to do the same. Brent imagined the bad things that might happen at the bottom of the steps. His brain transferred that information to his legs, and he froze.

"Brent?" Officer Hutch repeated.

Brent looked back up the staircase, toward his bedroom. Could he crawl into bed, close the door, and everyone just go away?

"Is he going to run?" Officer Hutch asked his dad, alarmed.

"No, no, he wouldn't. Brent? Listen to the police officer."

"Honey? It's okay," Mom said, wiping away tears. "Oh, dear, look at his face!"

Based on how he felt, light-headed and in the magical world of stars and flashing lights, Brent imagined his face looked something like Patricia Mendelson's pale bum.

"Out of the way, Ma'am." Officer Hutch climbed the steps, slid between Brent and his mother, and twisted him around. Brent felt cool metal around his wrists. "You have the right to remain silent—"

"No! Stop! You don't have to handcuff him!"

Mom pulled on Officer Hutch, but Dad intervened, hauling her off the steps and away from this travesty of justice. Officer Hutch continued with the arrest.

"Anything you say can and will be used against you in the court of law. You have the right to an attorney. If you can't afford an attorney, one will be appointed for you. Do you understand these rights, Brent?"

Brent studied the Miranda rights in school, but never thought in a hundred lifetimes they'd be read to him while being handcuffed in his own home. While his Mom bawled uncontrollably at the bottom of the steps and his Dad held her tight, Brent nodded his agreement to Officer Hutch.

"Running will only make it worse," Officer Hutch said, as he helped Brent down the stairs.

"He still has his PJs on!" Mom said.

Great, thought Brent. His pile of embarrassments was about to grow higher. It wasn't Christmas, but Frosty the Snowman and his little elf pals were about to meet the morning sunshine. His Frosty PJs were his favorite. They just weren't supposed to be seen outside his house, ever.

"Privacy breach is a misdemeanor," Officer Hutch said. "It'll go on your record, there'll be a fine, maybe community service, but I doubt you'll overnight at the jail unless more parents press charges."

"Is that a possibility?" Dad asked. More wails from Mom.

"I don't have that information, sir. You're welcome to accompany your son to the station."

The fine, the community service—those annoyed Brent, but they didn't scare him like the first item. *His record.* Would he have a criminal record now? How would that affect his college applications and his scholarships? Do Ivy League schools factor criminal records into their final admissions?

"Shoes! He needs shoes!" Mom broke free of Dad's grip and rooted through the closet like a druggie looking for her stash.

"Here are his sandals," Dad said, holding up the pair Brent usually wore.

"No!" she screamed. "Those won't match!"

God bless her, thought Brent. She had to find the one pair of shoes that matched Frosty.

A blast of cool morning air ran up his leg as Officer Hutch led him outside and into the squad car. His mom and dad locked the door behind them and rushed to their SUV. Brent squinted into the sunshine.

As the famous "Frosty The Snowman" story goes, Frosty melts away in the hot sun but promises to be back again someday. Brent wasn't sure he could make the same promise. His life was melting. How could anything ever be the same again?

Chapter 20

Rory
Pour Some Sugar on Me

Brent's old wound flared up easy, Rory thought, eclipsing even Todd's crotch bomb. Brent sometimes joked that if he'd seen Patricia Mendelson's breasts, the sting would have been less. But it was a hell of a sting. Rory remembered the hard days after Brent's suspension and arrest, the interrogations he and Todd endured to convince Brent they weren't responsible. He didn't want that inquisition to start up again, but he didn't hold out hope that Brent could find the unknown rat ten years later.

Todd retrieved one of his "Secret Life" printouts from the garbage and seemed to be admiring it, maybe reminiscing about his days on the Leelin High Leopards. Hockey was big in their town, but nobody made it anywhere, not even Tommy Hobson. Things went bad for Tommy after high school. He was a drunk now.

Rory watched Todd haul a Swiss army knife from his pocket and jab holes in the picture. That's not good, Rory thought. Why did Todd have a Swiss army knife at a ten-year high school reunion?

Crap. Now he was a witness. Whomever Todd killed tonight, Rory would have to testify that he saw him with the murder weapon. And he hated public speaking.

"You know this thing has scissors?" Todd said, waving his knife in the air.

Todd's current mood was unnerving. He had good reasons to be depressed, but watching him with that knife took the imagination to strange and siren-worthy places.

Todd pulled out the mini-scissors. "One night in high school, can't remember her name now. Shit, what was her name? Anyway, I had to use these." Todd clicked the scissors open and closed below his belt.

"Umm, I'll take places you don't put scissors for two hundred," Rory said. He laughed at his own *Jeopardy* joke.

Todd laughed too. Rory was surprised he got the joke. It implied he watched *Jeopardy*.

"She told me that if I didn't trim the hairs she wouldn't perform fellatio."

"Fellatio?" Rory said. That was funny. "Can't you just say blowjob?"

"If he can play professor," Todd stabbed his scissors in Brent's direction, who was still ignoring everyone, "so can I."

"Todd, you never went to college."

"Who's the expert? The guy who watched them draw a dick and a mouth on a chalkboard, or the guy out there every weekend with his pants around his ankles?"

Rory wished Brent were paying attention. He wasn't comfortable having this conversation alone with Todd. He needed the Brent buffer zone.

"I gotta use the can," Rory said. He gulped the rest of his rum and pineapple and picked a stall.

Rory sat down on the toilet and waited. He didn't really have to go. He just wanted to escape Todd and steal some quiet time to strategize. If his friends knew his plan was to avoid Alice and escape the reunion, they might drag him outside like a perp resisting arrest. Sometimes guy friends humiliated you in the name of what was good for you. You hate them for it, and so you do it right back the first chance you get. It's the cycle of abuse that all male friends perpetuate.

Rory's current state of mind mirrored how he felt on prom night. On that night ten years ago, he'd sat in his bedroom struggling to find confidence and to formulate a plan to ensure success with Alice. Coincidentally, that was the first and last time he trimmed, Todd-style.

It was all thanks to that porn he'd watched at Todd's place. To the seventeen-year-old Rory, his mass of hair down there wasn't sexy. It didn't meet porn standards. Half as a mental distraction and half as prep for potential sex, seventeen-year-old Rory locked his bedroom door and did the deed. Remembering his struggles made Rory smile.

Once he made the decision to shave, he faced a few issues. The first was tool choice: blade or electric? The last thing Rory wanted on prom night was a bloody crotch, so he opted to play it safe and go electric. He'd start with the sideburn trimmer and clip the anaconda hairs down to size, and then use the shaver to smooth it all down to nothing.

The second issue was position. Rory had a floor-length mirror that was perfect for this, but should he stand or sit? What was the optimal body position for penile grooming? Taking a good look at his "business," the answer was obvious. Standing was the only way to reach the undercarriage. Rory slid a garbage can between his legs and stood in front of the mirror.

The third issue was speed. He had to get ready and pick up Alice soon. How fast could he perform the operation and come out looking like a porn star?

Tool: Remington Micro Screen Electric Shaver.

Position: Standing half-crouch.

Speed: Five hairs per second.

Bzzz.

The electric shaver motored up.

He took a deep breath and the tightness in his chest eased. He imagined himself as a royal gardener shaping the palace hedges. The world around him grayed.

Bzzz, bzzz.

His shoulders relaxed, his knees steadied, his breathing leveled. It was just him, and *him*.

Bzzz, bzzz.

The wiry little hairs fell into the garbage can and with each hair that fell he seemed lighter, bouncier, stronger, faster. He started to whistle.

Bzzz, bzzz, bzzz.

When it was over, the procedure, or the distraction, had dulled his nerves enough to allow him to pick up Alice and make it to the prom without incident.

Ten years later, as he sat in his bathroom stall, Rory wished for another distraction like that. He wasn't about to borrow Todd's Swiss army scissors and repeat the procedure here, so what then?

And then he spotted it. A lone green cylinder on the floor. Could it be?

Rory dropped to his hands and knees and picked it up. Dust and dirt clung to its emerald body, but it was otherwise intact and medically sound. It was omega pill, the last and only survivor of his pill bottle eruption. Salvation. All he had to do was swallow. He couldn't rinse it in a sink without alerting his friends, so he decided to trust his mother and his dog.

Growing up, Rory was disgusted whenever he caught his dog drinking from the toilet, but his mother taught him that water was the same everywhere in the house, no matter which sink or bowl it came from.

Rory flushed, and then swirled the pill in the fresh, clean toilet water. As he scooped water from the bowl to chase the pill down with, he hesitated. What if it was a fake, a sugar placebo, as Brent said?

Rory sat down on the toilet with Brent's words in his head. *If you think it's working then it is, even if it isn't.* But what happened if Rory doubted the drug's authenticity, did that mean it wouldn't work? The only way to be sure was to analyze its powdery contents at a chemistry lab. Todd's nemesis, Lewis Tinker, worked at a lab like that. But there was no time to consult him, and that was probably a bad idea anyway.

Rory's anxiety increased as he debated what to do, which defeated the purpose of the drug, or sugar pill, or whatever it was. Take the pill or don't take the pill? If he took the pill, was that a cop-out?

Suddenly he had to pee. He did it sitting down.

For Rory, the stakes were huge, like the 1988 Summer Olympics and the famous 100-meter dash steroid scandal. Tonight could be his race, his dash for the gold. If Rory won, would his knowledge that he took the pill dampen his victory? If he got caught, would Alice think him a fraud?

No, he lectured himself. We live for the moments. Tomorrow is never guaranteed. Opportunities like these come around once every ten years. You do what it takes. Todd would agree with that. Rory's regret at losing another chance with Alice would outweigh any shame at taking the pill, a drug he'd now convinced himself was pure and potent medicine.

He popped it in his mouth.

Chapter 21

Brent
Walk This Way

Brent thought he was dry enough. He was sick of running the hand-dryer. Todd lounged against the sinks, playing with a pocket knife. Rory was back inside a stall, probably huffing and puffing through a faux heart attack.

"Can you tell?" Brent asked Todd, pointing to ground zero.

Todd glanced down and shook his head. "Naw, it's fine. And sorry, man. Are we cool?"

Brent didn't answer immediately. He wanted Todd to know that his asshole move might have been funny at seventeen, but it was not okay now. Brent looked him in the eye and held it for a second.

"Yeah. We're cool."

"You going out there?" Todd asked, pointing toward the door.

Brent nodded. "I'm on the hunt."

"Do me a favor. Scout Stacy for me, will ya? See if she's hanging around Tinker, and then come back and report."

"I said we're cool. Doesn't mean I'm doing favors."

The hours were creeping by and focusing on his friends' problems was sucking up Brent's night. He needed to start interviewing now.

"Just check it out," Todd said. "Watch her for a bit, that's all. But from a distance. Don't let her see you."

"And then what? What if I see her with Lewis? That breaks your agreement, right?"

Todd shrugged. "I guess I dump her."

"Just that easy, eh? After ten years? I don't think your agreement is iron clad, Todd. I think there's variables that could sink your ship, and they wouldn't be Stacy's fault, or your fault. My advice to you is—"

Brent almost stopped himself. Here he was again, getting involved in his friend's problems after promising himself he wouldn't.

"Do a good deed tonight," Brent said. "Get yourself out of the zone. Maybe cut Stacy some slack?"

"What zone?" Todd said. "Stacy has too much slack already."

"The karma boomerang zone." Brent pointed to his half-dry crotch. "Stuff like this comes back to get you."

Todd laughed and leaned against the sink. "Yeah, yeah, professor. I get karma. I'm the guy who beat up Buddha and stole his lunch money. I've been getting karma-fucked since high school."

Brent felt a twinge of sympathy and didn't want to. Todd deserved punishment for what he did, but the punishment should fit the crime. Maybe a ten-year loveless marriage and a social rebranding as a cross-dressing hockey fairy was punishment enough. Brent decided to let it go, and in the category of good timing, he saw, or rather heard, a way to lighten the mood.

Todd was about to say something else, but Brent raised his hand to silence him. "He's pissing in the stall," Brent whispered.

Todd cocked his ear. He heard it too. The tell-tale tinkle, tinkle sounds of Rory whizzing in his office.

"There's a lot of lonely urinals out here!" Todd yelled.

The sound of tinkling stopped abruptly.

"I'll buy you a drink if you finish standing up," Brent said.

One tiny, almost inaudible, splash. Then silence.

"Screw you guys."

Rory's answer set them off. Todd laughed and smiled, and Brent laughed too, but he wasn't in the moment. He was acting more fun than he felt. He had an urgent need to start interrogations.

"Maybe we should get Mickey?" Todd said.

"No, we meet Mickey at midnight, like we planned," Brent said. "Now is my best chance to find who wrote that piece of shit graffiti."

Before Todd could answer, the toilet flushed and Rory emerged. Something was different, Brent thought. Rory had a cooler vibe, a better energy. Had he mastered himself in that stall? One way to find out.

"I'm leaving. You coming?" Brent walked to the door.

"The reunion?" Rory asked.

"No, the bathroom. Goodbye, Rory." Brent chuckled and shook his head.

"Wait," Rory said.

Inwardly Brent sighed. "No, I'm not waiting, Rory."

"Promise you won't make me talk to Alice until I'm ready, and that you won't leave her alone with me until I say." Rory's words tumbled out like a Formula 1 racecar speeding around the track.

That was a lot, Brent thought. More than Todd had asked for.

"Pussy," Todd said, smiling. Rory ignored him.

"Okay," Brent said. "But you better close that deal with Alice, my friend, or it'll be ten more bitter years in the gloomy Land of What-Could-Have-Been."

"Just gotta wash up."

Rory washed his hands meticulously, taking long enough that Brent's optimism evaporated. He was about to leave without saying another word when Rory shut off the tap, plucked a rum and pineapple from the tray, and joined him by the door.

"You staying?" Rory asked Todd.

"Yeah. I'm giving it time to cool down out there. You guys go."

Rory took his opportunity for revenge. "Who's the pussy now?"

"Bite me," Todd said, less playful, but still in the ballpark.

"Later." Brent saluted Todd, and against all odds, Rory followed him out the door.

Chapter 22

Lewis
Burning Heart

Ever since he overheard Stacy's conversation, Lewis kept one eye on the bathroom door, drank bottles of liquid courage, and waited for his opportunity. He had to be sly about it. It had to look as if he were defending himself and not instigating the fight.

Lewis imagined him smoothly ducking Todd's swing and countering with a one-hit knockout blow. That was followed by a triumphant shoulder ride around the gym to cheers of "You da man, Lewis! It's about time somebody kicked his ass!" Then a teary-eyed Stacy would maul him with kisses and profess her secret love to the world. That was the best-case-scenario, but Lewis knew the odds of that storybook ending were slim.

He was up against a seasoned brute whose hatred for him rivaled his own. But no matter if it went the other way, if Lewis had to weather bruises and a broken bone or two, if what Stacy said to her girlfriends was true, the blood and pain would be worth it.

Stacy called him last night, so he knew the drill. He was supposed to stay away from her tonight, and she from him. If they did, Todd promised he'd never bitch about their relationship again. It sounded like a good deal to Stacy, but Lewis didn't think so. Todd would never keep that bargain. He just wanted to mess up Lewis and Stacy's night. Still, for Stacy's sake, Lewis agreed, and he'd had every intention of respecting her decision—until fifteen minutes ago.

Thirty minutes ago, while still following Stacy's no-contact policy, Lewis orchestrated his picture prank. To everyone else it was a funny memory; to Todd it was a kick in the nuts. Lewis was now the heroic comedian and Todd the too-sensitive asshole. Todd had railed at the bartender, demanding to know how those "drink coasters" got there. The poor girl pleaded innocence, more than earning the hundred Lewis paid her. Embarrassing Todd had always been Lewis's best revenge. This time it came with a bonus, a bathroom confrontation between Todd and Stacy that brought miraculous news.

Fifteen minutes ago, Stacy stormed out of the men's bathroom. She joined her girlfriends, the tears started, and she vented about Todd's jealousy and abuse. Music to Lewis's ears, which happened to be close enough to hear, but not so close that it looked as if he were eavesdropping. The glittering jewel at the end of her rant was a vow that if Todd fought Lewis tonight she'd leave him for good. That was a whopper, and the keys to the time machine back to Lewis's old life.

As Lewis watched the men's bathroom, wondering how long Todd and his buddies planned to jerk each other off, Brent Fleetwood and Rory Chase exited, but without Todd. Lewis slunk deeper into the shadows as the pair passed. He knew from his surveillance that only those three were inside, which meant Todd was alone.

A dark angel had answered his prayers. He didn't need to be subtle. He didn't need to make it look like self-defense. If he caught Todd alone in the bathroom who's to know what really happened? He'll say Todd started it, and maybe Todd will say he started it. Big deal. Who would Stacy believe? All he had to do was get him to fight.

Lewis opened the bathroom door and let it close behind him. Todd was nowhere in sight. He planted his feet shoulder-width apart, chin up, shoulders back, chest out.

"Bowman," Lewis said.

After a moment's silence, a stall door opened and Todd emerged, zipping up his pants.

There's the son of a bitch who married my girl, thought Lewis. He asked her straight out of high school when Stacy was still rebounding and too immature and impatient to wait four years for Lewis to finish college. Instead, she hitched her life to Todd's putz-wagon.

Lewis was sure he was on the juice. Todd worked out now more than ever, or more precisely, he worked out his shoulders, biceps, and chest. His skinny legs never got their turn. Lewis was surprised Stacy let him out wearing his too-small t-shirts. Even Todd's sport coat seemed miniature. He had muscle on him, he'd give him that, but if Lewis wanted to sacrifice penis-size and ten years of his life, he could look like an out-of-work wrestler too.

Todd was bald now, but lucky because the look suited him. In a candid moment, Stacy told him that she liked rubbing Todd's head. Lewis hated that. It made him shave his head too, hoping for a few rubs of his own.

Todd nicknamed himself "Todd the Rod" in high school. Lewis added "Nim" to make it Todd "The Nimrod" Bowman. He had fading looks and a high school reputation that had carried him for years. He also had Stacy trapped in an unhappy marriage, and it was Lewis's duty to save her by any means necessary, including dirty tricks, underhanded pranks, and manipulations of all types. Fate had messed up after high school. It was supposed to be Lewis and Stacy happily ever after.

"Tinker," Todd said. He stood opposite Lewis, about ten feet away. They were like gunfighters waiting for the clock to strike noon.

"I hear you cut a deal," Lewis said. "You don't mind if I take Stacy dancing tomorrow night?"

Todd stepped closer. He wanted to pop Lewis in the face already. This was going to be easy.

"You ever feel like a real shit, Tinker?" Todd said. "She's married. You know what that means?"

"Just because you *are* married doesn't mean you *should* be married. We're just friends anyway. What are you worried about?" Lewis grinned. Sarcasm dripped over the word *friends*.

Todd took another step forward. Good, thought Lewis, keep coming.

"We're going to have a straight talk?" Todd asked. "That's not your style, Tinker. Had a few too many?"

"I'm not in here to take a piss," Lewis said. "Let's say what we want to say. For starters, you could never stop her from seeing me, deal or no deal."

"I think she'll stop. She gets nervous around handicapped people." Todd slammed a fist into his palm.

Lewis smiled. He knew this was going to happen, knew it the

second he walked in, but it was amusing that Todd was this predictable. He braced himself.

"Please," Lewis said. "I'm supposed to be scared of a guy who wears women's underwear?"

That should have done it, but Todd held his ground. He just stared at Lewis and then stared some more.

"Are you fucking my wife?"

Lewis hesitated. He had to be careful here. He couldn't say anything that incriminated Stacy, so he ignored the question. "You remember prom night?"

"You slept with Stacy at prom?" Todd's eyes widened.

"No!" Lewis shook his head. What an imbecile. "I'm just asking, do you remember prom night? What happened to Rory?"

"I was there, yeah."

"He had a case of the blues, didn't he?" Lewis winked at him.

"The blues?" Todd looked perplexed. He wasn't getting it.

"Yeah, the blues, moron. Think about it. I was surprised you didn't get a case of the blues too. That was the whole idea."

"Why don't you fuck off and answer my question? Are you screwing my wife? Yes or no?"

"What can I say? I love your wife's tits." Lewis braced himself again.

Todd still didn't attack. "That wasn't the question. Yes or no?"

Lewis was unsure where to go from here. Todd displayed surprising scruples. He was holding on tight, and even digging for information.

"What's the matter, Lewis? You're man enough to come in here and talk, but not man enough to tell the truth? I asked Stacy too, and she said no. So either she's lying, or she doesn't want me to ever find out, which means she doesn't want to leave me. Ever think about that?"

"Oh, she wants to leave you," Lewis said. "For lots of reasons."

"Does she? Do you love her?"

"Yes, I do." Lewis didn't hesitate. It felt good to say it.

"That's helpful," Todd said. "At least I know you're not just friends, which means I'm allowed to kick your ass!"

Todd surprised Lewis with how fast he closed the distance. He raised his fists, blocking Todd's first strike, but the second struck his head, stinging his ear and rattling his brain. Lewis jabbed, trying to create distance, but Todd didn't back off. Lewis took multiple hits to the face because that was the only place Todd was throwing. He was relentless with his rabbit punches, bing, bing, bam, bam! Lewis ducked and moved but Todd got hold of his tux, keeping him close and flailing away with his right. If Lewis couldn't create distance, he did the next best thing; he closed the distance. He wrapped Todd up and took him into the wall. The punches stopped. Lewis stuck his left leg behind Todd's right and pushed. Todd tripped and they both fell. Lewis landed on top, but Todd twisted, slipping out from under him. Now Lewis was on the bottom and—

Lewis woke up. Why was he waking up?

His head throbbed. It was quiet.

Lewis remembered the fight. He just didn't remember the end of the fight. He sat up warily, swiveling around to see if Todd was still there. He touched his forehead—a goose egg, but no blood.

"Todd?"

No answer. He must have left to share his victory with the rest of the gym. Beautiful, Lewis thought. Mission accomplished.

Love is a subjective word. If Todd used that as his excuse for fighting him, Lewis could talk his way around that easy enough.

He tried to stand on wobbly legs. He was parched, and that dripping faucet tortured him. Tap water would be ambrosia.

There was a knock on the door.

"Todd? Are you in there?" It was Stacy! "Rory? Brent?"

Lewis had seconds to go one of two ways with this.

The door began to open.

Lewis flopped back down like a sniper hit him.

Chapter 23

Stacy
Need You Tonight

6 years ago.

Each summer after high school, when Lewis came home from college, Stacy knew. For four years, she knew. They had the same friends, so it was hard to avoid him, but she did. The most Lewis ever got was a quick doorstep chat, a cursory hug, or a wave from a distance. He chose college over her so why should he get both? But now Lewis was home for good, a college graduate with a chemistry degree. He landed a good job at a textiles plant, and was putting down roots. Things changed. He started calling. She agreed to one secret dinner, for closure. To avoid drama, she told Todd she was going out with the girls.

Lewis chose the restaurant, a new Chinese place, fancy, elegant, reservations required. Todd hated Chinese, so there was no risk of an embarrassing, what-the-hell, meeting. The waitress escorted her to a table and Stacy took the seat with her back to the wall, facing the front door. No surprises. She wanted to see him coming.

She drank her water, fidgeted with her napkin, and read the menu twice. After four years, she had her choice of speeches. Calm and indifferent with a realistic approach to their lives—that would be her tact. That would show Lewis that she was over him and not bitter. The "you're a selfish bastard" speech followed by a steaming bowl of wonton soup dumped onto his wontons was the other tact.

The two waters she drank bypassed her tummy and went straight to her bladder. The room was hot. She was sweating. Before Lewis arrived, Stacy rushed to the bathroom for maintenance.

As she touched up in front of the mirror, she realized her outfit might have been a misstep. Did she want him to drool and pant and beg? Yes; however, her look might send him the wrong message. He might think she wanted to look good *for him*, rather than look good *to spite him*.

In four years of marriage, she never made this much effort for Todd. Sure, she did herself up nice, and Todd always said how pretty she looked, but Stacy never fussed about details or bothered to accessorize perfectly. Yesterday, she spent three months' entertainment budget and an entire day shopping, all for tonight.

Her dress was a tight black cocktail number with a plunging neckline. Under that dress was a pushup bra with gel cups (essentially a second pair of breasts propping up the pair God gave her) and matching thong panties. The purple amethyst nestled between her cleavage was on sale, but still outrageous for a mall jewelry store. After buying the big gem it was silly not to buy the matching earrings and bracelet.

The black knee-high boots with four-inch heels was the most

expensive item. Every woman knows that when you find boots like these that don't wreck your feet, you buy them, whatever the price.

The mani/pedi/makeover was a three-for-one deal, so she'd saved on that. She needed a trim anyway, so the up-do was just a tiny splurge, though she'd spent an hour afterwards spritzing each curl until it complied with her commands. The fishnet stockings were a bargain, under ten dollars, and the white faux leather arm gloves were thirty percent off—all great buys. She looked like an expensive call girl. Perfect, of course, but he better not think she'd done this for him!

When Stacy returned to her seat, Lewis was waiting. He rose up like a gentleman and pulled out her chair. As soon as she laid eyes on him, she regretted coming. He was fat, not that she should care.

In high school, Lewis was stocky, but it was mostly muscle. Stacy liked beefy men, guys with poundage to them, and short men. She didn't understand the short fetish. It was a quirk of hers. What she didn't like were short, fat men. In the year since she'd last seen him, Lewis had become such a man.

She forced a smile and pressed forward to shake her ex-boyfriend's hand.

"You look amazing," Lewis said, ogling her up and down. He went for a hug.

Stacy patted his back and pulled away. "You too," she lied.

"Really? I look like a spare tire, but that's what a university diet of processed fishburgers, poutine, and exam stress does to you. Don't worry, I'm getting back in shape."

"I'm not worried," Stacy said, shrugging off his comment like an insult. She put her hands to her breasts as she sat, wishing she had a shawl. He didn't deserve the vista view down her top.

They nattered about the menu choices, the pros and cons of sushi, if the duck would be too greasy, and what all the different types of noodles were. Eventually they made their choices and ordered a bottle of red wine. About halfway through the first glass, Stacy started the conversation she'd come here to have.

"You're an asshole. You know that, right?"

Dammit, Stacy thought. That wasn't the speech she meant to go with. Now she had to order wonton soup.

Lewis laughed. Not the reaction Stacy wanted. Her eyes flashed murder at him and he got serious fast. "Sorry, sorry," he said. "I'm not used to your bluntness. Yes, complete asshole."

"Selfish, rotten, uncaring, insensitive asshole," Stacy said.

"Yes. All those things. Would it make a difference if I told you I'd choose differently, if I had the chance?"

Now it was Stacy's turn to laugh. "Sure you would. What did four years of college get you? A job? Big deal. I have one of those too. What did you give up for college?"

"Diaper changes?"

"You don't get to joke about that!" Stacy pointed a finger at him like a laser pistol. She choked off her next retort as their dinners arrived. Chicken Almond Soo Guy for her, and Pork Lo Mein for him.

"Another bottle of wine, please?" Stacy smiled at the waitress, who'd seen the laser pistol and was happy to scurry away. She poured herself another glass from the first bottle and set it back on the table. Fat boy could pour his own.

"Sorry," Lewis said. "We used to joke about anything, no matter how serious. But I guess things are different now."

"And why are they different, Lewis?"

"You married Todd. I left for college."

"Correction. You knocked me up, freaked out, ran off to college, and *then* I married Todd."

"Correction," Lewis said. "Yes, I freaked out, but I had my college plans before you got pregnant. Tuition paid, courses picked, residence booked, etc., etc. That was the plan *before* you got pregnant, and you didn't like it much then either. I did not 'run off' to college and abandon you. I asked you to do the long-distance thing."

"Long-distance mommy? Are you serious? Yeah, that'd work great, Lewis, you selfish prick."

"No mommy! We agreed on the abortion, didn't we? Group decision?"

"What choice did I have? Postponing college was never an option for you."

Lewis sat back in his chair, stricken. "Are you saying that you wanted to keep the baby?"

Stacy saw the exposed jugular vein and lunged like a starving vampire. "If you had stayed we'd be a family now."

Lewis kept quiet. All he could do was nod his head, look around the restaurant, anywhere but her, and pour himself another drink.

Stacy continued her attack. "I broke up with you because I loved you. I set you free. College was more important to you than our relationship, and more important to you than family and marriage. I gave you what you wanted and moved on."

Lewis got misty-eyed. He snatched the napkin off his lap and dabbed at his eyes. This is beautiful, thought Stacy. Cry, you bastard, cry.

"I loved you too," Lewis choked between sobs. "I'm sorry. I was scared. Everyone told me I had to go to college. I wasn't a dad. I was seventeen."

"So was I. Look, Lewis." Stacy switched her tact to calm and indifferent. "That's all over and done. You said you're sorry. Apology accepted. Now eat before this good food gets cold."

They had ignored their meal while walking over the hot coals of their past. Stacy grabbed the napkin away from him and handed him chopsticks. His red, bleary eyes made her happy.

"I can't eat with these," Lewis said.

"You can't use chopsticks?"

Lewis reached for his fork.

"No!" Stacy slapped Lewis's hand away. "Here, like this." She showed him how to hold chopsticks, and after a half-dozen dropped morsels, he got the hang of it.

"Thanks," he said, smiling. Stacy saw appreciation, admiration, and love in that smile, and ate it all up, enjoying it more than her Chicken Almond Soo Guy.

She stuck to small talk from then on, and Lewis seemed content to have a normal conversation. They caught up on everything innocuous and impersonal: friends, jobs, nutrition, and the weather. As the night neared its end and they polished off their third bottle of wine, Lewis asked Stacy the question she knew he'd wanted to ask for four years.

"So why Todd?"

Stacy shrugged. "Todd was good looking, athletic, popular, and he'd wanted me for a loooong time." She grinned, toying with him.

"Yeah, I know. I hated that guy. He didn't care that you and I were going out. He made plays for you all the time."

"You weren't nice to him either. What came first, the chicken or the egg?"

"You didn't pick him because you knew I hated him, did you?"

Stacy frowned. She didn't like that Lewis had that thought. She supposed he knew she could be spiteful, but still. That was rude.

"And did I marry him to spite you too? Is that what you think? You have a very high opinion of yourself, Lewis Tinker." Stacy sat up straight and looked around the restaurant. "Where's that bill? I'll pay for mine."

"Come on," Lewis said. He grabbed Stacy's hand. She pulled it away. "Of course you married him because it became something more, but back in high school, after we'd broken up? I mean, Todd Bowman? Rebound?"

Stacy stood up and pulled her wallet from her purse.

"Stacy, sit down, please. I'm paying, come on. Please? I'm just asking if you love the guy?"

She sighed and relented, sitting down, but kept her posture rigid and composed, or tried to. The wine had made her head fuzzy and her legs unsteady. Of the three bottles they'd drunk, Stacy drunk two.

"Maybe I didn't love him then like I loved you in high school, but he's my guy now, and more than you can ever be."

"I'm glad then. I'm happy for you. Do you know why?"

"No. I don't care."

"Because you loved me enough to let me go to college. I can love you enough to let you go. And I do. I still love you."

She hoped those words would spew out of Lewis tonight. The key was that she never say them back. "You're drunk, Lewis."

The bill arrived as Lewis protested. "You think I'm saying that because of the wine?" He dug for his wallet and found his credit card. "Look at her. Isn't she beautiful?" he asked the waitress.

"Whatever," Stacy said, ignoring the compliment. "Lewis, you're taking a cab home."

"So are you, Sissy." That caught her by surprise. Sissy was an old pet name that only Lewis used. He smiled. Yes, he was drunk too.

They tumbled into the backseat of the cab together. Stacy's panties peeked into view while she shifted to get comfortable. She was slow to fix the problem and Lewis's hand found her upper thigh. She let it go for the moment. They were on their way home.

"You live in town, right? Where?" Stacy asked.

"12 Argyle," Lewis said. He rubbed his hand slowly back and forth. "Apartment building."

"12 Argyle? That's three blocks away. You could walk." Stacy pushed his hand off her leg.

"I'm lazy," Lewis said. He put his hand back on her leg.

"12 Argyle," Stacy told the cabbie, "and then the Treestone Condominiums, please."

Lewis drifted to her side of the cab as they made the quick hop to his apartment. She allowed it, and gave him her leg for the rest of the trip. He'd be gone soon.

Predictably, when the cab reached his place, Lewis invited her up.

"It's a horrible apartment," he said. "You really need to see it."

"Why would I want to see a horrible apartment?" Stacy laughed. She enjoyed seeing Lewis flirty and tipsy. It reminded her of high school.

"Because you always had an eye for that kind of thing. My white walls and mismatched furniture need help. Don't punish them because of me. They're innocent."

"There's a unit free in my condo. If your job's so good maybe you can afford it?"

Lewis's eyebrows rose. Stacy regretted saying it immediately. That was a dangerous offer. "Actually, forget that," she said. "You living next to Todd and me would not be a good idea."

"It's settled then," Lewis grinned. "You come up for a night cap and I promise not to move in to your condo."

Stacy sighed. "Fine." There wasn't much she could do. She had to go up now to stop him from moving into her condo.

Lewis paid the cabbie and together they climbed the stairs to his apartment. Inside his apartment, which he was right, was undecorated and horrid, Lewis tried for a kiss before even pouring them a drink.

Stacy backed away. "No. Lewis, I'm married. Hello?"

"I know, I know." He tried for a kiss again.

Stacy turned her head and let him kiss her cheek. What could she do? She'd said no. The room swayed and her brain was all fur and softness. She was drunk. She knew that. She shouldn't be here, but she shouldn't be impolite either, should she? She'd been mean to Lewis the whole night and she did agree to the nightcap.

His mouth moved from her cheek to her lips, and his hand slid up to her breast. Again, she pushed him away. "No," she said. "You're being bad."

"I know, I know," he said. But didn't stop.

As Lewis's hands explored her body and he moaned her name, Stacy rationalized some more. She said no twice, and she was drunk. Whatever happened tonight was not her fault. She'd tried to do the right thing, hadn't she? This was Lewis's fault, and maybe something inside of her felt bad about lying. She'd told him she was pregnant to keep him from going to college. The lie hadn't worked, so no harm done.

As Lewis pressed into her, insistent, she repeated her mantra. She was drunk and she said no. This was not her fault.

Chapter 24

Stacy
Kiss You When It's Dangerous

Stacy stepped into the men's bathroom and saw Lewis sprawled on the floor. "Lewis! Oh my Gawd!"

Instantly, she knew what happened. She didn't have to ask, but she did anyway. "Did Todd do that?"

"Yes," Lewis said, raising his head. "You married an ape."

And there it was. Despite their agreement and Stacy's threat to end their marriage, Todd had done it. That pompous, arrogant, jealous, stupid ass! She had to leave him now, didn't she? If she didn't, Todd would have the upper hand forever. This was a genuine divorce moment. All thanks to her asshole husband!

"Stacy?" Lewis watched her from the floor. He still hadn't moved.

"Sorry!" Stacy pushed it all aside for the moment to tend to Lewis. She kneeled to examine him. No blood, just a wrinkled tux, an off-center tie, and a disgusting bubble on his head.

Stacy touched the bump. He winced. "Oh, stop it, you big baby," she said. "How did this happen?"

"I stood up for our friendship, thank you very much."

"Our friendship?"

Stacy and Lewis could never be just friends. They learned that six years ago at the Chinese restaurant. There was too much history, too much chemistry, too much emotion, too much comfort, too much heat, too much, really, for a woman married to another man.

"Can you get up?"

"I don't know. I need motivation." Lewis puckered up.

"Oh, no. That would be rewarding you for being a jackass."

He pointed to the lump on his head. "Kiss better?"

"That disgusting thing? I think not."

Lewis always made her laugh. Even at a time like this, with her world on edge and her emotions somewhere between nervous breakdown and axe murderer, he made her laugh. She did things, said things, and told Lewis things that she wouldn't do, say, or tell to anybody else on this planet.

His hand found hers, fingers moving slowly over her palm and the inside of her wrist. It was quiet. There was only the murmur of music in the distance.

She shifted his injured head onto her lap. He ran fingers up and down her arm. She was breaking the agreement, but Todd broke it first, so this wasn't her fault. What was good for the goose is good for the gander, right? Stacy's mind drifted back to her marriage crisis.

She'd been gossiping with the girls and someone joked that marriage should be like a sports contract. You agree to a number of years, and at the end of that term, both parties decide to renew, or not. If someone doesn't want to re-up, you go your separate ways and sign with new teams. So, the question put to Stacy was this: If your marriage contract were over, would you renew? She'd laughed and pretended to call a divorce lawyer. The girls got a kick out of that.

She could do it; she could make the choice right now, admit her feelings for Lewis and start the next chapter in her life. She knew Lewis loved her. And it wasn't as if she hadn't thought about it already. She and Todd had no children, they didn't "connect," they had no intimacy, and they argued. But they also had a home, a car, and ten years, dammit! What would married life with Lewis be like? It was fun and exciting with Todd in the beginning too. If she could hook up with one guy tonight, she'd pick Lewis, but in the morning would she want to stay with him or go home? The strange answer seemed to be go home, but how could that be?

"Hello?" Lewis tugged on her sleeve.

She knew she shouldn't kiss Lewis, but fuck Todd! It was just a little smooch, and she felt like it. A brief peck on the forehead, just to get him standing, that was her plan. But her face lingered for a second, and that was all the signal he needed. He pulled her lips down to his and they connected.

Make out.

Lewis wrapped his arms around her and pulled her close. Her legs felt awkward under her, so she shifted to lie down beside him, their bodies pressing together. Lewis's hand slid under her dress while another pushed down her top. She peppered him with kisses, oblivious to the world around her. And in that instant—

Brent and Rory burst in, engrossed in conversation.

"She was just dancing with him. Don't get all . . ."

Stacy and Lewis separated quickly, but she knew they saw more than enough.

". . . crazy," Brent trailed off.

Stacy couldn't stand as fast as she wanted. Her dress and heels wouldn't cooperate, so Lewis helped her up. She was already blushing, and that made it worse. She made a big show of brushing off, delaying the inevitable eye contact.

"Of all the places to screw around, you pick the men's bathroom at our ten-year high school reunion?" Rory said.

His expression made Stacy ashamed, and then angry, and since she was already confused, that was a mixed bag of emotions boiling in the kettle.

"It's a party, Rory. Everybody's flirting. Don't get all weird because Todd's my husband."

Stacy's preservation instincts kicked in. She was in defensive mode, shields up, innocent face on. Should the divorce come, she would not allow the world to think that she'd been the bad one.

"Flirting?" Rory said. "Don't think so."

Brent wagged his finger at her. "In every relationship there are three worlds, Stacy. Every couple is on one of them. The first is Flirtation, Planet of Innocent Fun. The second is Foreplay, Moon of Temptation and Exploration. That's where you were, on the moon, and preparing to rocket towards the sun, otherwise known as Fuck World, Star of Passion and Penetration."

What an arrogant ass, Stacy thought. Like he had any grasp of her relationships. "Oh, that's very clever, Brent. But I was most certainly on Planet Flirtation."

"Rory?" Brent said, as if the parrot would disagree with him.

"On the moon," Rory said.

"Planet!" Stacy said. "I was helping Lewis. Have any of you noticed he's hurt? Did you know Todd smashed him in the face despite our agreement? An agreement that if he fought with Lewis we'd break up? Huh? Anybody? No? Well that happened before this little mistake." Stacy met Lewis's eyes. There was an apology in hers. Lewis read it easily and nodded.

"Yeah," Lewis said. "I was knocked out for a second, didn't know who or where I was. That kiss, that was me. I was pretty out of it."

"I'm confused. What's your agreement again?" Rory said. "Because Todd got into a fight with your boy toy, you're allowed to make out on the bathroom floor?"

"Make out? Holy exaggeration, Rory!" Stacy said. "I'm not saying there wasn't anything out of bounds, but considering what Todd did, yeah. And I'm drunk."

"I can see that," Rory said. "Obviously none of this is your fault." Rory's mocking smile made another appearance. Stacy wanted to slap it off his face.

"So you were just helping him recover?" Brent said.

"Right. I was playing nurse. Look at that thing on his head."

"Interesting," Brent said. He paced and stroked his mini-moustache. "You were no doubt demonstrating the healing powers of the breasts. They say that a plump, firm breast pressed into the palm of a male has remarkable rejuvenating powers. Did you know that Rory?"

Sarcastic dick.

"Yes, I did, Brent," Rory said. "I also noticed that Stacy used her French assistant, Madame Tongue, to tickle Mr. Tinker's tonsils. A fine display of teamwork and a very effective technique."

She was not about to stay here and let them have their fun. "Come on." Stacy grabbed Lewis by the hand. "We're leaving."

Rory blocked her way. "You know we're going to tell Todd."

Stacy didn't want to play this card, but she wasn't sure about the future, and a deep-rooted fear of starting over gripped her heart. She played her ace.

"I don't think so," she said.

"I do," Rory countered.

"Brent won't, so you won't."

"What? Of course he will." Rory looked at Brent, expecting an immediate and emphatic "damn straight we're gonna tell him!"

Brent shuffled his feet and eyed the floor.

"Brent?" Uncertainty crept into Rory's voice.

Chapter 25

Brent
Our Lips Are Sealed

She was blackmailing him. It happened ten years ago, and that little witch was using it against him.

"He won't say anything because of that," Stacy said. Grinning, she pointed at Brent's damp crotch.

The irony was almost funny. Almost.

Everybody in the room, especially Rory, was baffled. "That's got nothing to do with it," Rory said. "That happened an hour ago. What are you smoking, sister?"

Stacy cleared her throat and answered with the exquisite calm that came from superior, first-hand knowledge.

"A boy with low self-control has something to do with it."

"I was planning on telling him tonight," Brent said.

"Were not." Stacy called his bluff, eyes squinting at him suspiciously.

"Was so." What a mature and clever response that was, Brent thought. Really put her in her place with that one.

"Brent? What the hell?" Rory said.

"Remember Mr. Beauregard's history class?" Stacy said. "All our desks were in columns. I sat near the back with Brent behind me?"

"Yeah?"

Fine, thought Brent, tell him. Tell everybody. Tell Tinker, he's here too. Why not carve it into the wall and make it official?

"I used to reach back, tease him, pinch him under the desk, whatever," Stacy said.

"And?"

Stacy smiled. "Care to *finish*, Brent?"

Oh, she's got all the good lines tonight, Brent thought, as he reluctantly took over. "One day we had a substitute teacher and the class was madness. The teacher had no control. That day she teased a little further."

"How much further?" Lewis crossed his arms and glared at Stacy.

He might not like how this story ends, thought Brent. "She rubbed something other than my knee, but just as hard."

"Stacy?" Lewis's eyes bugged out of his face. Add that to the gross bump on his head and he could be *The Fly*.

Stacy shared the dénouement. "He seemed to like it, so I kept rubbing, and then I felt the, umm, is *release* the proper term?"

"No way." Rory grinned ear-to-ear.

"What?" Lewis did not grin.

"Then there was a big wet spot, like that." Stacy again pointed to Brent's pants.

"Right in class?" Rory said, enjoying the revelation.

"Nobody saw," Stacy said.

"And you never told Todd?"

"What do you think?" Brent said. *Duh*.

"What? He'd be fine with it. It's not like it happened while they were going out."

The room went silent. Brent stared at Rory.

"I said," Rory cleared his throat, "it's not like it happened while they were going out?"

He made it a question. Stacy nodded. Affirmative. They were going out.

So there it was. Couldn't skip that little detail, could they? Fuck.

It was an over-the-pants hand job. No, not even that, thought Brent. It was a natural biological function resulting from hormones and friction. The fact that it felt good was not applicable. He supposed most guys sitting in class might think, holy shit, I'm gonna blow, better stop the fun before things get messy. Brent didn't.

Would Todd care, ten years later? A mature, secure, well-adjusted person wouldn't care. So yes, Todd would care. Should Brent tell Todd? Under the circumstances, also yes, because it was out there now and only a matter of time before Todd found out. It was better he hear it from Brent than Stacy.

"We made a pact never to mention it," Stacy said. "But Brent, if you tell my husband that I was on the moon with Lewis, I will tell him. And you know what? When I tell the story, you held my hand down there and forced me to do the job."

Ouch. "That's evil."

"It's called managing your marriage. Maybe you'll understand someday."

Lewis was quiet. He'd just seen a side of his lady love he didn't know existed. Process that, pal, thought Brent, and then see if you're still horny for her.

"We're actually not going to tell Todd?" Rory said.

"The guy lives in a fantasy land anyway," Brent said. "You heard him. He thinks he's the only guy who called the good time number."

"Oh my Gawd! Is that still here?" Stacy jumped and clapped her hands.

"You know about that?"

Stacy walked unerringly to the correct stall and exact spot where her number was written. "Knew about it? Who do you think wrote it?"

"Damn, woman." Rory shook his head and laughed.

"Wait a minute." A desperate thought struck Brent. He pointed to his graffiti. "Do you know who wrote that piece of shit?"

Stacy read it out loud. "I am the rat, the one who told, on that presidential prick, Brent, the lying asshole." She laughed. "Sorry, Brent. By the way, did you ever spy on me in the shower, you perv?"

Brent smiled. "How do you think I know you dye your hair?"

Stacy punched him in the arm. "No! You're kidding?"

Brent shrugged and said nothing. He enjoyed turning the tables on her.

"Brent," Lewis said. "I might know something about it."

Brent's smile disappeared as his gaze found Lewis. His heart beat faster. The name. He needed a name. "Who?"

Lewis motioned Brent to a corner, away from the others.

"Are you kidding me?" Stacy said. "We can't hear this?"

"Yeah, share with the group." Rory echoed Stacy's protest.

Brent ignored them. Lewis pulled him close and whispered. "There's a price for what I know. You tell Todd you saw Stacy and me making out. It's going to hurt your friend, but in the long run, it's the right thing for everyone. Stacy and I are better together. You know that."

In the interest of getting the information he wanted, Brent

nodded. Lewis continued. "And you also have to tell him about the high school hand job. It's got nothing to do with me, but it helps my cause. You tell him all of that tonight. I'll need your word on this."

Brent wanted to climb into bed with Lewis Tinker as much as he wanted to sleep with a boa constrictor, but again, he nodded. "Agreed. Now who wrote it?"

The bathroom door opened and Todd appeared. He began his apology before the door closed behind him.

"Stacy, before you get mad." Todd held one hand out defensively, as if expecting her to charge. "It was wrong, I know. Tinker, I'm sorry for kicking your ass. Stacy, I really am sorry. I know better. But he provoked me. He said he was in love with you. That's not friends, is it?"

Wow, this was a first, thought Brent. Todd Bowman admitting he acted immaturely and apologizing to his wife and nemesis? Was this a critical moment in Todd's evolution, a sudden spike of unexpected moral growth? Or was it the result of baser motivations: selfishness, uncertainty, fear? This was the kind of question Brent loved to delve into.

If he cared.

The name! That's all he wanted! The fucking name!

Todd and his heartfelt apology interrupted an important discussion. Brent didn't want to be a dick, and yeah, this might be an awkward moment with Tinker, Todd, and Stacy all here, but some things couldn't wait.

"Lewis? Who?" Brent hissed.

"I said I loved her." Lewis answered Todd and ignored Brent. "I didn't say I was *in love* with her. I meant like a best friend. There's a difference."

"You talked about her tits, dude," Todd said.

"My what?" Stacy said. She crossed her arms over her chest and blushed.

"That was just guy talk," Lewis said, waving off the accusation. "We were having a heart-to-heart, a mano-a-mano, and you flipped out."

"Whatever," Stacy said. "Todd, no matter what you and Lewis talked about, you started a fight. You broke our agreement."

"I know, baby," Todd said, looking pained. "I feel bad about it. Paranoia can drive a man insane. Can you forgive me?"

"Can you accept Lewis and me as friends?"

Todd was about to say something, then choked it off. He looked at Lewis, then Stacy, and then Brent. He wanted help, a sign, a nod yes or no. It was bad timing. Brent's entire being was focused elsewhere.

"Before anyone says anything else," Brent said. "Lewis has something to say to me. Lewis, finish what you were telling me."

"Brent!" Stacy flashed him a look like he was way out of line.

He was out of line? She's in a bathroom with potentially three guys she made cum. And he's out of line? Whatever.

"We got a deal, right?" Lewis said.

"I gave you my word."

"Mitchell Matthews." Lewis said it loud enough for everyone to hear. "We went to college together. We were drunk one night and got talking about high school. He spoke about that graffiti and the day you got caught. He talked like he had a secret, but changed the subject when I asked more questions. Mitchell's your guy. Talk to him." When he finished, Lewis turned to Todd, waiting for his answer to Stacy's question.

Brent had his name. The conversation in the room carried on without his awareness.

"Mitchell Matthews? What are you guys talking about?" Todd said.

"Is it more important than us?" Stacy said. "Answer the question, Todd."

"Uh, friends. Okay," Todd said, getting no help from Brent. "But no more tits talk. That's disrespectful."

"Come here, honey." Stacy hugged her husband. They kissed and made up while Lewis squirmed. "Now I will take my friend Lewis and get that nasty welt looked after."

Todd acquiesced with a polite nod to Tinker. As Stacy and her boyfriend exited, Lewis flashed Brent a look that screamed, "do it now. You gave me your word!" Brent got the gist, but he never promised *when* tonight he'd tell Todd, and Brent was busy at the moment. He was in the middle of a quick and dirty psychological analysis of Mitchell Matthews.

Faker. Ass-kisser. Wanna-be.

Mitchell was his vice. When Brent was school president, Mitchell was his number two, and the man who assumed the mantle after Brent's impeachment. He was Samwise to Brent's Frodo, or so it seemed. High school politics are different than real politics. In the real world, when you run for President you take your Vice with you. He's your running mate, your buddy, your pal, a man who knows his place. In high school, you get the vice job by losing the presidential election. Big difference. Not a system that promotes loyalty.

Mitchell's high school claim to fame was his house parties—that was his thing. Brent remembered one party in particular, a big bash a month before prom that might have changed their Frodo/Sam relationship. They'd talked about it already tonight.

Rory had ralphed all over Mitchell's parents' bedroom. It smelled like Rory had eaten tacos and tires all day. Mitchell was freaking out. "You gotta clean this up!" he kept hollering. They weren't exactly friends, but they had a good president/vice working relationship. Brent promised Mitchell that he'd clean it up after he made sure Rory was okay. Brent may even have given Mitchell "his word" that it would get done.

It did not get done.

The following Monday, Brent got the silent treatment from Mitchell, and shortly after prom he was ousted and destroyed. Did Brent's unfulfilled promise give Mitchell the reason to initiate his coup, the motivation to steal the crown he'd coveted? It made perfect sense.

Mystery solved, punishment pending.

Chapter 26

Rory
Only in My Dreams

"Holy shit. Thanks for all the help, assholes," Todd said.

"Help?" Rory said. "She forgave you. That's what you wanted."

"Did my wife just leave arm-in-arm with Lewis Tinker? Then I did not get what I wanted."

"Then why agree to her friendship deal?"

"What could I do? Tinker was right. I snapped. I broke the agreement. Man, it felt good though." Todd threw air punches, reenacting his battle.

"It was always going to end this way," Rory said. "Your agreement was for one night only. Tomorrow Stacy and Lewis get to be friends anyway. Look on the bright side. You got a few good licks in and stayed married."

"I wanted to say no!" More air punches from Todd.

Rory laughed. "That would have been ballsy. Saying no to her face after you broke the agreement?" Rory whistled through his teeth, imagining how that power struggle might have played out. "Was it worth a shot to see if she backed down? Maybe. Now you'll never know. I suppose you're actually worse off."

"What? Worse off how?"

Rory wanted to tell him about Stacy and Lewis's bathroom steamroll, but that would violate Brent's trust. Also off-limits was Stacy and Brent's high school vanilla pants-shake. Rory kept it simple. "You're worse off because she can hang out with Lewis tonight. Before, under the rules of your agreement, she couldn't until tomorrow."

"Crap, that's right," Todd said. "He's going to be all over her, and she's drunk. When she's drunk she might as well be single. She barely knows whose dick is whose! Brent, what can I do?"

"First, I'm gonna have a chat with Mitchell Matthews," Brent said, punching on the hand-dryer and shoving his crotch under the hot air. There was lots of punching going on, Rory thought. Mitchell Matthews might be next.

"You have three options," Brent said. "Do nothing and suck it up. Rescind the friendship accord and gamble your marriage. Or divorce her. Pick one and stick with it. Rory, I know you're freaking out about Alice, but—"

"She grabbed a guy's ass out there! You saw it."

Rory did the impossible. He broke free from his bathroom prison and joined the dance. He was a man of purpose, of confidence, of hope. Whatever psychological endorphin boost he received, it worked. Rory went from bathroom mole to gymnasium lion, prowling the savannah grass in search of his prey.

To help make it possible, he used a mind trick Brent taught him years ago. Brent told him, "Act like who you want to be, and you'll become that person." The trick was to ask yourself: if I were so-and-so, how would I act in this situation?

He picked Ace Plutonium.

Rory created *Earth Wars 2200* when he was fourteen, a comic book he wrote and illustrated on the pages of a Hilroy notebook. It starred Ace Plutonium, a crack starship pilot and war hero turned mercenary. Ace knew tactics, weapons, explosives, and women. He always got the girl. In the first and only issue of *Earth Wars 2200*, Ace got three, at once. When his mom found the comic, she rolled it up, beat him with it, and forced Ace into retirement.

But for a fleeting moment at his high school reunion, Rory *was* Ace Plutonium.

They made their way to the bar, the only place you can gawk at women and not look like a leering drool-o-saurus. That's when Rory saw her.

The Panther.

Dance floor.

Laughing.

Smiling.

Grabbing some guy's ass.

Picture the starship, *Anxiety 2*, seconds away from settling into space dock when a sudden surge in the plasma injectors rocks the ship. Electrical systems fail, including impulse power. It lists to starboard. The engines struggle to fire. They hiss, they sputter, but they do not reignite. Escape pods, like little tears of self-esteem, launch in droves from the dying ship. Shuttle bay doors open as a vessel packed with hope tries for an escape, but instead gets crushed by a giant celestial hand, squishing the rear of the *Anxiety 2* in its fist. Broken and powerless, the ship plummets through the atmosphere to the planet's surface, crashing into the bathroom with all confidence on-board lost.

"It's not like she kissed him," Brent said, "and we're not exactly dealing with a shy girl here."

If she liked him so much, thought Rory, why was she grabbing some other guy's ass?

"You better get back out there," Brent said. "You too, Todd. You guys want to make something happen, it's not going to happen in here. I may need your help too, so—"

Whatever words were forthcoming from Brent halted. Silence and darkness descended upon the bathroom as Mitchell Matthews, aka, dead man walking, entered, accompanied by reunion coordinator, Gary Bean.

Chapter 27

Mitchell
Beat It

If he didn't get some stall time soon, Mitchell would have to find the nearest convenience store or bush. Too many pigs-in-a-blanket had roughed up his colon; otherwise, he never would have turned to Gary Bean for help. But when a man knows he's about to unleash porcelain hell, he needs a modicum of privacy.

"Mitchell! Long time! How you doin'?" Brent said, smiling and friendly. He said nothing to Gary.

Rory and Todd stood quietly and barely looked at them. Todd leaned against a sink, sipping a beer and staring at the wall. Rory picked a yellow drink off a tray. The guys had set up their own bar in the boy's bathroom. Rules didn't matter to this crew, never did.

"Not so great," Mitchell answered with a smile. "You guys try the buffet?" He patted his stomach and winced. Nobody answered. Rude, Mitchell thought.

Beside him, Gary took a deep breath and launched into his

planned, non-confrontational speech. "Uh, listen, guys. I don't know what mischief's been going on—"

"Mischief?" Brent played dumb.

Mitchell shifted uncomfortably, sensing tension in the room. He caught thin smiles on Rory and Todd's faces, and still the pair had not acknowledged their existence.

Gary soldiered on. "You've been in the bathroom a long time and it's prohibiting people from comfortably using the facilities. As reunion coordinator, it's my job to see that everything runs smoothly."

"Mischief? What sort of mischief?" Brent asked.

Rory and Todd snickered. Mitchell thought this would be a simple, polite, in-and-out discussion, but it was shaping up to be something far different. Was this going to get ugly? Did they need backup? The only thing Mitchell worried about tonight was Rufus Pendergast. Any other high school baggage was cake compared to that.

Ten years ago there was an incident at the pool where Mitchell worked as a lifeguard. Rufus Pendergast pretended he was drowning. Mitchell knew he was pretending, so he ignored him and continued flirting with Heather Hotchkiss in her itsy-bitsy-teeny-weeny bikini. Meanwhile, Rufus carried on with his charade until one of his friends dragged him out of the pool and performed mouth-to-mouth, making it look oh-so-dramatic. Mitchell didn't buy it, so he stayed by Heather Hotchkiss in her itsy-bitsy-teeny-weeny bikini. Rufus took his BS theatre episode all the way to Mitchell's boss and got him fired. That pissed Mitchell off.

An hour later, after Mitchell cleaned out his locker and jumped into his car, life wasn't all bad because a sympathetic Heather Hotchkiss sat beside him in her itsy-bitsy-teeny-weeny bikini. As he tried to pull out of the parking lot, Rufus and his goons crowded in front, blocking his way. "Get out of the car, asshole," Rufus said. "I almost died because of you. I want you to know what that feels like." Rufus slammed his fist on the hood of Mitchell's father's car, denting it. Mitchell figured he had two choices:

1. Get out, fight, and maybe impress the hell out of Heather Hotchkiss while getting pummeled to death.

2. Drive.

Option 2 included an assumption that the assholes would, in fact, move out of the car's path. They did. But not fast enough. Mitchell hit the gas and roared away over Rufus's foot. He felt the car lurch as he steamrolled the appendage, and in the rearview mirror saw Rufus drop to the pavement in pain, his foot dangling in the air. Mitchell was so scared he kept driving.

"You ran over him!" Heather screeched. *Yup.*

Mitchell's official police statement was that Rufus threatened his life, and he was only trying to get away. Rufus's official statement was that Mitchell tried to murder him, twice, because Mitchell was in love with Heather Hotchkiss, Rufus's ex-girlfriend. The police were more inclined to believe Mitchell. Even after all this time, Mitchell still couldn't bring himself to admit that maybe, in hindsight, Rufus was, possibly, actually drowning, a little. Maybe.

"I don't know about mischief, Gary," Mitchell said, forgetting about Rufus and trying to help his suddenly sweaty companion out of a jam, "but for what I need to do," Mitchell patted his tummy again, "I need a little privacy."

"And I'm saying that it doesn't matter what you're doing in here," Gary said. "You guys are just having fun, I know. We need to clear the bathroom is all."

"No, really," Brent said. "What mischief specifically? I want to know."

Brent picked up a martini, drank, and never broke eye contact with Mitchell. His stare was so intense that Mitchell had to look away. This was getting weird, he thought. Brent was talking to Gary, yet he was staring at him. The whole scene had a gangster vibe.

"Well," began Gary, forcing a smile like this was all routine and not like poking badgers in their nest hoping they decided to leave peacefully. "Lewis Tinker claims he was assaulted in here, and apparently your wife, Todd, keeps coming in to speak with you? This is the men's bathroom."

Todd shrugged. He said nothing, just sipped his drink. Rude again, Mitchell thought, and very gangster-like.

"Mitchell has tried repeatedly to use the facilities, and he's not alone. I already told you about having liquor in the bathroom and what do I see?" Frustration grew in Gary's voice.

Rory and Brent clinked their glasses together. These guys were acting like complete douche bags.

"In conclusion," Gary said, "call it mischief, call it hanging out, call it whatever, I would like you fellows to exit the bathroom and join the rest of us in the gym. That is where the reunion is taking place."

Brent nodded his head but did not move. "What about graffiti?"

Strange question, thought Mitchell.

"Graffiti?" Gary repeated, making sure he heard right.

"Yes, if we were writing on the walls, would that be mischief?"

"That's vandalism. That would be frowned upon, yes," Gary managed to say with authority.

Brent put his drink down and approached. He stood over Mitchell, suddenly menacing. "What did you write, Mitchell?"

Mitchell was immediately confused. "Write what? What's your problem, Brent? You president of the bathroom now?" Mitchell was unwilling to back down and take this abuse.

Brent grabbed Mitchell by his lapels and hauled him towards a stall. Taken by surprise and in a state of shock, Mitchell went along for the ride.

"Stop that!" Gary said. But all he did was yell. Not much help.

Brent shoved Mitchell's face at a wall. "Read that!"

"Brent," Mitchell started, but his voice cracked. He was shaking, adrenaline coursing through his body. He was also outgunned. Three against him and Gary Bean, who wouldn't count for much in a fight.

"Read it!" Brent ordered.

Mitchell coughed and tried again. "I am the rat, the one who told, on that presidential prick, Brent, the lying asshole. Oh boy."

"Yeah, 'oh boy' is right. Why'd you do it?" Brent, still crunching Mitchell's lapels between his fists, tried to shake the answer from him.

Mitchell understood what was going on now, and he was in a pickle. He had information, but the timing could not have been worse. Whose side was he on? Whose side *should* he be on?

In one corner was Brent, his former leader, a role model for Mitchell for most of high school, and a man fallen from grace, unfairly banished to a pedestrian life. Brent was also the guy who didn't clean the puke off his parent's carpet after he promised he would. By the time Mitchell got around to it, the stink wouldn't come out. It clung to the fabric like a ghost unwilling to leave its haunt. His parents' sensitive sniffers picked up the scent as soon as they returned, which led to further questioning. Cornered and running out of lies, Mitchell wilted and confessed to the unauthorized house party. A hefty grounding followed, along with an end to staying home alone. He was the only teenager who needed a babysitter. It was humiliating, and it was all Brent Fleetwood's fault.

In the other corner was the man who killed President Fleetwood, a man Mitchell thought he knew, but whose motive for the diabolical deed he did not. Mitchell was happy the day Brent's peeping tom suspension rocked the school. He benefitted from Brent's downfall. Karma had its pound of flesh, and that was good, so he kept quiet about what he saw. Then Patricia Mendelson's father pressed formal charges and Brent lost his future as well as his present. That's when Mitchell's nagging doubts began.

Did Brent deserve such a damning punishment for peeking at some breasts? Had Mitchell known about that hole-in-the-wall he would have been right there beside his president. At least Brent got to see what most guys had to conjure in their minds. There was some reward in that, but still, Brent's future had been bright. To whom did Mitchell owe his loyalty? Should he rat out the man who gave him revenge and paved the way for Mitchell's rise to power? Or had the time come for another sort of justice? Was it time for Brent to learn the truth, to face his shooter and ask him why?

Brent twisted Mitchell around to look him in the eye. It was just the two of them in the stall, tight quarters. Mitchell could smell the liquor on his breath and see the glistening intensity in his eyes. This was life and death.

He made his decision. Let the unknown shooter choose his fate.

"Gary, you want to say something about this?"

Chapter 28

Gary
Moment of Truth

Nausea hit Gary, and he wasn't ready for it. What did Mitchell mean, "did he want to say something?"

"No!" Gary blurted. "Why would I want to say something?"

"I didn't write it," Mitchell said, still gripped by Brent's fists. "I thought you might know something?"

"No!" Gary said. "Why would I know something?"

He should have been used to this sensation, but it was years since Gary felt like the powerless kid in the room. He started to sweat. This wasn't the plan.

Gary organized this reunion, a job that's supposed to fall to their senior class president, of which they had two. Gary never consulted Brent, and Brent never contacted Gary. Mitchell was helpful, but not enthusiastic.

He wasn't rich enough to own a personal helicopter, so the dramatic parking lot landing was out of the question. But Gary was the guy driving the BMW and wearing a gold Rolex and Armani suit. He figured that should have been enough for his movie script to play out. The story should have gone like this:

Gary Bean, former nerd and social pariah, returns ten years later with impeccable fashion sense, a bulging wallet, tales of trips to exotic locales, and an infectious charisma that draws the popular girls to him like a ritzy downtown shoe store. Meanwhile, all the cool guys would say things like, "Hey Gary, why didn't we hang out in high school? Hey Gary, let's do shots!" And the shamelessly flirting beauties would all say, "Hey Gary, how come we never dated? You're cute. Here's my number, a list of my favorite sexual positions, nude photos, and a coupon for a free blow job. Call me."

Sadly, Gary got piss on his script, again, which was more than enough to snatch him back to nerd reality and confirm the natural hierarchy. Right now he was in trouble. All eyes were on him and he could see the wheels turning in Brent's head. He had to eliminate himself as a suspect, post haste.

"Look, Mitchell," Gary said, "Don't try and blame me for something you obviously did ten years ago. C'mon."

Mitchell choked on his next words. He managed a hoarse, "pardon me?"

Gary felt sick doing it, but self-preservation is a strong instinct. In order for Gary to survive, Mitchell had to meet the front of a bus.

"This is between you and the guys," Gary said. "In light of the situation, some bathroom privacy is warranted, but no fighting, okay? This is ancient history. I'm sure you gentlemen can settle this maturely while I attend to my duties." Gary walked towards the door.

"You passed a note to Mrs. Bobowski! I saw you!"

Mitchell broke free from Brent's grip and pointed at Gary like a pitch-fork-wielding villager yelling "Witch! Witch! You're a witch!"

Gary forced a laugh and kept moving. "That was a doctor's note. I was sick the day before. Give it up, Mitchell."

"Oh yeah? You slid it into her pocket like a weasel seconds after Brent left class. After she read that note, she left immediately, leaving you in charge as class watchdog. Just a coincidence, Gary?"

Gary should have laughed it off again. He should have said, "What of it?" and agreed that he'd shoved the note in Mrs. Bobowski's pocket. He should have played dumb, denying any knowledge of Brent's hole-in-the-wall. Without proof what could they do? But Gary was in a time warp. This was high school and he was the nerd accused of an act that would end in an ass-whooping. Instinct kicked in. He did what all wise nerds did when the cool kids went on the offensive.

He made a run for it.

Todd was quicker. He snatched Gary halfway out the door.

"Help!" Gary squawked, but the music drowned out his cry. Todd hauled him back inside and kicked the door shut. He pushed him into the center of the room.

This was his judgment, Gary thought. He'd been hunted down and revealed. He shrugged, not a whit remorseful.

"Okay, it was me," Gary confessed.

He braced for the attack. Gary waited for a punch in the face or the toilet plunge. Bathrooms always dredged up dark memories of drenched hair, water up his nose, and drowning.

"You're the guy?" Brent said. "Un-fucking believable. How'd you do it? How'd you know?"

Gary took a deep breath and tried not to stutter. "I overheard you talking about the 'crack.' Whatever that was, it was a big secret.

I was curious. I followed you around for a few weeks. I'd go to the bathroom after one of you went, and I even skipped class to stake out the boiler room. When I put it all together, I checked out the crack for myself. Never when the girls were showering. Idiot!" Gary smacked his forehead. "I should have! That would have been the only naked girls I saw in high school."

Todd laughed and shoved Gary in the back.

"But I didn't," Gary said. "I waited for my chance and ratted you out to Mrs. Bobowski. I wrote my graffiti poem after you got suspended. I was proud of that."

"Proud?" Brent hadn't moved from his spot. He looked confused. The rest of the room watched Brent too, waiting for his next move. Gary met his eyes, and in that second Brent's gaze became cold steel. His eyelid twitched and he stalked forward.

"I prided myself on something in high school," Brent said, talking as he walked. "That even though I was a popular guy, I always treated the geeks, dweebs, and not-so-cools with friendship, politeness, and respect, possibly sacrificing a portion of my own popularity to make you . . ." The word *you* slid off Brent's tongue like slime. He grabbed Gary's neck and squeezed. ". . . and guys like you, feel better about themselves. This is a stab in the back, Gary. A kick in the nuts. I never picked on you. I never made fun of you. But you ruined my life."

Brent's fist slammed Gary in the nose. Blood exploded into the air like a burst pimple. Gary staggered, crying out in pain. The sting made his eyes flood with tears. He cupped his face, but blood had already drained onto his shirt. Around him, cheers rang out, calling for the beating to continue.

Gary didn't see the next blow, but his chin cracked and his head slammed back from the force of the uppercut. His knees buckled and he crumpled to the floor. Gary braced for the fall but his hands were slick with blood and slid away from him. Blood ran freely from his nose as Brent loomed over him.

"Why?" Brent asked, but didn't wait for an answer. He reached down to pull him up, arm cocking back for another hit . . . but Gary lunged. He stood quickly and rushed the door, but Todd blocked his path again.

"Help!" Gary yelled, hoping someone would hear and come to his rescue.

"You're not walkin' out of here, Bean," Todd said. "But you might crawl."

"I'll sue you!" Gary threatened.

"Tell me why, Gary. Then you can go." Brent closed the distance between them. Rory and Mitchell followed a few steps behind, quiet and watchful, their bloodlust not nearly as high as Brent's and Todd's. There was a time Mitchell would have come to his defense, but not after Gary threw him under the bus.

"The short version?" Gary said. "You were an asshole. Said mean things and *lied*. I thought we were friends."

"Friends?" laughed Todd. "You and Brent? Since when?"

"We hung out in class."

"In class? You mean you were forced to sit together because the teacher assigned seats?"

"Whatever," Gary said. "The cops weren't my fault. It was just a prank before that. Payback."

"Payback for what?" Brent said. "What lie are you talking about? What did I say that could justify this?"

The old memory sparked in Gary. It filled him with anger, as it had many times before, and the anger gave him strength.

"Lies can do a lot," Gary said. He wiped his face, smearing

blood. "I ruined your life, you said? You treated me with friendship, politeness, and respect, you said? Is that the way you remember yourself in high school?"

It might have been the right cross, the uppercut, the blood, or maybe it was just his moment, but Gary felt his anger grow into something new, something unfamiliar. This must be what people feel like before a fight, he thought. This must be adrenaline! Until now, he wasn't sure his body manufactured that chemical. For the first time in Gary Bean's life, he put his fists up.

"Have you forgotten Spring Carnival, senior year?" Gary said.

"Spring Carnival?" Brent looked perplexed.

Spring Carnival. For Gary, the day the earth stood still.

Because of Spring Carnival, Gary's nickname at work was Mean Bean, the Jolly Green Asshole. There were times, usually during those long, boring status meetings, when Gary's mind wandered. As he daydreamed through the farm field of his life, Gary's foot would always land on that big squishy cow pie that was Spring-fucking-Carnival. It was like throwing a switch. Lightning bolts crashed and the mad scientist screamed, "It's alive! It's alive!" as Frankenstein rose from the boardroom table to throttle the closest victim. While in his Spring Carnival trance, Gary fired six employees, threw seven staplers, and spit his gum out fourteen times.

Chapter 29

Gary
Down Under

10 years ago. Spring Carnival.

Gary Bean never had it better. This is what it felt like to be popular. This is what it felt like to have attention, to be admired, to be liked!

Even underwater, with air bubbles swarming around his silly grin, he could see her through the glass. She stood tall in the crowd, arms in the air, jumping up and down. His ears were water-plugged, but the cheers were unmistakable and swelled him with pride. They were for him and his Spring Carnival date, the beautiful Peggy Sanders.

The glory days of Gary Bean's high school life occurred during a 30-hour stretch in June. They began during lunch period, Thursday, June 4, as he sat alone in the cafeteria summoning the courage to approach a girl and make words come out of his mouth.

Boys teased the object of Gary's affection, calling her a giant or a Sasquatch, but the 6'1" frame and long legs of Peggy Sanders mesmerized Gary. He could see what his short-sighted classmates could not; Peggy Sanders was a supermodel. When she left high school she'd be famous and beautiful.

They were opposites. Peggy was the tall, lanky blonde, towering over her friends and teachers like a giraffe. Gary was a short, portly, dark-haired hippo. Giraffes and hippos don't make the best slow-dance partners, but Gary was convinced the pair would fit where it counted most.

He was the new kid in school. His father had relocated for a job, and Gary hadn't made any friends yet. It's not easy moving during your senior year, especially when you're the fat, smart kid. In English and History, Gary sat next to one of the cool kids, Brent Fleetwood. He considered Brent almost a friend, though they only saw each other in class, and only talked for a minute before or after.

Something Brent said that morning helped. As they sat at their desks, Gary asked Brent's opinion of Peggy.

"Do you think Peggy Sanders is too tall for a girl?" he asked.

Brent grinned and said, "They're all the same height laying down."

Gary blushed. One step at a time, he lectured himself. First, he had to get the date! It felt good to have his feelings validated, though, and for someone not to insult Peggy for her height.

Gary hatched Operation Beanstalk two weeks ago when Mr. Beauregard asked for volunteers to work their Spring Carnival booth. At his old school, Gary had volunteered the two previous years, and each year he'd watched the non-volunteers and their dates having fun while he counted change, swept up their garbage, and went home alone. Not this time, he thought, not in my final year. This year he'd be on the other side of the booth, and maybe, with a little luck, he'd walk Peggy Sanders home.

According to the Operation Beanstalk Manifesto, Gary asked Peggy to be his date one week before Spring Carnival. But as he sat in the cafeteria today, on the *day* before Spring Carnival, he still hadn't asked. What he had done was plow through two fish burgers, two rice pilafs, four mini yogurts, two bananas, and two puddings. It was double his usual cafeteria spread—and he ate it all with no appetite. Peggy always took the entire lunch period to finish her tray, and usually left half of it. Gary could polish off his tray in five minutes, but food was his excuse to linger in the cafeteria and summon his courage. Courage was in short supply right now, which meant he required a large food supply.

He'd written his speech multiple times over lunch, and tried to steady his nerves by simplifying what he had to do. He had to walk and he had to talk. Babies could do that. Simple. Still, his butt remained glued to his chair.

When the bell rang signaling five minutes until class, and Peggy and her friends stood to leave, Gary accepted his fate and adopted a new life philosophy: Better to never try and never fail than try and get rejected. Life would be easier that way, if less exciting. There was always *Playboy* for those lonely nights. He gathered up his garbage and his speeches, and followed the herd to the exit.

As Gary waited in line at the garbage cans, he watched Peggy, laughing with her friends and throwing out an untouched pudding. How could he date a girl who didn't like pudding? It never would have worked. As Peggy placed her empty tray on top of the garbage can, she looked back.

"What?" she asked, concerned.

Gary's heart thudded to a halt. He looked left and right, then back at her. Was she talking to him?

"What, what?" Gary said, trying to understand why he couldn't feel his legs.

"You frowned at me," Peggy said. "Did I do something wrong?"

Yes, you threw out a perfectly good pudding and rejected me in my mind, Gary thought, but wisely did not say. Instead, he did what he had never done before. He did not retreat. He channeled his inner Marine, daring to do the most amazing, gutsy, and improvisational act of his young and uneventful life.

"I've got something for you," Gary said. Setting his tray on the floor, he turned his back to Peggy and shuffled through his papers. He chose the latest version of his speech, the one with the fewest words scrawled out, and folded it up like a note. Then he turned and handed the note to Peggy.

"Here."

Peggy took it with a "thanks," and together with her giggling friends made her way out of the cafeteria.

Gary did all of that while surrounded by gawking students. He saw envy in that garbage line from guys who wished they had the guts to do what Gary had just done!

As he left the cafeteria on the wings of the victorious, the first thing Gary wanted to do was share his triumph with Brent, but he had to wait until last period. Gary knew Brent would congratulate him where nobody else would.

Gary's victorious feeling lasted two minutes. Then came the sweat. When would she reply? Would she reply at all? How would she reply? By note, by face? Most importantly, what would be her reply?

Along with the sweat came self-doubt. That was Gary's first-ever high school note. He'd passed notes along for other people, so he knew they generally looked more polished than his. Had he left any speech annotations in the version he gave her? He hoped not. That'd be weird.

Hi Peggy,

You don't know me that well, but we're in two classes together. Do you know my name? [PAUSE FOR ANSWER.] Gary, yes [REMEMBER TO SMILE]. Anyway, are you going to Spring Carnival tomorrow, or are you working it? [IF GOING, PROCEED TO NEXT SENTENCE; IF WORKING, PROCEED TO LAST SENTENCE.] Great, me too. I was just wondering if you wanted to go together, like a date, you and I? What do you think? [TRY NOT TO SAY ANYTHING. LET HER THINK ABOUT IT.] Yes? Super, I'll pick you up at 5, sound good? Maybe? [REACT TO THIS ANSWER WITH A SMILE.] Well, let me know when you can. Bye for now. No? [DON'T FREAK OUT.] Okay, well if you ever want to hang out sometime you know where to find me. Bye for now.

When Gary arrived for last period there was no word from Peggy. He didn't want to share his triumph with Brent anymore because it might not be a triumph. Brent was busy with Todd and Rory anyway, whispering about things Gary's social status did not give him clearance for. What the hell was "the crack," he wondered. They were obviously trying to keep it a secret.

"Mind your business, Bean," Todd said. "Quit eyeballin' us."

Mrs. Bobowski walked in and Todd and Rory slunk back to their seats.

"You okay, Gary?" Brent asked. "You look sick."

Gary had ten seconds to spill his guts. He leaned over and whispered.

"I asked Peggy Sanders to Spring Carnival. Gave her a note. No reply yet. Looks bad. What do you think?"

Brent smiled and flashed the thumbs up. "Nice. Listen, she's got plenty of time. If you get a reply today, it'll be after final bell. Guaranteed. If you don't hear by then, tomorrow morning for sure. Peggy's not the kind of girl to play games and leave you hanging."

Gary never spoke to Brent again that day, but didn't need to. Brent's words returned the color to his cheeks, so when Gary stood in the bus line he didn't look like crap when Brent's prediction came true.

Peggy approached carrying a note. "Hi," she said, shyly handing him her reply before walking away.

Dear Gary,

Thank you for asking me to be your Spring Carnival date. I think it would be fun! And, yes, you can pick me up at 5:00. Do you know where I live? 110 Orchard Lane, green house, opposite the church. I imagine my parents will want to meet you first. Are you okay with that? Next time, you can talk to me in person. Judging from your speech notes, you would have done fine :)

Peggy

Gary skipped the bus line and ran home instead. He had to

burn off his double lunch so he could fit into his favorite shirt for his first ever date!

He was now in the middle of his glory days, the eye of the hurricane, but nobody, not even Brent, could have predicted the storm to come.

Friday, June 5. Spring Carnival. 5:15 p.m. Gary and Peggy passed under the balloon-covered archway into the school parking lot, the site of Leelin High's annual Spring Carnival. Peggy's presence beside him was like a lodestone, drawing him towards her. Gary fought the constant desire to "accidentally" brush against her. It was unbearably amazing.

The day was summertime hot with nothing but blue sky, perfect for the carnival. Peggy wore a yellow summer dress and makeup like Gary had never seen before. How could anyone not see her beauty today? Weirdly, that thought scared him. What if other guys noticed his prize? Peggy was Gary's hidden gem, but if she had other suitors, how long would she stay with him? Gary took a deep breath and smiled. He was barely a half-hour into his first date and already jealous of phantom rivals. I must love this girl, he thought, so don't blow it by being a jackass.

Gary starved himself since yesterday to fit into his cool clothes. He wore his favorite Hawaiian dress shirt—dark green with bright flowers, coconuts, and pineapples dancing across every inch. He left it untucked with a white shirt underneath. The first thing Peggy said when she answered the door was, "I love your shirt." Mission accomplished.

His shorts were cargo-style, wide and baggy and covered with pockets. Gary could fit whatever he needed into those shorts, and he had: comb, lip balm, sunscreen, tissues, contact lense solution, allergy pills, aspirin, breath spray, and a bus schedule. He was ready for anything.

"What do you want to do first?" Peggy asked, as they surveyed the carnival chaos around them.

Each homeroom had its own game or food station. Food was easy for Gary, but games were not. He broke carnival games down into four categories. 1) Sports games, which he did not do well. 2) Water games, which, if they required taking off his shirt, he would run from. 3) Games of chance, which required no real skill. These he could do. 4) Mind and puzzle games, which were his bread-and-butter. These he would focus on.

"Look!" Peggy said. "They have the egg race!"

Great, thought Gary. Category one. Although not an outright sports game like Hit the Hoops, Sniper Shot, or the Wheelbarrow Race, the Egg Race still required speed, balance, and coordination. Three things not in Gary's cargo shorts.

Peggy held her hand out for Gary.

Her hand.

Gary reached forward and squeezed her hand around his. She smiled and propelled him forward.

She held his hand the whole time they watched the egg races, which distracted Gary. He wasn't fully cognizant of the rules when Peggy handed the booth operator tickets for two, and shoved Gary into his lane.

"You go," Gary said, trying to back out. "I don't think this is my event."

"I hope not," Peggy said. "That gives me a better chance of winning." She put her egg on her spoon, and turned her eyes forward, ready for the race.

There were four egg carriers per race. Gary and Peggy were up against flat-chested Emily Neeman and her large-chested friend Patricia Mendelson. Gary chastised himself for noticing those details, but of all six boobs on the starting line, he thought Peggy had the best pair. That made him happy.

Someone handed Gary an egg. He reluctantly put it on his spoon and readied himself to be humiliated by three girls. He knew he'd hear about it tomorrow from some asshole with nothing better to do than recount Gary's unmanly failures.

"Racers ready!" hollered the booth operator. "Race!"

Gary moved along as fast as he could, eyes glued to his egg. Left, right, up the stairs, through the hoop, the tires, the jump rope, and then the finish line. He looked up. All three girls were behind him. He'd actually won!

People screamed at him. Gary couldn't help but gloat as Peggy ran up and plopped her egg into the bowl.

"Winner! Lane 1!" said the booth operator.

Gary was in Lane 2.

"You're supposed to put your egg in the bowl!" Peggy said, laughing. Gary looked down at his egg, which wobbled off his spoon and splattered to the ground.

"Gary!"

"The bowl? Oh. Guess I missed that part." Everyone around him laughed, which Gary was used to, but this time it felt different. This time it felt as if they were laughing *with* him, at least a little.

Peggy wrapped her arms around him and pecked him on the cheek. "You're sweet," she said.

"Do I have to pay for that egg?" Gary said, managing a joke in this surreal moment of cheers, laughter, and his first kiss.

Peggy laughed again. "No, let's go!"

"You may have won the game," Gary said, "but technically I won the race."

"Who has the bag of potato chips?" Peggy wagged her winnings in his face. She tugged him by the hand and off they went, rushing to the next station.

Just like that, after one egg race, Gary wasn't concerned about sports games, water games, or winning or losing. He was busy having the best day of his life. With Peggy by his side, Gary Bean was no longer Gary Bean. He had super powers. The power to try things he would never try on his own; the power to laugh when he failed; the power to see a brighter, less lonely future; and the power to feel worthy in his own skin. Peggy Sanders gave him all of this.

Like all Spring Carnivals, the dunk tank is the centerpiece. Never in his wildest dreams did Gary imagine he would take a turn, but here he was, hand-in-hand with Peggy, and she wanted to. The only question was which line would Gary get? One line was for the dunker, the one who threw the ball; the other line was for the dunked, those brave enough to sit atop the plank.

"You wanna get dunked?" Peggy asked.

"Do *you* wanna get dunked?" Gary repeated.

She laughed. "Not in this dress. You'd see my bra and panties." Peggy poked him in the chest as if to say, "not yet, but maybe later." At least that's how Gary interpreted it.

"I get three balls, sucka. Get in line!" Peggy stepped into the dunkers' line, which left the dunked line for Gary.

In all water situations, Gary kept his shirt on to save himself the flabby embarrassment, but based on his experiences today, he wasn't sure he should. Peggy's Nike-like "just do it" attitude had changed his perspective. He'd also noticed something strange.

Any guy who kept his shirt on—maybe he felt fat like Gary,

or had scars, a birthmark, a hairy body, or three nipples—looked wimpy. Any guy who took his shirt off, even the chubby guys, looked confident, no matter the jiggles and the extra flesh. Why? Shouldn't Gary, a fat guy, support guys who kept their shirts on? If other guys kept their shirts, Gary wouldn't look out-of-place. Why, all of a sudden, did he think taking off his shirt would impress Peggy, and not repulse her? That was a big switcheroo in the Gary world view.

When it was their turn, Peggy smiled and tossed the ball back and forth in her hands, teasing him while she waited for Gary to climb the steps to the top of the dunk tank.

When Gary reached the top, he had to make a decision. The confident route, or the safe route? He knew the right answer, but did he have the guts to pull it off? He looked at Peggy. She winked at him.

Gary ripped off his Hawaiian shirt and tossed it aside. That was followed by his white t-shirt, which he whirled around his head like a propeller. He didn't care how much his fat jiggled.

Peggy and the crowd roared its approval. This was the act of a confident man. For the first time in history, a shirt-less Gary Bean stood in public. Peggy had given him another super power.

Gary tiptoed onto the plank and sat down.

"That's gonna be a big splash," jeered someone. Laughter followed.

Rather than take the comment as an insult, Gary joined in. "Don't worry about it. You think she can hit the target? C'mon."

"Oh, really?" Peggy said. "That's what you think?"

Gary gestured to the target, daring her to prove him wrong.

Peggy threw.

Bullseye.

Gary's perch disappeared and down he went. Ka-sploosh!

Submerged, Gary pressed his face against the glass, playing to the crowd. Peggy got him with her first shot. She was perfect. Together they had done it all, every Spring Carnival event, even the unforgiving dunk tank. It was a life-changing day for Gary. To celebrate, he wanted another kiss from his date.

Gary pulled himself out of the tank. When he stood up, he raised his arms high in celebration. The crowd roared. "Gar—!"

The roar stopped, replaced by a collective gasp. Peggy covered her eyes and turned away.

What happened next on June 5 at 6:33 p.m. happened in under a minute.

Gary turned to see what everyone was looking at. There was nothing behind him. The water left his body feeling cool, and the breeze felt nice on his legs and his . . .

Gary looked at his penis. That shouldn't be there. A shrunken and shriveled slug dripping wet like the rest of his naked body.

Naked.

His soaking wet cargo shorts lay piled at his feet, their cargo still inside their pockets. He'd forgotten about that stuff. The weight of it all must have pulled them down!

Gary tried to haul his shorts back up, but they clung tight to his thighs, refusing to budge. Screams and screeches rang through the air around him. Stuff spilled out of his pockets, splashing into the water. It was a worse-case scenario for males around the world, and it was happening to Gary.

But was it happening to Gary? Wasn't he *Super Gary*?

With his penis dangling in front of him, Gary gave up on his shorts. He faced the crowd and yelled at Peggy. "You know it shrinks in cold water, right?"

Peggy screamed with laughter and so did the crowd. She clapped for him, staring right at his manhood. Super Gary put his fists on his hips and posed.

Mr. Beauregard yelled from the side of the dunk tank. "Gary Bean, pull up your shorts and get down this instant!"

It was hard to resist the urge to cover his nuts and run, but his classmates' cheers fueled Super Gary. He was living a dream. Who was this unmasked man, this new legend of Leelin High? Gary wasn't sure himself, but as he waved at Peggy, penis wiggling back and forth, he knew it would all be different from now on.

"He peed! Oh my God, that's so gross!"

What? Gary checked his dick. It didn't feel like he was peeing. His body dripped water and so water was also dripping off of *it*, but he wasn't peeing.

"I saw some come out! Holy shit, he peed in the dunk tank!"

"I'm not peeing!" Gary said, suddenly desperate to get his shorts back up, which he managed this time. His eyes searched the crowd for the heckler and landed on . . . Brent.

His supposed friend, Brent Fleetwood.

Cries of disbelief and disgust broke out through the crowd, taking up Brent's lie.

"Was he peeing? Really?"

"Gary Bean pissed himself in the dunk tank!"

"How could you tell? He barely has a penis!"

Gary's eyes met Peggy's. Watching her face was like watching glass break. Her friends whispered in her ear, and one of them shoved her finger down her throat, pretending to puke.

Strong hands grabbed a shaken Gary and helped him down. It was Mr. Beauregard.

"That's quite enough, Mr. Bean," Mr. Beauregard said. He handed Gary a towel.

"I wasn't peeing!" Gary wiped his eyes, trying to stem the tears before they took over.

"I've got your shirts when you're dry. You sure you didn't pee? Not even a little? I need you to be honest with me, Gary. It's a hygiene issue."

"No! At least it didn't feel like it. Water was dripping off me, but it was just water. I'm sure of it."

"We can't take that chance." Mrs. Bobowski joined their huddle at the base of the dunk tank. "We'll have to close the dunk tank just to be sure."

"I said I was sure! I'm not a child."

How could this be happening to him? He knew he hadn't worn underwear, so that part he understood. He'd had no cool pairs and didn't want to risk an old ratty pair in case he and Peggy made out.

Gary looked for her amongst the crowd, a sea of grimacing and grossed-out faces watching the Gary Bean train wreck. But no Peggy.

"All right, the dunk tank is now closed!" Mrs. Bobowski addressed the crowd. "Everyone move along. Nothing more to see here."

As the crowd dispersed, some called out to Gary.

"Thanks for contaminating the dunk tank, Bean!"

"Next time get potty trained first!"

"Make him drink it!"

Gary turned his back and put his shirts on. Mr. Beauregard put a hand on his shoulder.

"It'll be okay, Gary. These kinds of things, well, in time they'll just . . ." He turned to Mrs. Bobowski. "I don't know what to say to him."

The looks of pity on his teachers' faces said it all. Gary would never live this down. For the rest of his miserable high school existence he'd be forced to remember this moment.

"Maybe you should go on home now, Gary," said Mrs. Bobowski.

Gary nodded. He looked once more for her, but Peggy Sanders was gone, and so were his super powers. The man he almost was had been destroyed by someone he thought of as a friend.

Brent Fleetwood had ruined his life.

Chapter 30

Brent
Like a Virgin

B rent listened to Gary's tale of woe, but it was all wrong. The implications were mind blowing.
"I didn't say it," Brent said.

"Yeah, right," Gary said. He wiped more blood from his face and looked in the mirror. The flow had stopped. He ran the water and cleaned himself up as he talked. "You can stop denying it, Brent. It hurts to learn you're responsible for this shit story, doesn't it? Maybe you've repressed the memory."

"I didn't forget, Bean," Brent hissed. "I didn't say it."

Brent turned Gary around, forcing him to look him in the eye. "Do you understand, you prick? It means you shot the wrong guy. You fucked up!"

Brent shoved Gary aside, his thoughts a jumble. Everything that had happened to him, everything that he'd lost was all a case of mistaken identity? Life couldn't be that fickle, could it?

"You think I'm stupid?" Gary said. "I saw you say it. I wasn't peeing, you asshole. But thanks for that. It was bad enough my dick was hanging out, bad enough that my only high school date couldn't speak to me again, but I got all those shitty nicknames on top of that. Gary Beansprout? Waterboy? Drip? The Urinator? Remember those?"

That got laughs from Todd and Mitchell.

"Funny, isn't it?" Gary said. "All year long it was, 'Hey, Gary, is that a wet spot on your pants?' Or the classic, 'Want to come to our pool party, Gary? Oh, wait.'"

"Come on," Todd said. "You were peeing! You didn't mean to pee, but all the same, stuff came out your wee-wee. I saw it. Why can't you admit it? You owe Brent that much."

Gary's face trembled with anger. "I owe Brent for lots of things," he said, "but acknowledging that lie is not one of them. I owe him for digging spitballs out of my hair—"

"Yes!" Todd said. "I had the best spitball shooter ever. I called it the bazooka."

"And pulling the wedgie out of my ass," continued Gary, "and sometimes from over my head, that was interesting. And let's not forget pounding on the inside of my locker after school, praying the janitor wasn't too drunk to hear."

Todd, Rory, and Mitchell were all laughing now, but Brent stayed quiet.

"I still avoid locker rooms. I'm still scared of a football. I'm still a virgin. And it's all your fault!" Gary pointed his finger in Brent's face, inches away, like he wanted to stab it through his eyeball.

"Spring Carnival wasn't your reason," Brent said, glaring past Gary's finger, unfazed. "That dunk tank mishap might have been the catalyst, but you had other motives."

"Oh, did I?" Gary said, backing away. "Pray tell, Brent?"

When he learned Gary was the one, Brent did a quick and dirty psychological analysis of Gary Bean.

Loser. Geek. Backstabbing punk.

Gary fit the nerd stereotype. He couldn't get a date in high school, but had enormous academic success. Gary wasn't valedictorian. You had to be mildly attractive or quasi-popular to get that political prize, but he won all the medals, awards, honorariums, and scholarships. This was the kind of guy who itched to graduate because making buckets of moolah was supposed to solve his women problems. But they wouldn't. Even if he got one, she'd control him, and soon he'd be paying the professionals: hookers and marriage counselors. So why did Gary Bean attack Brent? He shot him in the back to keep the better man down.

Brent was Gary Bean's high school hero. For starters, Brent was just as smart. His academic efforts fell short of 100 percent commitment, but that didn't mean the IQ test result would be any different. The x-factor was girls. Brent got some; Gary didn't. If a person searched deep enough and truthfully enough, he'd find that the primordial emotions ruled him. Survival instincts. Competition. Greed. Gary Bean's actions were proof of Brent's dystopic world vision. The source of Gary's heinous deed was the reason human beings were inherently evil—the ugly green monster, jealousy.

"You were jealous," Brent said. "You wanted to be like me—"

"Oh, screw off!" Gary said. "Don't make this about you, you egomaniac. Did I wish I had friends in high school? Did I wish I had some girls? You're fucking right I did. So, sure, I'd switch my high school experience for yours, or Todd's, or Rory's. I'm a top bank executive. I make good money. But would any of you change places with me? Anybody trade places if it meant giving up your high school memories, the good times, the girls, the glory?"

Gary was right. Nobody in this room wanted to be him no matter how rich he might become.

"Dammit, Brent!" Gary said. "Let's end this right here and now. I'm sorry my revenge went further than I intended. I didn't know Patricia Mendelson's parents would press charges. But just admit that you said it, let's shake hands, and move on with our lives. What do you say?"

"I said I didn't say it, Bean. I'm not a liar."

"I saw you! I remember every second of that moment, and I saw you."

"Did you?" Brent said, pacing the room. "You saw the words come out of my mouth?"

"I heard them and looked up right where the voice came from. That's where you stood. Right there."

"So you didn't see me say the words?"

Rory whistled through his teeth. Brent wondered if they were thinking the same thing, that eyewitness testimony was unreliable. In psychological testing, when people looked at photos of a car accident and were later asked to recall the vehicle colors, they were positive of their choices, but were often positively wrong.

"Did I see the actual words come out of your mouth? No, but that doesn't mean I'm wrong. It was you, Brent. It was."

"Maybe it came from my general direction? Who was I with that day?" Brent turned to Todd. "You. We were at the dunk tank together, right? Who was around us?"

Todd gave it some thought, but came up zeros. "Don't remember. But he peed. I saw it too."

"No!" Gary shouted. "Shit." Inexplicably, he started to laugh. "Can you believe this? Here we are ten years later. Did he pee? Who said he peed? My nose is probably busted. Brent has a criminal record. Man."

It suddenly struck Brent as funny too. He couldn't help it. A snort of laughter snuck out.

"And you," Gary pointed at Todd. "You did not see piss. You saw water drip off my dick. You're telling me that you can distinguish between water and piss from fifteen feet away?"

"It's the way it comes out," Todd said. "Piss has force to it. Water just drips. I saw it project, man. As soon as I saw it, I yelled, 'He peed!' because I knew it."

"Wait," Gary said. "You yelled, 'he peed?'"

"I think so, yeah. I'm sorry, but it was funny."

Brent and Gary stared at each other. Gary's eyes widened. No way, Brent thought. Todd?

"Those were the words," Gary said. "That's what I heard. Those exact words."

All eyes turned to Todd.

"What?" Todd said. "You think *I* said it now? I know I said something, but . . . hold on a minute." Todd's brow furrowed. He rubbed his chin, thinking hard. Then his face split into a grin. "Son of a bitch. I think it *was* me. Can you believe it? How messed up is that?"

Very, Brent thought. He didn't know where to start.

"Wow. There are minds blowing all over this room," Todd said. "I guess you owe Brent an apology, Gary."

Gary leaned against the counter, his hand over his mouth, his eyes focused somewhere in the past. "Brent," he said, "sorry is not going to cut it. You were the one cool kid that was good to me. I wanted to be your friend, but I was never jealous of you. I thought you were the best. You tell me what I can do to make it up to you. It's done. I don't care what it is. Just say it."

Brent knew Gary was a shitty actor, and he looked as if he was about to puke.

"Sorry's good enough," Brent said. The truth was out but it did nothing for Brent. He'd been denied his revenge. All he ever wanted was someone to point to and say, that's the guy and this is why. How could he blame Gary now? Gary wasn't jealous. Nothing was like he thought.

"It should have been you," Gary said to Todd. "You're the one who should have got all the shit that Brent got."

Todd shrugged. "You got it wrong, Bean. Look what you did to an innocent man."

CRACK!

Gary's fist smacked Todd. The unexpected punch took Todd by surprise.

Rory rushed to get between them before a fight broke out.

Todd bared his teeth at Gary and clenched his fists. A red welt formed on his cheek.

"You probably deserved that, Todd," Brent said. "You heard his story. Take a deep breath and back off. Karma, remember?"

After a moment, Todd took his advice and backed away. "We're even now, Gary. I'm going to forget that."

"Even? How can we be even? Thanks to you I ruined Brent's life."

"Thanks to me? You blamed the wrong guy. How's that my fault?"

"He's right, Gary," Rory said. "This sucks from every which way, but it's not Todd's fault you did what you did."

"Like hell! It's Todd's fault that any of this happened. If he wasn't such a dildo, then I wouldn't have accidentally spoiled Brent's future."

"Wow," Brent said. "Is this the bromance version of *Romeo & Juliet*? Of all the bad assumptions and crappy choices in that story, I never thought I would see it repeated at Leelin High."

"Yeah," Gary said. "If we could turn back time."

The conversation trailed off and everyone got lost in their own world for a moment. Brent was thankful for the respite. He needed to figure out his next move. He had his long sought-after answers, but where did he go from here?

"That was quite a purge," Mitchell said. "Not exactly the purge I was hoping for. You guys work it out. I'm getting a ginger-ale. It's supposed to be good for stomach problems."

Mitchell left, and the quiet descended again.

Brent knew there was a lesson here, a moral, but it eluded him. The great mystery of the graffiti was solved, and like all great mysteries the killer was not the butler, so to speak, or any other obvious suspect; and the motive wasn't jealousy, competition, or greed. It was simpler than that. It was justice, or revenge, or both. It made sense. Brent needed more time to analyze and process, but in the meantime, in the here and now, he was experiencing a new sensation. Gary's heartfelt remorse had infiltrated Brent's dystopia. With a hail of machine gun fire, Gary's apology had blown the heads off ten-year skeletons and planted alternate world theories among the weeds of Brent's sour logic. The world might actually be different than Brent imagined.

"You know what, Gary?" Brent said, changing the topic. "It wouldn't be so bad to be a virgin. I might switch places with you."

"Pardon? What are we talking about?" Rory said.

Todd made that dismissive horse noise with his lips. "Sure, Brent. Yeah."

Ever since Gary named it number three on his list of nerd nightmares, the virgin topic struck a chord with Brent.

"There's not one girl I've slept with whom I couldn't wipe from my brain, pain-free, except my first," Brent said. "Anybody know what that means?"

"You haven't read *The Joy of Sex*?" Rory said.

"The blow-up dolls aren't working?" Todd said.

Brent ignored their idiot comments. "Who's the horniest guy in this room?"

Three sets of eyes focused on Gary.

"Right. When's the last time you were that horny?"

"You don't mean your first, *first* time?" Rory said. "Everyone's scared to death their first time."

"I wasn't scared," Todd said. "I lasted two strokes. I wanted to tap that soooo bad."

"You're both right," Brent said. "Whatever that emotion is, fear or lust, it's strongest in the beginning. Drives you crazy one way or the other. That's love."

"Love?" Todd spat the word. "Did we switch topics? Sex is not love."

"Love and sex; chocolate and peanut butter. Is there a better combination? How many times have you been in love?"

Todd snorted and looked away, but answered. "Even if you married your first love, married couples get bored in the sack too."

"Passion fades. It's normal," Rory agreed.

"Does it? Should it? Wait, wait," Brent said. "Two women. There's two that I couldn't wipe from my brain, pain-free. I had a long dry-spell once. She broke it; she was great. But that dry spell kinda made me a virgin again, so the theory still applies."

"I guess I'm a virgin too," Rory said, raising his hand. "Two year dry spell."

"Losers," Todd laughed. "Look, marrying your first is scary. What if she only liked missionary? What if she had weird tits? What if she wouldn't go down on you?"

"It's simple psychology," Brent said. "Positive reinforcement. Sex only in a marriage is positive reinforcement for that marriage. If you had sexual knowledge of only *one* woman, you wouldn't think her tits were weird because they'd be your *only* tits."

Gary nodded his head. It was encouraging for Brent that someone could comprehend what he was saying, as opposed to his blockhead friend.

"One pair your whole life?" Todd said. "How is that positive?"

"Your theory is sound, Brent," Gary said. "But it only works in a perfect group society, one where everyone's only seen one pair of tits."

"Agreed," Brent said. "If you see two pairs of tits, one pair becomes less desirable. See three pairs of tits and you're handing out gold, silver, and bronze medals at the Bazoom Olympics."

"Soon you'll have a favorite shape and size, and hope the next girl you're with has that exact pair," Gary said. "If she doesn't have your magic pair you could be unsatisfied. That's just one example of perfectionism in partner selection. There are potentially hundreds."

A bell went off in Brent's head.

"Perfectionism. Yes! Great word. That's what happens when you keep screwing a lot of random chicks. You're cursed for life with a set of sexy puzzle pieces, compelled to build and rebuild your fantasy for eternity. That's why sex isn't as good as it used to be. We all wanna fuck a mythical jigsaw puzzle! Can we love a girl who's not the answer to that puzzle?"

"Depends," Gary said. "There's a formula for that. If she has eighty percent of the pieces, maybe that equals love for somebody? But the more complicated the puzzle, the less chance at completing the formula."

"Who does, really?" Rory said. "How many married couples do you know who are truly in love?" He cocked his head in Todd's direction. Todd didn't see.

Gary shrugged. "Without the magic formula it's an economics argument, cost-benefit analysis."

Cost-benefit analysis, Brent thought. How many poets wrote about that?

"Sure, everybody wants the one, but she's hard to find, hard to catch, and hard not to screw up with," Rory said. "But what can you do? If you can't land her, you take the logical runner-up, right? You compromise and accept the consolation prize. Sure, some people reach for the dream . . ." Rory rolled his eyes and trailed off, grumbling to himself.

"Which is why I want to be a virgin again!" Brent said. "I'd be starting over, deconstructing that perfect jigsaw-puzzle-princess in my head. Then I could fall in love again and avoid shitty robot sex."

"So take a few years off," Todd said. "Go on a voluntary dry spell. Just don't whack off every day."

"Believe it or not, that's good advice," Brent said.

"Voluntary dry spell," Todd said, chuckling. "I was joking. Like that's even possible?"

"*Weird Science*," Rory said. "Remember that movie?"

"Loved it," Gary said.

All men did. It was an 80s teen flick about a pair of computer nerds who build the perfect girlfriend and bring her to life.

"Here's my original hypothesis again," Brent said. "A virgin like Gary is not plagued by perfectionism like the rest of us casual fuckers, so it's easier for him to find the one and have good, hot sex, yes or no?"

"I'd like to do some field research," Gary said.

Brent laughed and clapped Gary on the back.

"Why does my jigsaw princess always look like The Panther?" Rory said. He sank to the floor and hugged his knees.

"The Panther? Who's that?" Gary asked.

"Rory," Brent said, ignoring Gary for the moment. "You know what you have to do. Invade Alice's wonderland. Tonight. Don't procrastinate in here any longer. Gary? The Panther is Alice Green."

"Alice Green? I thought Panther was slang for older women who patrol bars for younger guys?"

"Those are cougars," Rory said.

Brent decided to educate Gary on a secret known only to him, Rory, and Todd. "As it pertains to Alice Green, Panther is short for Panther Chameleon."

"Does this have something to do with prom?" Gary looked at Rory and winced. "And that thing she did?"

"No," Rory said. "She got this nickname long before prom. You ever watch her closely?" Rory's eyes brightened as he talked about Alice.

"Only class I didn't get an A+ in had her in it."

"Then you probably noticed her little quirk?"

Gary shrugged and grinned. "You gotta help me out here."

"She has an alluring habit, or *had* I guess, not sure if she still does, of licking her lips. Constantly, all the time. And not quick either."

"Oh my God, yes. She did it slow, like in a porn or something. And her tongue was so long. It was—"

"Hypnotic," Rory said, finishing Gary's thought. "Alice's habit snared guys like the Panther Chameleon traps insects. We came up with the nickname in biology class."

Rory looked at Brent, and together they went back in time, sharing the same memory. They were seated side-by-side, forced to watch a boring science movie. With their heads resting on their desks, barely resisting the urge to sleep, this lizard-ish creature launched its tongue across the screen to devour a bug. In unison, Brent and Rory rose from their lazy positions, heads whipping around to stare at each other. "Alice," they whispered at the same time.

They all laughed except for Todd. Brent wondered why he hadn't said anything or insulted anyone lately. His friend seemed sullen and removed. Brent guessed what was on his mind. Since they were all sharing hard truths, it was time he shared with Todd. Todd deserved payback for what he'd done to Gary, but Brent would rather not be the one delivering the karma. He wasn't sure how it would all play out once Todd knew everything. They might all get bloody over this.

Chapter 31

Todd
Bad Medicine

Are we all done playing with Gary Bean? Todd wanted to ask. How'd they go from busting Gary's face to clapping him on the back? The fat rat may have apologized, but he still did it. Do the crime, do the time.

"Todd? We should talk," Brent said.

"About what?"

"You're still on board with the plan, right?"

"What plan?" What Todd thought he was doing tonight was getting all mixed up with what he should do, wanted to do, or couldn't do. He was in one of those freaky, time-altering movies where one event sets off a chain reaction that alters everything you thought was true for the last ten years. Todd couldn't keep up.

"Mickey," Brent said. "We agreed we'd have a ceremony with Mickey tonight. We're still doing that, right?"

"Right," Rory agreed.

"Of course," Todd said.

"Mickey Rifken?" Gary asked.

"No," Todd said. "You, just—" Todd motioned Gary to stay quiet.

"Okay, that takes care of some housekeeping," Brent said. "The next piece of business is Lewis Tinker."

"What about him?" Todd said.

"Before I tell you, I want you to know that it's going to piss you off." Brent looked to Rory for confirmation.

"Yup," Rory agreed, "definitely going to piss you off."

"What the hell is this?" Todd said. "Spit it out."

"No," Brent said, "I won't 'spit it out.' For your own sake, you need some context. You don't want to make a rash decision you'll regret."

Todd felt his stomach twist. "Does this have to do with Stacy?"

"We'll get there," Brent said, "but I'll need a safe zone promise."

"Fine, safe zone. Tell me."

"Seriously, Todd. Safe zone. Can you do it or not? You also have to promise to stay and talk it through. That's part of the deal."

"How bad of a story is this? Holy fuck, you guys."

"In some ways, this could be a good story," Brent said.

Rory looked at Brent as if he'd gone off script.

"Really, it could. Depending on the decisions Todd makes and how he moves forward."

Rory thought about it. "Okay, well, if we're talking about the future, maybe."

"So, talk," Todd said, trying to stay calm. "We're in the safe zone. What did Lewis Tinker do?"

"He wanted me to tell you," Brent said.

"Wanted *you* to tell me. What?"

"This whole story, this whole thing we're gonna talk about. Lewis wanted me to tell you. Keep that in mind."

"You're giving me a message from Lewis? Seriously?"

"Look, just remember that Lewis thinks what I'm about to say is good for him and bad for you. In his opinion, when you know the story, you'll do something he wants you to do."

"Why didn't the asshole tell me himself? Why use one of my best friends as a messenger?"

"A few reasons." Brent cleared his throat. "One being opportunity. He didn't have any because it happened tonight, right after your fight."

"Here? At the reunion?"

Brent nodded. "Yeah."

Todd took a deep breath, steadying himself. "Okay," he said, then fell silent. He looked around the room at everyone, even Gary Bean, but said nothing more.

"You all right?" Brent asked.

Todd smiled. "This reunion's one for the books. What else can happen?"

"You got what Brent said, right?" Rory asked. "Lewis expects you to follow your gut, so maybe don't do that this time."

"Yeah, I heard," Todd said. "I know what you're going to say. I don't need a degree to connect the dots, but there's one thing I don't get. How did my wife and Lewis Tinker cheat at the reunion and I miss it?"

Gary sucked in a breath. At least one person didn't know, Todd thought.

Brent and Rory exchanged a surprised look. Did they actually think he wouldn't figure it out? After all of that preamble it could only be one thing. The two questions remaining were how did it happen and how far did it go? Todd pretended to be in the safe zone so Brent would tell him. He would avoid punching walls and Tinker's face for a bit longer.

"Cheating's a subjective term," Rory said. "Some people might not think it was cheating."

"Okay," Todd said. *If Lewis smelled her perfume it was cheating.*

"This is a good start," Brent said. "You're calm. Anger leads us where? The dark side."

Brent was good with his Jedi mind tricks, but Todd was too far gone. No clever *Star Wars* reference would save Lewis Tinker from Todd Vader.

"Here's what happened," Brent said. "You beat up Tinker and left to find Stacy. Meanwhile, Rory and I are at the bar. We come back to the bathroom and find Lewis and Stacy together."

"Together how?"

"Intertwined."

"On the floor," Rory added.

"On the floor?" Todd dropped his false serenity.

"They got up fast," Brent said. "We only saw a second, but enough to do the Planet F's test."

At the mention of the test, Todd regained his composure. This was the proof he needed. In high school, they had a binder devoted to each Planet. Rory even drew pictures. It sickened Todd to apply the Planet F's test to his wife, but the test was 100 percent accurate. Todd held no illusions that his wife stayed safely on Planet Flirtation.

"Let's do the test backwards," Brent said. "Was there any sex?"

"No," Rory said.

"Is that a Bill Clinton answer? BJs count in this universe."

"Understood. No oral."

"Okay, was there nudity?"

"No."

"Was there penetration?"

Rory hesitated. "I don't think so. Did you see any?"

Brent sighed. "Hand was up her dress. No way to tell how far."

"He fingered her in the bathroom?" Todd Vader reached out for an imaginary Lewis Tinker, choking the life from him.

"We don't know for sure," Brent said. "Let's table that one and finish the test. Was there kissing?"

"Yes," said Rory.

Todd bent over and put his hands on his knees. He was Rory all of a sudden, trying to avoid puking.

"Was there groping?"

"Yes."

"By whom?"

"Him."

"Where?"

"Breasts."

"Did she touch his privates?"

"Not that we saw."

"Done!" Brent rubbed Todd's back. "How are you doing, buddy?"

"Conclusion?" Todd asked, standing back up, feeling light-headed.

"She argued that she was on Planet Flirtation," Rory said, "but clearly—"

"Foreplay. The Moon," Todd said. "Docked at the first space station heading east. Two hyperspace trips away from the sun. And to top it off, she picks the men's bathroom at our ten-year high school reunion as her launching pad. How's that for sticking it to me?"

Todd knew he and Stacy lacked a certain something, call it affection, call it magic, call it fuckin' fruity tooty shmooty, whatever. He didn't know the right word. They could hang out and have a good time, but the way she talked to Tinker, the way she looked at him, or tried *not* to look at him, Todd had his clues. Having proof didn't make it a surprise. It hurt, though, and knowing his friends saw, that they knew and didn't tell him, that stung too.

"You saw them and didn't tell me right away?" Todd asked.

"We wanted to tell you," Rory said, "but there were complications." Rory looked at Brent. It was easy to tell who caused the complications.

"Like what? What complications kept my two best friends from telling me some guy's finger was inside my wife?"

"We didn't see that," Rory said. "At least I didn't."

"And why did you do what Lewis told you to do? Are you guys pals now?"

"Tinker had information about my graffiti," Brent said. "It was him who put me onto Mitchell, who put me onto Gary."

"Sorry again," Gary said. "Brent, if there's anything I can do—"

"Not about you right now, Gary," Todd said. "And the price for that info, Brent?"

"I make sure to tell you what happened."

Todd stared hard at Brent while Brent did his best to look anywhere but Todd. Truth was important to Brent, which made him one of the world's worst liars. There was something more to this. Brent wasn't the only one who could Sherlock Holmes his way around a conversation. Todd dug deeper.

"You've told me what you *can* tell me; what is it that you *can't* tell one of your best friends?"

"I'll tell you, but we wait for Mickey. That was the plan."

"Whatever," Todd said. "Why did Lewis have to make you tell

me? How did Lewis know that you wouldn't tell me anyway because that's what best friends are supposed to do?"

Todd moved closer to Brent, tracking his eyes and forcing Brent to look at him.

"We've barely seen each other in ten years, Todd. That's not what best friends do."

"So we're not friends anymore? That's your excuse?"

"We're getting off-track," Rory said. "Todd, we should be talking about you and Stacy. You need a plan."

"I have a plan," Todd said, keeping his eyes on Brent. "Are we friends or not, Brent? Because time doesn't change true friendship. Or am I wrong about that?"

"Of course we're friends, but we're not in high school anymore either. Look, there's one thing I need to talk to you about, but I'm saving that for when Mickey makes his appearance."

"And it's bad news? Like all the other news I got tonight? Will that piss me off too?"

"I hope not."

"But it's the reason you couldn't tell me Stacy cheated on me? It's that big?"

"I'm hoping it's not big at all."

"So am I." Todd swigged the rest of his beer and started pacing. "Todd Bowman," he said, talking loudly to the room like a museum tour guide. "High school tough guy and legendary partier. Where is he now? Headed for a divorce with an unfaithful wife who'll squeeze him for every penny his minimum wage job ever got him while screwing her lawyer the whole time. Probably be in jail or rehab in a year."

"Divorce?" Rory said. "Are you sure about that?"

"Rory Chase. Girl magnet. Stud muffin. For three years strutted down high school hallways like a king." Todd waved his empty glass in Rory's face. "But the emperor has no clothes. Guy's a pussy."

"Pussy?" Rory took a step towards him, but Brent wisely held him back. All Todd needed was an excuse. He didn't care who the punching bag was now.

"Professor Brent Fleetwood. The Renaissance man. Voted most likely to succeed, and that, my friend, makes you the biggest failure of all. What have you done? All that promise? All that potential? Two lousy degrees in psychology and philosophy. BAs in Boring and Useless. If you're so right all the time, what happened to you? You hang around offering your theories and BS into our lives. Well whoop-dee-doo, I'm bored of you."

Todd turned to the last person in the room. He was there, so Todd did him too. "Gary Bean, a good target for spitballs."

He was done. Done with the reunion, done with his marriage, and done with his so-called friends. He felt like a cartoon character walking over a chasm, not realizing the cliff was ten years back the other way. A night like tonight could make a man look down.

"Goodnight, gentlemen!"

"Todd, wait," Brent said.

Todd lifted an arm in farewell and slammed the door behind him.

Chapter 32

Rory
Centerfold

"Why didn't you tell him everything?" Rory said. Brent had botched his confession, leaving out the high school hand job.

"Todd's shit plate was piled high enough," Brent said. "I didn't want to serve it to him all at once."

"What's a vanilla-pants-shake compared to Stacy's moon landing? It was the perfect time to tell him."

"The difference is that I did it. Me! One of his best friends. That's a big difference, Rory."

"Guys?" Gary interrupted. "I'm concerned about what Todd's going to do out there. How about we check it out?" Gary headed for the door, but before he reached it . . .

Two long, shapely legs swayed into the room. A pink tongue snaked out between full, red lips. It moved slowly, seductively, from one side of her mouth to the other.

The Panther had come.

Rory's heart expanded like a balloon, rising into his throat with a surge of zeppelin-sized love. Then it constricted like a raisin, shriveling up to match his frightened testicles.

Alice Green.

The Panther.

She who controlled the contents of his stomach. Like a snake charmer, she could make what was left of Rory's supper rise or fall with a twist of her lips.

Natural blonde hair, straight and shiny, fell past her shoulders. Her face was so perfectly oval it would make Humpty Dumpty horny. Lips blazed with too-bright, too-red hooker lipstick, and her teeth were dentist-office white. She carried a stylish purse and wore a short, silky dress with spaghetti strapped shoulders tied in little knots that teased with the ease they could come undone. A gold anklet twinkled above a three-inch heel, and an emerald choker nestled in the hollow of her throat.

Gary was closest to her and the first who could speak. He managed a feeble whisper, almost to himself. "The Pan . . ."

He lost it on the "th" and ended with a gurgle that could have been the "er."

Rory unconsciously backed into a stall. Before he could yell "freeze, you bastards," Brent grabbed his last martini, and propelled Gary from the bathroom.

They were alone.

The Panther.

And her bug.

"Do you have a nest in here?" she asked.

It was the sweet, innocent voice of Bambi's mother (God rest her soul). But it had that naughty Catholic-school-girl-hangin-out-at-the-mall-food-court-lookin-for-trouble twang.

He didn't answer. He couldn't.

She approached slowly, circling wide like a predator sizing up her prey.

Rory hovered in the open door of his stall. It was like a cave, somewhere he could find shelter with the rest of the herd of pussies.

When she got close, as close as his beef tortellini was to the back of his throat, she stopped. "You're not scared of me, are you?"

Rory choked down the marinara sauce. "What?" He acted cool. "Yeah, you're real scary." He tried to laugh, but choked instead, coughing for breath. A half-digested mini tortellini flew from his mouth like the space shuttle.

"I'm fine," he said hoarsely. Tears streaked his cheeks and his face was a beautiful shade of doofus.

"You sure? I was waiting for you to come out."

"I was out!" Rory said, too loudly. "You were dancing with some guy."

"Who?"

"I don't know." Rory shrugged, trying to appear disinterested but failing. "You had your hand on his ass. Remember that guy?"

Rule number one with women. Never appear jealous. If you're jealous, you're weak. Rory knew this. But here's the problem. If you're lucky or unlucky enough to fall in love, you're essentially Peter Pan off course. Instead of Neverland you've flown to Needyland. You packed your suitcase with obsession and chocolate-covered-strawberries, and left your old pal, rational thought, behind. Stay in Needyland too long and you'll need binoculars to see where she fled to after telling her you loved her fifty times.

Rory didn't want to be jealous. He wanted to be carefree and aloof. What he should have said was nothing. But the imperial forces of don't-let-Rory-get-laid pushed their advance. They added a whiny ass-grabbing part to his sentence.

She surprised him by stepping closer, as in the front of her body grazed the front of Rory's body. She smiled, teasing him with a tongue dart.

"That's how I dance," she said.

Her scent, vanilla and coconut, drifted up Rory's nose like opium. When it reached his brain it was like a hot-oil massage, kneading his gray matter with muscle-relaxing ease.

She grabbed his ass, gripping it hard.

Rory tried to tell himself to breathe, but that was a message sent from the brain, and right now his brain was flat-out, buck-naked on a massage table being asked if he wanted a "happy ending."

"I like the feel of that big wad of man-flesh in my hand," Alice said. She kept a straight face, eye contact, and her hand molded into Rory's ass. "There's nowhere else on the body you can squeeze like this. Although men think breasts are fair game." She released his ass.

Rory's feet sank back to the floor. He'd risen up on tippy toes during the ordeal.

"Are you mad at me?" Alice asked. "About prom?"

"No. Are you mad at me about prom?"

"No." Alice looked him up and down. "You've got five minutes."

"Until?"

"Until I'm not horny anymore."

Rory had that feeling lottery winners get when their numbers show up. You want to trust it so bad, but you can't.

Alice checked her watch, which made Rory check his. Five minutes to midnight with the second-hand moving like a bullet train.

She tapped her high-heeled toe. "Tick-tock, Rory."

His brain rewound and scanned her last words. Did she really say *horny*? Rory zipped through the alphabet. A-orny, borny, corny, dorny, e-orny, forny, gorny, *horny* . . . i-orny, jorny, korny, lorny, morny, norny, o-orny, porny, ha ha, q-orny, rorny, sorny, torny, u-orny, vorny, worny, x-orny, yorny, zorny.

She must have said *horny*. But to be absolutely certain.

"Are you suggesting we? In here—?"

Alice pushed him into the stall until he fell onto the toilet seat. She closed the door.

And then the lottery winner accepts the impossible. He has stumbled upon the golden ticket inside Willy Wonka's chocolate bar. He is on his way to the fun factory. Nerves? What nerves? It was the perfect scenario, another time limit just like Mitchell Matthew's house party ten years ago. Rory could do five minutes. He *would* do five minutes.

Alice dropped her purse and hovered over him, stroking his hair. She took deep, sensuous breaths. "The last guy I screwed in a bathroom had my panties off by now. Don't you like me anymore?"

Rory's mind detoured to a dark place, to a Jamaican place. But he forced himself to ignore the "last guy I screwed in a bathroom" part and answered like a good soldier.

"Yes."

She pouted. "The way you've been acting tonight makes me think you don't. If we don't hurry, we could get caught."

That was a good point. Why wasn't he moving with a sense of urgency? Why hadn't he touched her? Why were his pants still on?

Lift your hands, Rory told himself. They're right in front of you. Come on, buddy. He reached up, palms open. He was going in for a two-hander . . . .

The bathroom door SQUEEAAKKED open. Alice stopped his

hands, inches from contact. She put his finger to her lips, kissing it and shushing him at the same time. She kept a firm hold on Rory's hands, preventing him from doing anything.

With a smile, Alice slid Rory's finger into her mouth. All the way in, then all the way out, sucking hard for the whole trip. None of Rory's vacations felt that great.

Alice leaned in close, her cheek next to his. The feel of her skin forced Rory's eyes closed. She whispered in his ear.

"Four minutes."

His eyes snapped open. Alice showed him her watch. The second-hand screamed around like a Concorde jet.

Rory tried to wriggle his hands free, desperately wanting to grope her body, but she held tight, not letting go. Alice shook her head, motioning outside the stall where some noisy, dream-destroying asshole threatened to ruin his magical moment.

She knew he was getting hot. If she looked down, she could *see* he was getting hot. Her tongue slid out again, massaging her lips. She released his hands but warned him with a raised finger to leave them where they fell. They twitched with desire, but Rory kept them tethered to his side, as ordered.

Alice pushed a spaghetti strap off her shoulder, like you would a ribbon before tearing away the wrapping paper. Her dress fell, but she caught it before it showed too much. Then she lowered it, inch by inch until—

"Peek-a-boo," she whispered.

Nipple.

Pink and perfect as the sunrise. Rory took a mental picture before the dress went back up. "Watch," she said.

Alice reached under her dress and slid her panties—wait, no, she paused. Her eyes closed. Her hand moved under her dress. This was weird, Rory thought. Was she . . . no way . . . was she? . . . no, c'mon . . . touching herself? She moaned. Holy shit, she was!

Her eyes opened, glazed and shiny. She slid her panties off, and then draped the glorious white cotton with green polka-dots on Rory's shoulder. He'd been knighted.

How much time had gone by?

Alice took one of his hands and massaged it gently, rubbing and caressing. She kissed the inside of his wrist, his palm, each of his fingers, and then guided Rory's hand under her dress, drawing it up the inside of her thigh. The anticipation was intense. As she brought him closer, he felt heat, like his hand was nearing an open flame.

Contact.

"Am I wet?" she said, peeking at him from behind a curl of blonde hair.

Was that a rhetorical question? Rory thought. She could tell, couldn't she?

"Do you want me to touch you?"

Now that's a rhetorical question, Rory thought.

Alice pulled his hand away from the heat, returning it to his lap. She unbuttoned Rory's pants and shoved her hand inside, squeezing him gently.

While Alice stroked, she nibbled his ear, her breath hot and loud, and then she kissed him. Rory felt her lips, her tongue, and "it." It was building inside him, coming. He had to get control.

The bathroom door slammed. Her stroking stopped. All was quiet. The dream destroyer was gone.

With her hand still gripping him, she said, "Do you have a condom?"

"Yes!"

Rory stood up. He held his pants, bashfully trying to hide his boner. "Just a minute."

Rory shuffled out of the stall with Alice's panties still on his shoulder. He balanced carefully as he made his way to the condom machine, his cargo too precious to be tarnished by the floor. She was behind him, he knew, waiting outside their stall, watching.

It was hard to buy a condom and hold your pants up at the same time. He managed to get his wallet free, but then it got impossible. Screw it, he thought. He let his pants drop.

Rory shook the change from his wallet and prayed as he counted quarters. Yes!

He plugged them into the slot and pulled.

Nothing.

He pulled again.

Nothing.

Rory turned around, keeping a confident look on his face, like the machine was just taking time to process his order. Alice leaned against the stall, legs spread wide.

Oh, so hot.

Dammit! He pulled again.

This time something happened. An "empty" flag appeared in the window.

Rory reeled as a horrific memory hit him like a punch to the gonads. Brent holding up the condom he got from this machine. The *last* condom.

He faced Alice. "It's empty."

She shook her head and sighed.

Please, God, don't let it end this way, Rory thought.

Alice looked disappointed, but wasn't saying anything. Rory posed in front of the condom machine, trying to look sexy with his pants bunched around his ankles and his wood poking through his drawers. He begged her with his eyes to think of another fun option.

She pursed her lips.

Not good, Rory thought. The sentence, "I can just pull out, right?" crept dangerously around his brain.

Alice smiled and rolled her perfect tongue over her lips. "I'm sure I can think of something."

Rory shuffled back into the stall, careful again not to lose his panty epilate. He re-assumed his place on the toilet seat, nudging his hips forward to the optimal position.

Alice shut the door, knelt in front of him, and reached into his undies.

With no blood left in his brain, Rory's chronic nerves shrunk to a whisper. For once, his desire drowned out the background noise. It was a powerful and freeing moment, the kind Rory only had in wet dreams. He wanted another five minutes, and another five minutes, and another until the deed was done. He could do this!

"We can go longer, can't we?" Rory said. He figured she must be joking about her five-minute cut-off anyway.

"Can we?" She stroked him with light caresses, but Rory was prepped already. Give him a running start and he'd bust through the Great Wall of China with his battering ram.

Alice stared deep into Rory's eyes, smiling her perfect smile. "Have you dreamt about me since prom?"

She was fishing for love, Rory thought. She wanted him to say something that translated as *you are special to me*. With a beautiful woman on her knees with her hands down his pants, Rory's self-confidence soared.

Rory wanted to say something clever. The unvarnished truth was that he'd thought about her every night for ten years. Throw in dreams, and Alice owned the lion's share of his life. But Rory couldn't say that, so he pulled out his mental paint brush, swept it across that thought a few times, and out came:

"I had a dream once about you and Mrs. Bobowski. You both got drunk one night and came over to confess your nasty desires."

"Shut up," she laughed, but kept a steady stroke. Here was a woman who could pat her head and rub her tummy at the same time. "So you have been fantasizing about me?"

Unvarnished truth: There aren't enough bathroom tissues in twenty high school bathrooms to cover the amount of times he'd fantasized about her.

Varnished statement: "Only on your birthday."

"When's my birthday?"

He answered without hesitation. "July 11th."

She smiled again. Her stroke increased, smooth and steady, up and down. "Tell me what I do to you in your fantasies."

Unvarnished truth: This! This is what she did to him in his fantasies. Alice doing anything to him *was* his fantasy. He'd been in love with her since high school.

Varnished statement: "This is my fantasy."

Whoops. That came out unvarnished. Rory's penis had knocked the mental paint brush from his brain's hands.

"Good." She glanced at her watch again.

Rory's nervous choir sang louder from a corner of his brain. With a beautiful woman on her knees with her hands down his pants *checking her watch*, Rory's self-confidence plummeted.

"Why don't we get a hotel? Like we planned at prom?" Rory said.

"I better get started," Alice said.

She pulled Rory's undies to the floor and there he was. Out for some air. Poking his little nose to the ceiling.

"Wow," she said, surprised at the view. "Retro-look. 1970s." Alice laughed. "You don't like to trim, do you?"

Rory suddenly felt like a dirty caveman. His mighty club softened as thoughts of Todd's Swiss army knife crept into his mind. He should have trimmed when he had the chance!

"Relax, baby." Alice increased her stroke to compensate for Rory's sudden anxiety. She rubbed it with both hands.

Rory hardened again.

"Preparing to dive, captain," she said, as if she were the sexy first lieutenant on Rory's imaginary starship. "Close your eyes."

Rory complied and felt her hot breath on the tip. She rubbed her cheek against it and murmured, "Why didn't we do this ten years ago?"

Rory's hands went numb as all the blood rushed to the center. "I don't know."

He waited in silence, listening to Alice's rustling movements, anticipating the arrival of that warm, wet sensation, the feel of Alice's amazing tongue on his—

A biting pain seized him. He gasped and doubled over.

Rory's eyes popped open. He stared first at the toy teeth clamped to the top of his penis, and then to Alice's smug face as she stood over him.

"Surprise, you bastard."

Chapter 33

Alice
A View to a Kill

Rory's hands darted for the teeth, but she slapped them away.

"You like rumors, Rory? This one ring a bell?" She wiggled the teeth.

Rory screeched. "Ow! Fuck! Get it off!"

"You know why we didn't do this at prom? You dumped me, asshole! *At prom*! You ruined my life!"

Rory had that I-just-woke-up-and-don't-know-where-I-am look. It was beautiful to see. Alice plowed onward with her speech.

"A girl gets one prom, Rory. One! And you shit all over mine, you selfish prick. I know what you call me, I know why, and there's nothing on this green earth of ours like a blowjob from *The Panther*."

Alice licked her lips slow and seductive. Rory's jaw moved, but no words came. She hoped he was having a stroke.

Alice ripped the fake teeth off Rory's penis, making him yelp in pain. She loved that sound. Then she grabbed her purse and left the stall. She had done it.

Before she reached the bathroom door, Rory burst out. "Alice!"

She heard the crash behind her. The imbecile was on the floor with his pants down, looking up at her with pleading eyes. At least he pulled up his underwear, she thought. Alice wondered if she could make him cry.

"You don't know the whole story," Rory said.

Alice crossed her arms and soaked in the moment. This was the guy she fell in love with?

In high school Rory was popular and good looking, and Alice liked him for all those reasons. She was a teenage girl; that's what they all like. He was one of the guys who asked her to prom, and she thought, great, that's the cute, popular guy I'm going to prom with, one thing off her to-do list. But weeks before the big night he said something, did something, whatever trick the magician pulled, hypnotism maybe, Alice developed actual *feelings* for the jerk. They walked the hallways holding hands, made out in the bus line, snuck out to see each other after their parents went to bed, and like lots of stupid, naïve, love-struck teenagers they made *the plan*.

Let's do it at prom, they thought. That'll make their first time together extra special. Yay! I love you. I love you too. Smoochy, smooch.

They rented a hotel room and bought condoms. But because Alice was actually falling in love (gag) with this bastard, she made the extra effort he had no idea about. She bought rose petals, candles, champagne, three smutty lingerie outfits, flavored oils, lubes, sex toys, a video camera, and a porno tape. How's that for girlfriend of the year? Rory was the last boy/man Alice did that for.

Days before prom, Alice shared her erotic plans with her girlfriends, and somehow fell deeper in love with the loser the more open she was about her feelings. Right about that moment, the son of a bitch got distant. He wasn't quick to hold her hand, not so affectionate in the bus line, and his parents were suddenly going to bed later and later. Alice accused him of cheating, but he denied it. Rory swore his love up and down and over and over. He even cried. She believed him.

They marched into the prom together, arm in arm, and then Rory went to the bathroom. Did she see Rory again that night? Once, as he flew by, drunk, to tell her it was over.

She was dateless at the prom, embarrassed, angry, and heartbroken. The rumor mill started fast. The fickle masses were quick to tear her down. All they needed was a whiff of gossip. These were the reasons Rory dumped her:

He caught her picking her nose and eating it.

She snapped at dinner and came at him with a knife.

She freakishly keeps her eyes open when they kiss.

She made out with an eighth grader.

Her hootchy smells like mothballs.

She bit his penis on purpose—that was the rumor that stuck.

Alice could have gone to prom with any number of cute, popular guys, and she might have fallen in love with any one of those cute, popular guys, but Alice picked Rory.

What did a rejected, suddenly alone beauty queen do for the rest of her prom night? She salvaged her flagging self-esteem. Alice got totally smashed, took the fawning Jamaican foreign exchange student back to her hotel room, screwed his brains out, and made a video of the whole thing.

In the morning, hung over, Alice realized she may have overreacted. She burned the videotape with a pack of hotel-supplied matches and breathed a sigh of relief for that. Then her surrogate boyfriend woke up.

"Hoo, dat was a heck of a night, Al-eece. When we do dat again? Now?"

Alice calmly explained that it was a one-night thing and she'd appreciate it if he kept it just between them. He agreed, as long as he could have the video. Not possible, thank God.

So now he didn't agree. He thought they should be boyfriend and girlfriend. The man was suddenly a traditionalist. To his credit, he didn't come right out and call it extortion. He just said, "Well den, what do I git? You use me, right? I give you good time?"

So much for chivalry.

They left the hotel together. Alice felt like everybody in the lobby was watching and screaming, "Slut! Look at the slut!" In her haste to plan the ultimate romantic evening, she forgot to pack clothes for the next day. There she was in her rumpled prom dress with Jamaican Bob beside her in his creased white tuxedo wearing a "yeah, I did her" grin. Alice never knew his real name. Everyone just called him Jamaican Bob.

He followed her home and waited on the back porch while she, with tears streaming down her face, avoided her parents and crept into her room. She opened her money jar that contained everything she'd earned working at the shittiest job ever at the mall, counted out five hundred dollars, snuck back outside, and handed it to Jamaican Bob. It was like paying him for fucking her. By his amused smile, Alice knew he thought the same thing. Then the little mafia creep kissed her goodbye! She should have slapped him, but she needed him to keep quiet, so she held her peace.

Jamaican Bob told the world anyway.

Next came five years of depression, breakdowns, anger, resentment, a litany of failed relationships, a botched college career, and intense psychotherapy.

What if.

What if Rory hadn't dumped her at prom?

What if Rory hadn't dumped her at prom and made everybody gossip horrible lies about her?

What if Rory hadn't dumped her at prom, broken her heart, and made everybody gossip horrible lies about her?

What if Rory hadn't dumped her at prom, broken her heart, made everybody gossip horrible lies about her, and driven her into the arms of another man who made her a whore?

What if.

"It was a lie," Rory said from the bathroom floor. "You gotta hear me out. This is what happened."

Chapter 34

Rory
The Kid Is Hot Tonight

10 years ago. High school prom.

In school, Mr. Scolnecki taught him that fear was an evolutionary response. Millions of years surviving predators, the elements, and starvation wired it into us. Fear made us smarter. With it, we made it to the 20th Century. But now we have guns, meteorologists, and fast food—there's nothing left to be scared of. Fear is an irrational response; therefore, Rory's fear that he might puke on Alice was stupid. However, Franklin D. Roosevelt, who's a President and gets paid more than a high school teacher, once said *we have nothing to fear, but fear itself*. Rory understood what he was saying. Fear could make you puke, and that could be embarrassing.

"Ugggghhhh!" Splash.

There went the rest of Rory's beef tortellini dinner. He vowed never to eat that again. Outside his stall, he heard them talking about him.

"Did he drink before we got here?" Todd asked.

"I don't think so," Brent said. "Rory? How ya doin' in there?"

Rory emerged to face their questioning stares. He saw himself in the mirror, and for a second some good vibes hit him.

He had clouded the hairspray on at the critical moment; his hair was frozen in time and perfection. The ends half-curled above his shoulders, the feathered sides swept back evenly, and the front hung a fraction into his eyes, gently moving as he walked. Rory thought he looked good in his tux too, but it wasn't enough. He was prepared to barricade himself in the boy's bathroom rather than face the apocalypse.

"Don't know where that came from," Rory said.

"Better hope it doesn't come again," Todd said. "Spewing chunks on Alice is a mood killer."

"Drink," Rory demanded, reaching out a hand for Brent's flask. He took a mouthful, swished it around like mouthwash, and let it burn its way down, napalming any vomit residue in its path.

Brent eyed Rory. "You sure you're okay?"

"All good," Rory lied.

"Make sure she blows you first," Todd said. "She won't do it after. Latex taste. They hate it." He stole the flask from Rory and took his turn at the well.

"Give it a sponge bath in the sink," Brent said. "Keep it fresh. She'll think you're a considerate lover."

Todd laughed and shoved the flask at Brent. "A considerate lover? He'll be lucky if he finds the hole!"

Brent choked on his drink and passed the flask to Rory.

Rory guzzled as much nectar of courage as he could, far more than his share. Despite Mr. Scolnecki's assurances, Rory's stomach behaved as if the last T-Rex on earth was about to break through the bathroom wall like the Kool-Aid Man. He thought about Mitchell Matthew's house party, and Todd's words of wisdom that night:

. . . you should drink a lot more before you jump between the sheets with Alice. Tommy told me once that if he drank five beers he wasn't a stall guy anymore. That's your test, buddy. If you can piss outside a stall next time, if you ever get a next time with Alice, you'll be ready for your big game.

Rory didn't have any beer, so he was trying to drink the vodka equivalent before they ran out. It was Todd's turn next. Rory handed him the flask knowing what would happen.

Todd wiggled it and frowned. "You liquor pig! Brent? He took the rest. I had, like, two drinks, max." He glared at Rory. "Dude, that's bad karma."

Rory didn't care. For the moment, he'd dulled his panic. Surrounded by a mild vodka haze and good hair vibes, Rory took action. He stepped up to a urinal, closed his eyes, breathed deep, and five seconds later, peed. He smiled as the trickling flow increased to full stream. He was ready.

"Wow, Rory's drunk," Todd said. "He's pissing at a urinal."

Rory flushed and led the way to the exit. "Let's roll!" He opened the door and let the sounds of "Wishing Well" wash over him.

Brent rushed past, punching him playfully in the arm. "He's right. You get limp dick now it's your fault."

"Limp dick?"

"Yeah," Todd said, on his way by. Rory had stopped moving. "Watch out."

The door closed behind them. Rory stayed in the bathroom. He thought getting so nervous that he'd puke on Alice was the worst possible scenario. Now there was a new contender: Limpus Penisoftilus.

Drugs. They all had side effects. Alcohol was no different. In

Rory's mad quest to cure his nerves, had he OD'd? How long did limp dick last?

Brent opened the door. "What are you doing?"

"What if I already have it?"

"Have what?"

Todd stuck his head in behind Brent. "What's going on?"

"Limp dick!" Rory yelled, annoyed at having to say it.

Brent stepped back inside. Todd came too.

"You're not serious?" Todd said.

Rory was sure his grim face looked as serious as a pimple breakout on picture day.

"It was a joke!" Brent laughed. "C'mon." He waved Rory towards the door.

Rory wasn't budging. "Seriously, dude. What if?"

"Oh my God, look," Brent said, "limp dick is a progressive disease. It requires many drinks over many hours before it strikes, and the other two key factors."

"What key factors?"

"First, you have to drink a ton."

"Okay." That one Rory knew already.

"You have to be exhausted."

Rory hadn't slept right for a week.

"And you have to be wearing a condom. Avoid any one of those three and you're good to go."

"Dude! Hello? I did drink too much. I am going to wear a condom. And it will be very late by the time I pull it on!" Rory was a triple threat.

They laughed. Big surprise. What were the chances they'd love to hear his limp dick story at breakfast tomorrow morning? A thousand percent.

Brent managed to stop laughing and pat his back. "Relax. You're just nervous. It's a big night."

"I'm fine," Rory said, shrugging off Brent's hand. "I cured that problem. This is a new problem."

"So test it," Todd said. "Get in there."

He grabbed Rory like a bouncer and hustled him into a stall, slamming the door behind him. "And pull it out."

"Sure, Todd." Rory banged on the door, but Todd held it from the other side. "I'll jerk it in here, blow it on the walls, and do some painting."

"If you can jerk and blow you don't have limp dick." Brent, the voice of reason.

Hmm, that was true.

He'd pull it out for a piss anyway, Rory thought. All he needed was full stiffness, vertical wood. Think happy thoughts and see what happens?

"Give me some space!" Rory said. "Go to the other side of the room."

Sounds of fading laughter indicated they followed his orders. Rory sat down, unzipped, and pulled it out.

WHOOMP! Something crashed into his head.

"Hey!" Rory went into fight mode, fists up and one leg raised for either a kung-fu kick or jewel protection.

"See if that helps," Todd said from behind the door.

The invader was a *Playboy* rolled up like a pepperoni. Todd must have stuffed it in his jacket.

"Thanks, asshole." Rory flipped it open to the centerfold.

Miss April. Bridget, a 34-22-32, 5'7, 110-lb blonde from Montreal, Canada. She carried a red umbrella and wore a transparent yellow raincoat.

Ambitions: To make the world a better place.

Turn-ons: Fresh air, animals, confidence, and sunshine.

Turn-offs: Pineapple pizza, wake-up calls, fingerprints on windows, and bad breath.

Rory held the centerfold in front to block any peeping toms. He heard his friends' snickers in the distance. That was good, he thought, in the distance.

He took a mental snapshot of Bridget, closed his eyes, and started the procedure. Rory imagined himself in his bedroom, his castle, with Alice. They were making out.

Stroke, stroke, stroke.

Alice wore a transparent yellow raincoat. Nothing else.

Stroke, stroke, stroke.

He slid it in. She moaned with delight.

Stroke, stroke, stroke.

He hammered away. She screamed his name.

Stroke, stroke, stroke.

Rory opened his eyes. It wasn't hardening. He adjusted his grip and tried again.

Stroke, stroke, stroke.

Doggy-style.

Stroke, stroke, stroke.

He spanked her. She cried out for more.

Stroke, stroke, stroke.

Rory's eyes snapped open. Still no wood. He switched hands, going lefty.

Stroke, stroke, stroke.

Back to missionary.

Stroke, stroke, stroke.

She smiled encouragingly.

Stroke, stroke, stroke.

He tried to put it in but it bent, repelled at the gate.

STROKE! STROKE! STROKE!

She was talking. No talking!

STROKE! STROKE! STROKE!

He slapped it against her furry parts like a belt.

Stroke.

stroke.

stro—

It was like those witch movies when a magic spell changes an adult into a child. All you see is the top of the kid's head peeking out of his huge adult clothes. That was Rory's penis. All he could see was the top of its head. Not only did Rory not get hard, but his penis sensed his fear and retreated, flinching away from the master's hand. Was that possible? Could he strike out with himself?

Apocalypse now.

He zipped up slow, swallowed his dread, and emerged from the stall. He whipped the door shut with a BANG! It clanged back and forth like a bell heralding the death of Rory Chase, and his little friend too.

"I'm infected!" Rory announced.

"Did you look at page twenty-seven?" Todd asked.

Todd grabbed the *Playboy*, flipped to page twenty-seven, and held a blue-eyed brunette with big breasts under Rory's nose. Rory ignored her, and him.

"Brent? What do I do?"

Brent smirked. Rory could tell his friend wasn't taking him seriously. "You just need to chill. I guarantee that won't happen with The Panther. In fact, I say you pop a woody first slow dance."

"And if I don't? What do I get with that guarantee? This is a once in a lifetime night."

"It's all in your head. It's not the booze."

"Even though you were a liquor pig," Todd added.

"Oh, shut up. I'll buy you a drink at our ten-year reunion."

"Although, if you're convinced you've got limp dick," Brent warned, "you might give yourself limp dick. Like a self-fulfilling prophecy."

"So I just need to chill?" Rory said.

"Exactly. Chill."

"Great! I can't be nervous, so now I'm nervous about *getting* nervous. Prom's over!"

Rory lashed out at the stall door, kicking it repeatedly.

The bathroom door opened. Mitchell Matthews took in the scene, and smartly exited. Everyone ignored him.

"Look," Brent said, "even if you can't perform—"

Todd turned away to muffle his laughter. Brent paused to gather himself too. Todd's laughter was contagious, but not for Rory. He wondered if limp dick was contagious. Rory had an urge to sneeze on Todd.

"Even if the worst happened," Brent continued, "and the night wasn't perfect, you still have to go for it. *A life spent making mistakes is not only more honorable, but more useful than a life spent doing nothing.* George Bernhard Shaw."

"George Bernhard Shaw? C'mon."

"What then? Are you planning to stay in here all night?"

"I may have a solution," Todd said. He removed a small, circular tin from his jacket pocket.

"What's that?"

"Boner cream," he said, grinning. "You rub it on and it keeps you hard."

"Says who? Where'd you get it?"

Brent snatched the tin and eyed it skeptically. It was a nondescript silver tin about the size of a shoe polish container with no markings or branding of any kind.

"College guy," Todd said.

"It works? For real? You've tested it?" Rory asked.

"Nope, haven't had a case of limp dick yet, but all the college guys use it. I carry it around for special events because ya never know."

Rory took the tin from Brent and popped the top. Inside was a neon blue cream.

"Don't double dip," Todd said. "Take enough with the first scoop to cover the whole shaft. Don't ever touch your dick and dip again, okay? Let's be hygienic."

"Don't you have to have a boner first?" Brent said.

"Rub it on and it gives you a boner."

"Does it absorb into my skin?" Rory asked. "Or will my dick turn blue?"

"He said you have to really rub it in, like hand cream or something, but yeah, it absorbs."

Was he actually going to do this? Rory thought. Rub blue boner cream on his dick? "Wait, if this gives me a boner now, how long am I walking around with a boner?"

Todd laughed. "That, I don't know, but check it out." He pulled on the end of Rory's oversized sport coat. "That can block a woody."

Todd was making a lot of sense. That scared Rory. Brent was usually the ideas man.

"Brent? What do you think?"

He shrugged. "You don't need it, but if it helps your confidence that's never a bad thing."

Sold. Back into the stall Rory went.

Next, he did as Todd suggested. He scooped out a big glob of cream with two fingers. It felt like toothpaste. He stuck the whole wad on the shaft, and squeezed his dick and the cream in his fist. Blue slime oozed between his fingers. He started the procedure again, not for the procedure's sake, but because it was the best way to rub the cream in.

"Is it working?" Todd asked.

"Shut up for a second."

The cream was warm and slick.

Warm.

Stroke, stroke, stroke.

And slick.

Stroke, stroke, stroke.

His hard-on was instantaneous. Beautiful, vertical wood. It felt great. Rory kept rubbing it in.

Rubbing.

Rubbing.

Oh, boy.

Oh, boy.

Oh, boy.

oh, oh, oh.

Stop!!

A little came out.

A couple drops.

Don't touch it again, Rory thought. He'd blow his load with one more stroke. "It's working!"

Cheers from outside the stall.

Rory emerged victorious with a boner still in his pants. Todd was right. His sport coat covered his woody.

He handed the cream back to Todd. "I owe you one, buddy."

"Told you it would work."

"It worked?" Brent asked, as if he had zero faith in black market blue boner cream.

"The proof's in the pudding," Rory said, laughing at his own disgusting joke.

Brent groaned. "Didn't need to hear that."

"They should make a pill for this stuff," Rory said.

"What should I charge?" Todd said. "Ten, twenty, fifty a tin?"

"It's tingly and warm," Rory said. "Feels like . . ." he trailed off.

"Feels like what?" Brent said.

"Hot."

"Hot? Like warm pussy hot?" Todd said.

Rory grabbed his crotch, and then looked at his throbbing hand, now bright red.

"Fuck!"

"What's wrong?"

"It's stinging! Like really bad!"

Todd eyed his cock cream critically, but offered no help.

"Wash it off!" Brent said.

In a panic, Rory, the stall guy, whipped his suddenly flaccid pecker out right over the sink. He didn't care. The pain was that bad.

"My dick is red, not blue!"

Bright, screaming red, like a—

"Like a sunburn," Todd said.

Rory ran the tap and splashed water over his radioactive dick. Bits of soggy cream-flakes careened into the sink as he rubbed it down.

But they weren't cream flakes.

It was Rory's skin.

"I'm peeling!"

It was agony. Every touch flayed Rory's penis. Pain like that should be reserved for when you're dying because you know the end is near.

"Oh shit," Brent said. "You're—"

"Bleeding! My cock is bleeding!"

The last thing Rory remembered as he faded into oblivion was Todd dropping his cream like a hot potato . . . .

. . . Rory woke on a pony, galloping through the gymnasium. His body bounced up and down and his arms hung loose around the pony's body. *Whose birthday was this? How long is my turn? Pony rides hurt my crotch . . .* a fresh wave of agony swept through Rory, ripping his eyes open and returning him to reality.

Laughing faces and questioning stares blurred his vision as Todd piggy-backed him at high speed towards the exit. Vaguely, Rory heard "Glory of Love" playing. Slow song, he thought. He should be with Alice.

"Out of the way! Coming through!" Todd said, plowing through the dance floor, laughing.

Laughing? He thought this was funny? Through his haze of pain Rory debated strangling his pony ride.

A hand gripped his shoulder.

"Rory? You okay?" Brent said.

Rory turned his ashen face to Brent, who ran beside him.

"Smile," Brent said. "We're making this look like a game. Try not to scream."

"My cock," Rory said. "Where is it?"

"Where is it?" Brent glanced at the floor back the way they'd come. "It's still in your pants, isn't it? Did it fall off?"

Rory let go with one arm and reached down. Pain flared as he touched his penis.

"Ow!"

Todd slowed, twisting his head to look back.

It stung like an open cut after you poured peroxide on it, and what Rory imagined fire ants would feel like if they attacked your penis. But it was still there.

"Keep going!" Brent said. "We're almost out."

When Rory gripped Todd's jacket again, he smeared it with blood.

"What are you guys doing?"

Todd skidded to a halt. Rory's eyes focused on a purple prom dress blocking their path. It was Alice, her smile questioning, but playful.

Todd looked at Brent. Brent looked at Rory. Rory forced an innocent smile through the pain.

"Have you been in the bathroom this whole time? Quit clowning around and come dance. Todd, let him down." Alice grabbed Rory and tugged. Rory held on.

A flurry of thoughts raced through Rory's brain: Love, sex, how a bleeding penis was not good for either of those things . . . .

"Go!" Rory panicked and slapped Todd's shoulder, urging his mount onward. Todd burst forward. As Rory flew past, words of explanation tumbled out.

"I can't do it, Alice. It's over tonight. Sorry."

He watched her face turn from shock, to anguish, and finally to anger, all in a matter of seconds. And then the night sky appeared overhead, and the gym doors closed behind him.

Chapter 35

Rory
The Never Ending Story

10 years ago. Hospital. Morning after prom.

Rory spent the morning convincing his parents they weren't allowed to tell anyone what happened. Not uncles, aunts, cousins, grandma, friends, co-workers, or other doctors or nurses they might know—nobody. To hammer home how important this was to his reputation and future, it took threats of never speaking to them again, words like loyalty and betrayal, and the phrases "if you loved me" and "if you want grandchildren." Rory had begged the nurse not to call his parents, but a seventeen-year-old minor has no rights in this land.

When Brent's car roared into emergency and Todd carried him inside fireman-style, Rory still figured some pills, moisturizing lotion, sleep on it, and he'd be business-as-usual in a day or two. The attending nurse's unprofessional look of horror and the doctor's diagnosis of second-degree burns with areas of "mutilation" changed that. After the doctor wrapped his penis like a cocoon and the painkillers kicked in, he fell asleep.

"Where did you get this blue cream?" His mom's voice woke him.

"From a college student. Darrin." It was Todd's voice, unusually fearful. "Tall guy, skinny."

"Darrin what?"

"I didn't know him, Mrs. Chase. Just Darrin."

"Where's the cream now?" His dad's rumbling voice.

"I threw it away, sir. Maybe we can find it."

"I think he's waking up," Brent said.

His mother's face loomed over his, full of concern. Her anti-Todd voice changed to a more soothing tone. "Oh, honey, how are you?"

Rory couldn't feel anything from his waist down. The only sting came from the I.V. protruding from his arm. He'd had nightmares with one terrifying thought controlling his brain.

"Did they amputate?" Rory said, fighting tears.

His dad laughed and squeezed his leg. "No, your little pal will heal just fine. You won't die a virgin."

Todd and Brent laughed too, though Rory could tell it was fake. They weren't comfortable here. That made three of them.

"He *is* still a virgin, correct?" His mother's anger targeted Todd again.

"Uh, yes, Ma'am," Todd said. "I think so."

Rory smiled at how scared Todd looked. "Mom? Dad? Can I talk to my friends alone?"

"You haven't told us what we're supposed to say," Dad said. "If we can't tell the truth, we need something."

"After I talk with Brent and Todd," Rory promised. "I'll know then."

"We'll be right outside," Mom said, stroking his forehead.

"Not *right* outside, Mom. Don't eavesdrop. Dad? Make sure Mom doesn't eavesdrop, please?"

"We'll go get a coffee," Dad said, leading Mom out the door.

Immediately, Rory grilled his friends. "Who knows and what's the damage?"

"We got out fairly clean," Brent said. "Nobody knows for sure what happened. That's good news. Although don't ever make me dress you again."

Rory laughed. He felt a wave of relief. If nobody knew, that was incredible! That was the big issue.

"Thanks for pulling up my undies," Rory said. "You guys saved my ass. Whose plan was it to piggy-back me out?"

Todd raised his hand. "I wouldn't want paramedics playing with my pecker at the prom. Figured you would feel the same."

"Good thinking. Thanks, Todd."

Todd nodded. "People asked about you though. Where'd you go? Are you coming back? We had to make something up."

"What'd you say?"

"We started with alcohol poisoning," Brent said. "We told everyone it was a precaution, but you felt sick after the piggy-back ride."

"Good, great," Rory said. "I'll take that. Hope my parents will too. So is that it? The secret is safe?"

"Yes, but like I said, we got out *fairly* clean, not perfect. Someone must have seen blood on the way out because a rumor started."

"What rumor?"

"After you broke up with Alice—"

"What?" Rory propped himself up on his elbows. He felt a sting down below. "I never broke up with Alice. Who said that?"

Todd and Brent exchanged a puzzled glance. "I heard you," Todd said. "You told her it was over."

"I said, and I quote, 'I can't do it, Alice. It's over *tonight*. Sorry.'"

"Yeah," Todd said. "That wasn't a breakup?"

"No! Didn't you hear me? I said *tonight*! I wanted to get out of there fast, but I also wanted to give her an explanation. I told her I couldn't do the prom thing. The night was over for me and I was sorry."

"You never meant to break up with her? Really?" Brent said.

"No! Does she think I broke up with her?"

Brent took a deep breath, looking at Todd. "Oh, man," he said.

"Shit," Todd said. "That sucks."

"What sucks? What happened?"

"There's no easy way to tell this story now," Brent said.

"Nope," Todd agreed.

"Guys?" Rory said, imploring them to get on with it.

"Alice got drunk and hooked up with Jamaican Bob," Brent said.

Rory felt machine gun fire hit his heart, each word slamming into him in a killing burst.

"She cheated on me with *Jamaican Bob*?"

"Well, not to defend her or anything," Todd said, "but we all thought you broke up, so in her mind it wasn't cheating."

Rory didn't want to yell at the guy who carried him to safety, so he said nothing. Instead, he turned to Brent. "How do you know they hooked up? Planet F's test?"

Brent nodded. "Teachers had to separate them on the dance floor. It was disgusting. They were all over each other. Stacy said she caught them in the girls' bathroom too, so who knows what happened there. I'd say Moon for sure. Todd?"

"At least, but that's not the worst of it."

"That's not the worst of it?" Rory said. "What do you mean? There's only one place worse than the Moon and—no? They didn't? Fuck off."

Rory's head whipped back and forth between Brent and Todd. Alice wouldn't do that. "She and Jamaican Bob . . . in the girls' bathroom . . . at prom?"

"Not there," Brent said, wincing at his words. "At the hotel you and Alice booked. Jamaican Bob's spreading the story. Lots of details. I think we have to assume the obvious. The Sun, Fuck-World."

"She totally crashed and burned," Todd said. "Once you dumped her—"

"I didn't dump her!" Rory yelled.

"I know, I know," Todd said. "Sorry. I meant after that miscommunication?"

Rory nodded his acceptance of that word.

"She went psycho. Total derailment. Not sure if the rumor had anything to do with it."

"What rumor?" Rory said.

"Yeah, I was trying to tell you earlier," Brent said. "Someone must have seen blood on the way out. A rumor started that she bit you during a BJ, on purpose. That's why you broke up and why you went to the hospital."

"What? Holy shit. This is totally messed up. I gotta call her. Pass me the phone."

"Wait," Brent said. "There's more. At first we ignored the rumor, or said it was BS, but the more she screwed around with Jamaican Bob, we said what the hell, the rumor works. So, your official cover story is that Alice was angry with you and bit your cock during oral, you broke up, drank too much in the bathroom drowning your sorrows and the pain, maybe got alcohol poisoning, but definitely needed stitches for your bite wound. Looking long-term, it's the perfect alibi. Totally explains a penis injury. You should write that all down when you get a chance."

It was impossible for Rory to process. His dick, brain, and heart hurt. It was worse than the truth. People knowing he got burned by dick cream, but still being *with* Alice was better than Brent's cover story *without* Alice.

She seized her opportunity, Rory thought. He was a pussy with limp dick, and Alice secretly needed wild Jamaican Bob to satisfy her. She knew he hadn't really broken up with her. It was just convenient; she took her "out" and hooked up with that big-dicked Jamaican girlfriend stealer.

"Rory? You want to call her and straighten this out?" Todd held the phone for him.

Rory tabulated the damage. His penis was out-of-commission and his girlfriend fucked another guy. How exactly does one straighten that out? The truth? The only thing the truth could do was embarrass him more. The truth couldn't erase what she'd done.

"Naw," Rory said, pushing the phone away. "We stick with the cover story."

Chapter 36

Alice
Mad About You

"Wow." Alice wasn't expecting that. "That wasn't a birthmark on your thingy?"

Rory shook his head. "Scar." He leaned against the sinks in his tightie whities, peering up at her with puppy-dog eyes.

"They gave me an I.V. with a morphine drip. I was in the hospital for a week. It took three months for the skin to heal."

Alice wasn't sure what to say. He didn't mean to dump her? It was all a misunderstanding? All these years? Really? Or was that another load of BS?

"You told everyone that I bit your penis, Rory. Not accidentally, but pre-mediated like I was a psycho chomper girlfriend. For years afterwards, every guy I dated tensed when I went near that area."

"I didn't start that rumor."

"You didn't stop it either. And you knew the truth, asshole."

"You cheated on me. Technically—"

"Technically not! We were broken up. As soon as you heard that rumor, misunderstanding or not, you should have come clean, but you didn't. All because—"

"Because you slept with Jamaican Bob! Let's say for argument's sake that you did think I broke up with you, and I'm not totally buying that, but let's say you did. What ex-girlfriend fucks another guy the *same night* as the breakup, at *prom* no less, and in the hotel room I half paid for?"

"I was drunk." Alice looked away. For the first time in ten years, she felt a twinge of guilt. Nobody had painted it like that before.

"That's your excuse? You were drunk?"

"And single, dumbass. My boyfriend dumped me *on prom night* no less! What's your excuse for slathering dick cream all over yourself? Needed a little help, did you? Jamaican Bob didn't."

She watched Rory's face wilt. That stung him.

"Okay, I should have squelched the rumor. I'm sorry," Rory said.

"Not just a rumor, a lie. Let's call it what it was. It may have started as a rumor, but you and your pals said it was true. You lied about me, Rory."

Rory hung his head. "I'm sorry. That was a crazy, shitty night. Are you sorry?"

Alice knew Rory wanted her to understand and forgive him, but should she? Did what he went through equate to what she went through? Did his teenage nerves and impotence fears match her humiliation and years of depression?

"Alice?"

She held up a hand to silence him. Alice counted in her head, building a pie chart of whose life ate the biggest slice of crappola. She added it all up and made her decision.

"You ruined my prom because you had butterflies in your tummy?" Her lips twisted into a sneer.

"But—"

"You chicken-shit loser! Three months for your skin to heal? Big deal three months! Try forever. I wish I could have been your nurse. I would have turned that I.V. into an enema real quick!"

Alice stuck out her thumb and jabbed it into the air, emphasizing how far she'd have shoved Rory's I.V. "My life sucked for years after prom. Years! Did you know that, Rory?"

Rory shook his head.

"Did you even care what happened to me after prom?"

"I thought you'd hate me, so I never called."

"Right! I do hate you. I have never loathed somebody more in my entire life. The thought of you gives me migraines and tremors. You're the reason I joined kick-boxing!"

She took a threatening step forward. Rory slid a few inches away, like a dog sliding his tightie whitie butt across the carpet.

"Do you know the courage it took for me to come in here? The willpower to let you touch me?" She shivered, the memory giving her the heebie jeebies. "For me to touch your scarred and hairy little thing? It is amazing what a person can endure for revenge. Truly amazing."

"So all of that," Rory gestured at the stall, "and the note. It was all for revenge?"

"If there's any justice in the world, those teeth marks on your penis will be permanent."

With that, she stormed out. She'd said her piece.

Alice passed Brent and Gary Bean returning with drinks. She flashed them a big Panther smile as she swept by.

Chapter 37

Brent
Broken Wings

Brent opened the bathroom door and saw Rory on the floor, pants down, motionless. Gary bumped into Brent from behind, spilling his beer.

"Rory?"

He lifted his head, but said nothing.

"Right on the floor?" Brent said. She must have put him on the tilt-o-whirl. This would be a story for the ages.

Rory pulled himself up with the help of a sink, but he was wobbly. He grabbed his last rum & pineapple from Todd's tray, and drank with a shaking hand. Brent knew what this was. It happened when you were less than a hundred percent, dehydrated, and you blew a load that could smother a campfire. Alice had left Rory bone dry.

"What happened? Speak!"

Rory hauled up his pants. "We were in there," he started, pointing to the stall, but then seemed to lose focus. Brent guessed what happened. She had sucked out some brain matter; hence the origin of the phrase, mind-blowing BJ.

"The stall?" Gary said. "You were in the stall?" His face beamed, much like his own Brent suspected.

Rory nodded and took another drink, keeping both Brent and Gary in agonizing suspense.

"How did you wind up out here?"

Rory leaned against the counter, rubbing his head and saying nothing.

"Breathe buddy, breathe. Take another sip." Brent lifted Rory's drink to his lips as if he were assisting an invalid. He figured the pineapple juice would do Rory some good, replenish his sugars.

Gary bent down and picked something up. He rose with the object cupped in his hands like a handful of Spanish gold doubloons, his eyes wide with awe.

"Are these?" Gary said, holding a pair of white cotton panties with green polka-dots.

"Yeah," Rory said.

"Oh." Gary raised them higher, presenting them to Rory like a priceless offering laid out on a silk cushion. Without a word, Rory took the panties and set them on the counter beside him.

Brent clapped him on the back. "She walked out of here with a smile on her face. Whatever you did, she enjoyed it."

"She gave me a tongue lashing," Rory said.

"You lucky bastard," Gary breathed.

"This calls for a celebration," Brent said. "We need more drinks!"

"No, no celebration," Rory said.

"What? The prophecy has been fulfilled. You are the chosen one." Brent dipped his fingers in his martini and anointed Rory's forehead. "You have been marked by The Panther."

Rory rubbed it off, annoyed. "You don't get it. She chewed me out."

"Chewed?" Gary said. "You mean like . . . prom? She did it again?" Gary frowned and stared at Rory's crotch.

"No! She never bit my dick. That's a prom myth."

That took Brent by surprise. Rory telling the truth about prom? What could make him do that?

"She bitched at me for ruining her prom," Rory said. "Nothing happened."

"Nothing?" Brent said. "Then why were your pants off?"

"Well, not *nothing*. She stroked it and teased me, but it was all a ruse to mess with my head. The note, everything. She hates me and she let me know it."

"Wait, wait," Brent said, confused. "Back up. She was stroking it and then what happened?"

"She rips into me. I destroyed her life. I'm a liar. I'm an asshole, blah, blah, blah. She put this thing on my . . . anyway, so I told her the truth."

"The real truth?"

"Yup, all the while keeping in mind your sensitivity theory. Remember that? Mature women appreciate a sensitive guy, you said? And you know what? Your theory sucks. She called me a chicken-shit loser. This isn't funny, by the way."

Brent and Gary sported amused grins.

"I know the theory sucks," Brent said. "I only proposed it to make you feel better. I didn't think you'd put it to the test."

"Thanks for that, buddy." Rory gave him the finger.

"I'm not Freud. Even Sigmund said: *The great question that has never been answered, and which I have not yet been able to answer, despite my thirty years of research into the feminine soul, is what does a woman want?"*

"Revenge," Rory said.

"You're not actually mad about this," Gary said.

"Did you not hear the story, Bean? The girl's a cock tease."

"I heard that a gorgeous woman came into the guy's can, and basically, if I'm following the story right, played with your dick for a while?"

"She hates me," Rory said.

"Yeah? Where's the hot chick who hates me enough to stroke my dick?"

A wave of self-pity hit Brent as he listened to Gary. Chicks were Gary Bean's bane, his big life dilemma. In this, Brent knew he was wiser and more experienced, but in all other things he had not been smarter than Mr. Bean. Gary had the job, the money, and a great future. Yet here he was, bemoaning his life's lack of muff and titty. That was sad, but sadder still was Brent. His overreaction to the loss of his presidency and scholarships, and his subsequent lifelong trust issues should be sent to the Guinness Book of World Records, Dumbass Category.

Boiled down, what Brent had done was throw a ten-year tantrum, and who had suffered the most for it? Him. A tantrum is a crazed moment of negative emotion, the same force that drove Gary to carve his revenge in the bathroom stall. When you wake from a tantrum and look upon all that you have wrought, you realize two things. One, you were wrong. And two, there is no taking it back.

Todd said it best. His final speech put the shit in the bag, laid it on Brent's doorstep, and lit the match. Brent was the biggest failure of all. Bigger than anyone knew. Those degrees Brent had? He didn't have them. He never officially graduated. Psychology and philosophy encompassed the bulk of his courses, but a college graduate he was not. It was a secret much like Rory's prom nightmare.

The bathroom door opened and Todd stepped inside. "This party sucks. We're getting Mickey now, so I can get the hell outta here."

Chapter 38

Todd
Mickey

Todd walked by Brent and Rory without waiting for them to agree. They didn't need to agree. He was doing it. And why was Bean still here? Seeing him made Todd feel guilty. For some reason, Gary's sad pee-pee story stuck with him. Guilt was not an emotion he liked, so he smothered it.

"How'd it go with Stacy?" Rory asked.

Todd wanted to ask what happened to Rory. He looked like he escaped from rehab, got hung up on the fence, and pulled down by Dobermans.

Todd answered as he walked to the back stall. "I told her I knew and called her a whore. Couldn't find Tinker. Probably a good thing."

"Probably," Rory said, as Todd disappeared inside the stall. Brent stayed quiet.

Todd lifted the toilet tank lid and peered inside. He figured Brent was wrong, but he wasn't. The little bugger was still there.

He rolled up his sleeve, plunged his hand into the water, and tugged. The old duct tape released easily. It was rusted as all hell, not a glint of shining silver remained, but it was him.

Todd stepped out of the stall and displayed the remains of their sunken treasure to Brent and Rory. Gary watched, confused.

"This," Todd said, explaining to Gary's duh-face, "is Mickey. A flask of cognac we planted on our last day of high school."

"I can't believe he made it," Rory said, taking Mickey from Todd. "Don't they clean the toilets around here?" He wiped his hands and passed Mickey to Brent.

"How about some glasses?" Todd said.

Rory gathered three empties and rinsed them.

"What happened to your no liquor in the bathroom policy?" Todd asked, eyeing Gary's beer.

Gary smiled. "Policy change."

Rory handed out the glasses, skipping Gary. From the corner of his eye, Todd watched as Gary fidgeted, unsure what to do with himself.

Brent twisted Mickey's cap. It loosened in grinding steps, throwing rust dust with each turn. "We waited ten years for this," he said. "Glad we all could make it."

Brent didn't look at Todd, but Todd figured the last part was for him. Brent was probably surprised he came back after his dramatic exit. Todd was too.

He'd left. He was out in the parking lot, in his car, with the engine on. He sat there thinking, where am I driving to? For his whole life, it was either Brent and Rory, or Stacy. Stacy had failed him, and it wasn't looking great for his friends either, but was he prepared to let them go too?

Brent began his speech. "I remember what we said ten years

ago. 'This is so we never forget.' We knew things would change after high school, that we might lose our way. But Mickey's here to remind us of our teenage jackass selves!"

Everyone laughed except Todd, who forced a smile.

"Ten years later are we better men? Are we better friends than the boys who buried this treasure? No."

The room grew quiet as Brent's speech took a serious turn.

"Why? What happened? Friends aren't perfect. Friends fight and friends let you down. The truth is there are parts of both you, Todd and Rory, that I could do without. Parts I'd like to fix, and have tried to fix many times. I'm not perfect either. I know there are parts of me that you'd change if you could."

"Amen," Todd said.

"But back in high school," Brent said, "our imperfect parts were never enough to separate us. When's the last time we hung out like this since high school?"

Todd knew it'd been a long time. They all knew. They spent their first summer together, but not much after that. Days turned to weeks, weeks to months, and months to years. Todd had his reason. Stacy didn't like it when he drank with his friends, and he didn't like it when she was out of his sight for too long. That plus fifty hours a week of work didn't leave much time for old friends. Todd wondered what Brent and Rory's excuses were.

Nobody answered Brent's question. Todd figured they were like him, embarrassed to admit their priorities had changed despite the solemn vows they'd sworn in high school.

"It's been awhile," Brent answered for them, "probably six or seven years. What's our excuse? That I live a couple hours away and Rory lives, what, forty minutes away? We might as well be living on separate continents."

The circle grumbled its agreement.

"I know it can't ever be the same. That's the beauty of high school. We spent every day together. We were all in the same boat. But unless we get the same job, or go to the same college, or live next door to each other, that shared life is impossible. Fair enough, but can we do a hell of a lot better? You think Mickey is proud of us?"

More grumbles and frowns from the circle. Brent held up Mickey. "It's been ten years too long, but we have this moment. A time to clear the air, to say what we need to say, and reforge the bonds of friendship. Who wants to go first?"

Todd raised his hand. "I can. This has been bugging me since it came out. Gary?"

Gary looked up, wondering if he heard right. "Me?"

"Yes, you," Todd said. "If there's anything I can sympathize with it's losing a potential score. If my comment at the dunk tank cockblocked you in any way, and made you lose that action—"

"You know it did," Gary said. "Peggy Sanders, if you didn't know, is a New York model now."

"For real?" Rory said. "A model?"

"Yup. Gorgeous, like I always knew she would be."

Shit, that's a double suck, Todd thought. "Look, what I'm trying to say is that I can't imagine not getting laid, ever." That was a tough one for Todd to wrap his head around. "All I can say is I'm sorry, and if there's anything I can do, let me know."

"I'll think about it," Gary said.

"Think about what? Forgiving me?"

"No, I forgive you," Gary said, smiling. "But I'm sure I can think of a way you can make it up to me."

Todd didn't expect Gary to take his offer. He wondered what a rich banker would ever need from him.

"Brent," Todd said. "The same goes for you, about what I said at the dunk tank. It fucked you up too. I guess shit I say has consequences I can't see."

Brent nodded. "Apology accepted. Anything else?"

"Yeah. You pricks moved away. You left me here with a bitchy wife and nobody to hang out with. I got a problem with that."

He said it jokingly, but Todd meant it. It was selfish; selfish of him to feel that way, and selfish of them to leave. When Todd lashed out at his friends tonight, it was mostly for BS reasons. A real reason was that they abandoned him. It all seemed to go bad for Todd after his friends left. He didn't expect them to take his comment seriously, and they didn't.

"You could have visited us anytime," Brent said. "Think of it this way. You have a good excuse to leave town whenever you want."

Yeah, sure, thought Todd. Brent knew nothing about marriage. He was supposed to leave his flirtatious and booze-loving wife alone for a few days? Wonder what would happen? Nope, he was stuck in town. His friends would have to come to him, which they never did.

"I'm the married one, Brent. You and Rory should be coming to me."

"We should do that," Rory said. "Take turns visiting each other. I like that idea."

"Me too," Brent said.

"Yeah," Gary agreed.

Todd smirked, but said nothing. What was Gary thinking? That he'd hang out with them?

Todd rattled off one last item. "We already talked about you and Rory keeping secrets. You think you guys could do better with that? How about no secrets? We're supposed to be a trio. That's all I have to say for now. I'll wait until it's your turn, Brent."

Todd made sure to look Brent straight in the eye. Brent's turn would be a doozy.

"You missed something while you were gone," Rory said. "There's one story I need to catch you up on."

"Yeah, I can tell," Todd said, looking Rory up and down. "Good enough. It can wait. Who's next?"

"I don't have much to say," Rory said. "I can't look at you guys and say my life is your fault. Yes, it was Todd that gave me the blue death cream at prom." Rory paused. "Okay, I'm a little pissed off about that."

"I didn't know what it was," Todd said, pleading innocence.

"I realize that, but you never officially apologized for it either."

"You don't blame me, do you? It was an accident, Rory. I was trying to help."

"It's not about 100 percent blame. It's about taking responsibility for your part in it, accident or not. What did you just say? Shit you say has consequences you can't see? Same goes for shit you do. You gave me the blue death cream."

"I carried you out, remember? I thought that made us even?"

"That was cool, and I thanked you for that, but no, it does not make up for almost burning my dick off. If not for me, you might have used that stuff first."

"I always felt bad about it. But when you put it that way, I feel like shit. Consider this my official apology. And I guess I owe you one too."

"Alright, we're doing good here," Brent said. "Anything else, Rory?"

"Yeah, I had some pills tonight. Todd, you kicked in my stall door and knocked them in the toilet. Why did you do that? Why kick in my door when you knew I was in there sick? How is that being a good friend?"

"Pills?" Todd said. "I didn't know you were taking pills."

"Lots of people take pills. Doesn't matter. I know you didn't mean to knock them out of my hand, but why kick in my door for any reason?"

"It was funny," Todd said. "I didn't think—"

"About consequences," Rory said. "You don't care. You're unpredictable. That makes it hard to hang out with you. Since we're talking about reforging friendships, I gotta tell you. Unless you start acting more like a friend, someone who cares about my problems too, I can't be your friend."

"Jesus, Rory. That's heavy, don't you think?" Todd said, taken aback. "The pills were an accident."

"It's not just the pills," Rory said. "I care about your problem. You and Stacy. I'm trying to help. But do you care about my problem? Prom was bad for me, you know that. It's been downhill ever since. I don't know how to fix it. But do you give a shit? Or do you only give a shit when it's convenient for you?"

"I guess I think it's small potatoes," Todd answered truthfully. "You talk about prom like it's the end of the world. I don't see it that way. An unhappy marriage heading for divorce, that's a real issue. You try dealing with that. You've always had stuff handed to you, Rory. You've always been a drama queen. That's your problem. If you'd see your shit for the silly crap it is then maybe you wouldn't be so uptight about me kicking your door. But okay, if your stuff is as serious to you as my stuff is to me, then you're right. I can do better for a friend. I get it."

"Okay," Rory said. "Good to hear."

That was hard for Todd to say. Rory was right. He didn't need to kick in his stall door. That was a jackass move and had nothing to do with Rory. Todd was pissed off at the world and just wanted to kick something. He made a promise that he'd do better. His friendships were important to him. He couldn't lose his wife and them.

Brent cleared his throat, breaking an awkward silence. "Good stuff. Rory? Done?"

"Done," Rory said.

"Can I go next?" Gary asked. "If I'm allowed? I'm not sure I should be here. Mickey's your thing, not mine. I want to be here. I promise that even though I don't understand what you're saying, like what is blue death cream and why is it on Rory's dick, that everything you've said is in the vault. Sealed and padlocked."

"I can't speak for everyone, but it's okay with me," Brent said.

"Me too," Rory echoed.

Todd wasn't so sure. Did Gary belong here for the Mickey ceremony? No. Was it a big deal that he was here anyway? Probably not. Todd could either be a hardass about it and make a scene, or go along with his friends.

"Up to you," Todd said. "If you've got something to say, say it."

"Thanks," Gary said. "I want to talk to you, Brent. Did you ever consider us friends in high school?"

Brent sighed. "Not really, Gary. We never hung out."

"But we did. In class. We had good talks. You always gave me advice and helped me out."

"I did that for everyone. It might have been what got me elected class president. That's just me. When I think of high school friends, I think about the three amigos, Rory, Todd, and I. But that doesn't mean I didn't like you in high school. I did."

"Okay, let's forget about high school. Let's talk tonight. In the two hours I've spent with you guys, I've been a part of some cool things. I like that. I can earn my place. I could be a heck of a fourth amigo if you give me the chance?"

Todd laughed. "We don't do this stuff every day. Didn't you hear what Brent said? It's been six or seven years. After tonight, the seas will calm and your exciting evening will be a distant memory, and so will we."

"He's right," Brent said. "Don't think hanging out with us is like this all the time. It's not. In high school maybe, but not anymore."

"But that's what Mickey is about, right? You want to recapture those good times."

"Yeah, that's kind of the point," Brent said, "but not exactly. The three of us lost touch. I don't want that to happen again. The hope is we can schedule a monthly get together or something."

"That's what I'm talking about!" Gary said. "You mentioned visiting each other. We're young. You're cool. I can learn to be cool."

Todd laughed again. Gary Bean was surprisingly entertaining.

"I'm talking about some wild weekends. Doesn't that sound like fun?" Gary said. "Just call me if you're heading out for drinks. I've got connections. I could arrange some stuff. Don't dismiss the fourth amigo idea completely."

"All right, all right," Brent said, smiling at Gary's pitch. "When I'm in town I will give you a call and we'll go for beers. Sound good?"

"Great," Gary said. "But you," he pointed at Todd, "and I are going out for drinks next weekend, even if you have to fake it. You're going to help me land some babes. That's what you're going to do to make it up to me."

The fourth amigo, Gary "The Urinator" Bean? That'll be the day, Todd thought. Still, he was a man of his word. "Done. But first round's on you."

"Done. Yeehaw!" Gary twirled an imaginary lasso above his head.

He must be drunk, Todd thought. Nobody could be that excited and still be sober. Gary's ridiculous mood was infectious. He had the room in stitches.

After the laughter died down, Brent spoke. "I guess it's my turn?"

Nobody disagreed, so Brent prepared to say his piece. Todd perked up. This is what he'd been waiting for. Brent seemed pale all of a sudden. This was going to be hard for him, and it damn well should be.

"First," Brent began, "none of you should listen to me anymore. I don't have any university degrees. I never graduated."

"Never graduated?" Rory said. "Why not?"

"I'd need a real psychologist to answer that, Rory, but it seemed like getting ahead was pointless, that even if I climbed the ladder, someone would pull me down, so what was the point in trying? That's what I used to think, but I'm getting better. Anyway, I'm sorry I didn't trust you guys with the truth."

Todd shook his head for all the times Brent paraded out his fake degrees and made him feel stupid. But he held his tongue and waited patiently for the doozy.

"Wait, wait, wait," Gary said. "Are you saying that because of my mistake at the dunk tank, you got suspended, impeached, arrested, *and* never graduated from university?"

"It's okay, Gary. I'm thinking I'll go back now. I've got time."

"No, no, no," Gary said. "Well, I mean, yes, go back, for sure, but what do you do for work now? What do you make?"

"Na-da. Currently unemployed."

"Since when?" Rory said.

"I got canned this week. I'll get another. Would you guys relax?" Brent laughed.

Todd watched but said nothing. Brent seemed happy. The unemployed, college dropout was happy? How was that possible?

"You listen to me," Gary said. "You have a job at my bank. Junior something. We've got this education support thing too, so you can go to school at the same time. It's gonna work. You come see me Monday morning."

"I don't live here, Gary, but thanks."

"So move back! What the hell? Come out for drinks with me and Todd next weekend."

Brent kept laughing, and Todd kept watching and waiting.

"I'll think about it, Gary, but for now," Brent faced Todd, "there's something I've been waiting to tell you."

"Yup." Here it comes, thought Todd.

"It happened in Mr. Beauregard's history class. Stacy used to screw around with me, reach back and pinch me under the desk, that kind of thing."

"Okay," Todd said, playing dumb.

"One day she reached back and accidentally found a woody." Brent coughed and looked down, embarrassed. "Instead of flinching away, she rubbed. And kept rubbing until it was done."

"You went in your pants?" Todd said.

"Yup, in my pants. You two had just started dating, but I should have told you. I'm sorry." Brent looked straight into Todd's eyes, trying to make it look like he meant his apology.

This was unexpected and it pushed Todd beyond his limits. He had planned to forgive Brent for the hand job. But now there was a problem.

Todd knew the truth.

Before Todd came for Mickey, Stacy confessed the hand job, trying to show him that she was more honest than his so-called friends. It might have worked if she hadn't sucked on Lewis Tinker's face. She was lost to him now, but Todd realized he didn't want to lose his friends too. He would forgive Brent. But that was before Brent's lie. In Stacy's story, Brent secretly slipped his cock out first, and when she reached back to pinch him, thinking she'd get his leg, he surprised her with his dick. Then he held her hand down there, forcing her to do the job. Todd would have forgiven him if he'd told the truth. But not now.

It was quiet in the room except for the leaky faucet. Drip, drip; drip, drip.

"I am sorry, Todd," Brent said. "I didn't mean for it to happen. I'm glad you know. I'm hoping you can forgive me."

"Just pour," Todd said.

"Todd?"

"Pour."

"Are you okay?"

"Pour!" Todd grabbed Mickey and poured an ounce of clear liquid into his glass.

"Wait a sec," Gary said. "You guys aren't really going to drink that? That flask has been in the toilet for ten years."

"It's Mickey," Todd said through gritted teeth.

Gary flinched at the venom in Todd's tone.

"Doesn't cognac age well?" Rory said. "Wouldn't it be better in ten years?"

"Here we go then," Brent said, holding out his glass. Todd poured an ounce in his, and then Rory's.

Todd sniffed his glass. Toilet water.

Brent and Rory did the same. "Doesn't smell like cognac," Rory said. "I'm no chemist, but this is toilet water."

"That's Hepatitis A," Gary said. "I wouldn't drink that."

"We're all drinking," Todd growled. "You too, Bean. You wanted to be the fourth amigo? Here ya go."

Todd found a glass for Gary and poured the toilet water. Gary didn't protest under Todd's baleful stare.

"Todd's right," Brent said, nodding to him, a lame attempt at making peace. "This is Mickey. To the glory days and to even more glory!" He raised his glass.

"Cheers!" Only Rory echoed the toast.

Todd hesitated. None of them drank. Pussies, he thought.

"Toilet water, huh?" Brent swished it around his glass. "What do you think?" he asked Todd.

"I think we'll talk later," Todd said.

"Good."

Awkward silence. Drip, drip; drip, drip.

"Which Hepatitis was that again?" Rory said.

"You know," Gary said, "in ancient Greece they used to toast their gods by spilling some on the floor. It was a mark of honor and respect."

Brent brightened. "That works, doesn't it?" He looked from Rory to Todd.

Todd didn't say anything. Rory raised his glass. "To the girls of Leelin High?"

"To the girls of Leelin High!"

Brent, Rory, and Gary tipped their glasses, sending Mickey to the floor. Todd didn't hesitate this time. Mickey represented friendship, so he threw his in the face of his fake friend, Brent.

Ten years ago, while the rest of the school buried pictures, essays, and other assorted crap in a ceremony commemorating their graduating class's "official" time capsule, Todd, Rory, and Brent snuck off to the bathroom. Back then, Brent had said, "What better way to remember high school than with the very thing we used to forget it?" True enough. Brent's flask had been a steady prop for three years, the centerpiece for many fun-filled nights. Usually they'd fill it with rum, vodka, peach schnapps, or jagermeister, but they wanted something special to salvage after ten years, so Todd stole a bottle of cognac from his dad's liquor cabinet.

But it was all bullshit. Because as Todd lowered Mickey into the tank, and all three of them shook hands and shared a dude moment, Brent knew that Todd's future wife had rubbed him off.

"I didn't know you were serious about her," Brent said, wiping toilet water from his eyes.

Rory tried to calm him down. "Take it easy, Todd. It was a long time ago."

Todd squared off with Brent, cornering him between the stalls and urinals. "You pulled it out, didn't you? You held her hand down there and forced her to do the job."

"What? No!" Brent said. "Did she tell you that? She said she might. That woman is incredible. Rory? Tell him."

"It's true, Todd. She said that if Brent ever told you she'd make it sound like he forced her to do it."

"Bullshit. She has no reason to lie. I already told her it was over. And she told me first!"

Brent wasn't acting nearly apologetic enough for Todd. If he didn't start groveling immediately, this was going to get ugly.

"She asked me not to tell you," Brent said. "It seemed logical at the time. She didn't want your relationship to end before it began."

"Logical? I'll tell you what's logical, professor. Kicking your ass is logical!"

Todd punched Brent in the gut. Brent crumpled, doubling over, his breath coming in gasps.

"Todd!" Rory yelled.

Todd ignored Rory like the bull ignores the flies.

"Look where you are, Brent," Todd said. "The karma boomerang zone."

It was the same speech Brent gave him earlier, about the consequences of Todd's repeated fuck-ups. Brent thought he was perfect. Todd used to think so too. Now he knew different.

Todd shoved him to the side. Brent hadn't said anything since the punch. The wordsmith had nothing to say, thought Todd. He knew Todd was right.

Rory again tried to come to Brent's rescue. "Todd, she's lying to you, come on! It went down like Brent said. It might be hard to hear, but at the time Stacy was known to be—"

"Slutty?" said a shaky voice from the doorway. Stacy stood there, her mascara smudged from crying.

Todd didn't want to look at her. He turned away.

"Was that what you were going to say, Rory?" she asked.

Chapter 39

Stacy
Every Rose Has Its Thorn

Stacy waited for Rory's reply and for Brent to stand. She knew what the fight was about. "Well, Rory? Was that what you meant or not?"

"If it walks like a duck, quacks like a duck, and fucks like a bunny, it's a slutty duck." Rory stung her with his wit.

"Todd and I are going through some stuff, Rory. I don't expect you to understand. Todd?"

Todd stared at the condom machine, his back to everybody. He didn't answer and he didn't turn. This was what he did at home. He shut off and then exploded. If Stacy kept talking, she'd eventually say something that provoked a response.

"I pulled out my cock, held your hand down there, and made you jerk me off?" Brent said. "That's the story you're going with?"

"It's the truth," Stacy said, sticking to her guns. "I suppose I could have torn my hand away, but it happened so quick I was in shock." Her eyes drilled into Brent's. *Remember what I told you? It's called managing your marriage.* If it served her cause and the greater good then a little white lie was worth it.

"You've put your husband in quite the pickle," Brent said. "Now he has to choose who's lying and who's not. What are the odds that the married woman grinding her ex on the bathroom floor isn't telling the truth?"

"Yes, guilty of kissing another man, thank you, Brent. Would you like to brand me with the letter *A*?"

Brent didn't answer.

"Todd? Can we have this conversation alone, or should I have it with your friends?"

Todd didn't answer either.

Fine. She'd talk to Rory.

"Rory, did you know that Todd has been lying to me for ten years?"

"About what?" Rory said.

"Prom. Every year I ask him what happened with you three in the bathroom, and every year he tells me the same tired story about Alice biting your penis, you getting drunk, blah, blah, blah. That's a lie though, isn't it, Rory?"

"What do you know about it?" Rory said.

"It's easy to lie when it serves your purpose, isn't it? Every year I hoped Todd would be honest with me, but every year he lied. I know about the blue cream. Lewis told me how he created it in chemistry class. It was a prank meant for Todd, of course, and I was mad at Lewis for doing it. I never spoke to him again for four years. It's sad that you were the one who suffered, Rory. Did it leave a scar? I suppose you should be proud of Todd. He stayed true to the lie, even though it meant betraying his marriage vows to me."

It was like a stink bomb exploded in the room.

All faces, Todd included, turned to stare at her. Rory's jaw hung open.

"Lewis Tinker made the cream?" Rory said.

"For me?" Todd said.

"You want me to kick him out of the reunion? I'll do it. I'll kick his ass out right now!" Gary said.

"You knew this and yet still you cavort with that maniac?" Brent said.

"I said I didn't speak to him for four years. That was punishment enough. Now we're friends again."

Stacy barely finished the word "friends" before groans echoed from every corner of the room.

"Yes! The chemist! Lewis Tinker! Of course it was him!" Rory said. "How could we not see that?"

"Sorry, Rory," Todd said. He turned his back again and faced the condom machine.

"Todd!" Stacy yelled, trying to get him to turn around again. "The point is you've been lying to me too, just like I've been lying about Lewis. You're right, we're too close. But what happened tonight has never happened before. I tried to say no."

"You may have said no," Todd said, making a slow and deliberate turn to face her, "but your tits, lips, and hips were saying yes, yes, and yes."

"You were my first, Todd. My first and only."

More groans from everyone. Stacy began to cry.

"You wrote your number in the guy's can," Rory said.

"It was a joke. Teenage boys are so pathetic and desperate. It was fun listening to them beg."

"Them? Boys?" Todd said, emphasizing the plural.

"It was high school. You weren't the only boy to call. There were lots. Gary called."

Gary sagged as all eyes focused on him, especially Todd's. "She said no!"

"Todd, listen. I teased, but I never did it. Except with you. And I swear, I didn't rub Brent for more than ten seconds before that boy creamed himself."

Brent laughed. "That part's true. It didn't take long." The mood lightened in the room, but not in Todd's bubble.

Stacy stepped towards him. "But you came over later that night, remember? And something happened. For me, anyway. I was so scared of screwing us up, I made Brent promise never to tell."

"I should have told you anyway," Brent said. "Then we wouldn't be in this mess a decade later."

"Yes, *ten years* later. Can we get past this at least?" Stacy said. "The future is more important."

"Would you rather be married to me or Tinker?" Todd said.

Stacy knew the question was coming and was ready for it. If she loved Lewis, this was the perfect opportunity to say goodbye to Todd and move on. She'd fantasized about that very thing often enough, but tonight, when she could exchange husband for old boyfriend, the prospect seemed rather blah. Why?

She wanted to have her cake and eat it too. Screw it, why not? She was allowed to have a little fun. She loved Todd. She despised him half the time too, but she still loved him. Lewis, on the other hand, made her fires burn. She got her passion from him. The bedroom flames had long since cooled with Todd. But, weirdly, "just" Lewis seemed rather boring. If they didn't have to steal kisses and plan clandestine meetings, she was just a pathetic divorced woman living in the past with her pudgy ex-boyfriend. Where was the romance in that? No, she needed both men. And since preserving a marriage is a good and godly thing, Stacy could lie about anything she wanted to make that happen.

She cleared her throat and answered Todd. "Lewis and I have a connection. You know that, and I don't hide it, but I chose to marry you."

"If you had to do it over again, you'd still pick me?"

Stacy's eyes darted to the floor, and back up quickly. "Yes," she lied.

If she took Todd's question literally, she knew the truthful answer was no. If she knew then what she knew now and could go back in time, she'd do things differently, like not get married at all. Or she'd marry Lewis and screw around with Todd. She smiled inwardly. That's what would have happened if she'd married Lewis. Perhaps there was something to that destiny crap after all.

The room was quiet while Todd mulled over her answers. There was only the drip, drip of the leaky faucet.

"Give me a second with the guys," Todd said.

"Why? You need to consult with the three wise men about our marriage? How about talking with your wife?"

"I just need a minute," Todd said.

"Is it a second or a minute, Todd? Fine."

Without another word, Stacy walked from the room, not meeting any of the eyes she knew were staring at her. Had she done enough to keep Todd? She wasn't sure. Stacy hated herself right now, but she was proud too. She had done the right thing, hadn't she? She would lecture her heart day after day until it submitted and agreed.

Chapter 40

Todd
If I Could Turn Back Time

"Why am I married?" Todd asked the room, but Brent in particular.

"Because you signed a document surrounded by candles. Never sign something ringed by open flames," said the prick.

Todd glared. "You're not allowed to be a smart ass right now."

"What am I allowed to be? You want to hit me again?" Brent challenged him, pointing to his chin. "According to you I'm the biggest failure of all. Isn't that what you said? I said I was sorry. I'm not lying. You still want to be friends with the big failure or not?"

"You owe me a hand job," Todd said.

"Here ya go." Brent put his hand out to shake.

Clever bastard, thought Todd. He shook hands anyway.

Brent pumped his hand up and down. "Should I keep going for ten seconds, or is that good for you?"

Todd didn't punch him. "Not a hand job from you, idiot."

"Unbelievable," Rory said. "Lewis Tinker and the blue death

cream. Doesn't that blow your mind?" He looked at Todd and read the room. Wrong topic. "Anyway, forget that. We're talking about you. If this was high school and she was just your girlfriend, what would you do?"

"I'd kick—"

"Besides kick Lewis's ass."

"I'd dump her."

"And now that she's your wife?"

"I don't know! That's why I'm asking you guys."

"So you'd stay with her for fear of losing your car, your condo, half of everything you own, and by the way, thank your turtle sperm you don't have any kids," Brent said.

"We own a lot of crap."

"All right, so if a genie popped out of this toilet and said, 'Yo, Todd, you wanna be married or not? All I have to do is snap my genie fingers and it's like it never happened.' You'd take the deal and be happy?"

"Do I get three wishes, or just the one?"

"Just one."

Todd thought about it. With two more wishes, he might do it. He'd wish for one night with Stacy in high school, no, three nights. That should cover every sexual position. Wish number two would be for a beautiful second wife with a guarantee that he'd be happier with her. Todd had seen enough of those "what if" movies to know that different is not necessarily better. His dad used to say, 'do you pick the devil you know, or the devil you don't know?' That's what made answering Brent's question so hard.

"That's a tough question," Todd said.

"Are you religious?" Rory asked.

"A little."

"You didn't get married in a church. It was in the park, wasn't it?"

"So? I had a priest. It still counts, doesn't it?"

"In the eyes of a lawyer it will. Do you love her?"

"I guess so. And don't ask me that again."

"Do you like her?" Brent said.

"I just said—"

"That you loved her, yeah, I heard that. You probably always will on some level, but do you roll your eyes every time she says something annoying? Do you hug and kiss her when you leave for work? How long do you spend picking out her Christmas card?"

In Todd's head he rattled off the answers. Yes, no, 5 seconds. "You heard what she said. We're going through some stuff."

"Look, we're cool about everything and we're still friends, right?" Brent said.

Todd nodded.

"Then I'm going to ask you something hard."

"Okay."

"Are you being a hypocrite?"

"About what?"

"About condemning Stacy for cheating with Tinker. Are you being a hypocrite?"

"What are you saying?"

"You know what I'm saying. I'm just saying it without actually saying it."

It was like Brent had a drill that could bore into Todd's head and make a peephole only he could see through. "If the answer was yes, would your advice be any different?" Todd said, dodging a direct answer.

"No."

"Bullshit. If I said I'd done it too, then you'd say we're even, get past it, move on."

"No," Brent repeated.

"Then what? What would you say?"

"I'd say it doesn't matter. It doesn't matter if you've done it too, or if she's right, or if you're right. What matters is if you're happy."

"I think about it, okay? All the time. But the answer is not yet. I've never cheated on Stacy. I'm not a hypocrite. I'm an asshole sometimes, but I'm working on that. But now I'm thinking that because she cheated, I should too. Not just because it might be hot and fun and all of that, but because it would make us even. If we were even, then we could stay married because that's fair."

"What if she keeps cheating with Lewis?" Brent said.

"Then I keep cheating with somebody."

"And if the cheating goes further?" Rory said. "You know what I mean. Maybe it already has?"

"Yeah, I know what you mean. Then I do the same thing."

"Maybe she starts seeing more guys, and not just Lewis," Brent said.

"Fine, same here. Maybe we'll be happier. As long as we know what the other is doing, maybe it's the best of both worlds?"

"You don't want to be a swinger," Gary said. "That's what you're describing. I had a friend who did that. He tried to make it sound cool, but the guy was miserable. There were rules, and favorites, and more fighting than you could ever squeeze into one relationship. Swinging is the *worst* of both worlds. You're not in love, so you don't get that benefit, and you don't get to sleep with whomever you want, that's a myth. Stacy will start approving or vetoing your partners. It's the most ridiculous situation, and it never lasts. I'm a virgin and I wouldn't do it to get laid. Save yourself the headache and go right to single."

Todd listened to Gary and then turned to Brent.

"I agree with Gary. Single or bust, buddy. Now what?"

"Now I either find a hotel and call a lawyer in the morning, or we go home together and one of two things happens. We pretend we were never here, or we argue about it the whole night and come up with a plan."

"What kind of plan?"

"I don't know. A way to fix it."

"How long have you guys been going through this stuff?" Rory said.

"A while."

"Have you made plans before?" Brent said.

"Yeah."

"And?"

"And it hasn't been the right plan."

"Have you tried counseling?" Gary said.

"Yeah, it never works. Fuck it."

When Stacy appeared and begged to take him back, Todd knew what he was going to do. This debate was a big charade. What did he have in his life besides her? What prospects? He didn't believe his friends would visit like they promised, and he wasn't the big-shot high school tough guy anymore. How much more of a loser would he be if he was divorced? Could Todd "the Rod" come back from the standing eight-count? He could hear his old coach's voice in his ear: "Take a seat on the bench, son, you're done."

"Tell you what, you get hold of that bathroom genie and then we'll see. Until then, I think I'll call it a night and go home and argue with my wife."

Todd grabbed Mickey and toasted his friends. "To me!" He shook the flask dry, spraying its last drops all over the bathroom.

Behind him, the door opened and Stacy stepped inside. Tears poured down her face.

"What?" Todd asked.

"I didn't want to tell you like this," Stacy said, her voice cracking. "But before you decide to stay or go, you should know." She took a deep breath and exhaled slow. "I think I'm pregnant."

Todd's mind froze. Nothing that came before those words mattered. Nothing beyond those words existed. Those words were his entire world.

"Is it mine?"

"Of course it's yours," Stacy said. "I told you that you were my first and only, didn't I?"

"Oh my God." Todd looked at his friends. They all gaped at him. Everyone, that is, except Gary, who had a sour look on his face.

"I'm calling shenanigans," Gary said. "She's not pregnant."

"Excuse me, asshole?" Stacy said. "Do you have a uterus? Maybe you do because you don't have a penis, Beansprout!"

"Why'd you say that, Gary?" Todd said, annoyed. He was just starting to tolerate Bean and then he said this?

"She's been drinking all night," Gary said. "What kind of mother does that? Look at the timing. I may not know much about women, but I've been in enough boardrooms to recognize a desperate bluff when I see it."

"How dare you!"

THUNK!

Stacy kneed Gary in the crotch. Gary doubled over in pain.

"Stacy! Holy fuck. Get away from him." Todd dragged Stacy away. "But why are you drinking?" he asked.

"It's not a big deal in the first trimester," Stacy said. "In the second trimester, if we decide to have the baby, that's when I should stop."

"That's not true!" Gary said. "Todd? Don't buy—"

THUNK!

"Shut up and mind your business, Drip!" Stacy said, kneeing Gary again. Gary dropped to the ground, hugging his crotch.

"Stacy! Stop it!" Todd said. "What do you mean 'if we decide to have the baby'? You don't think we should?"

"That's something we need to discuss, so let's go home and do that." She held out her hand. "Coming?"

Todd grabbed her hand.

"Todd." Brent's voice. "I think you should listen to Gary. He's saying she's lying. I'm saying she's lying. You don't need to wait for that bathroom genie. You can be the genie right now."

Todd knew Brent couldn't lie to his face. It was easy to tell when he tried. He'd looked Todd straight in the eye when he told him the hand job story. Stacy, on the other hand, had been lying to him since "I do." That left Gary. Would Gary sabotage Todd's marriage to get revenge for the dunk tank fiasco? He seemed happy at the prospect of bar-hopping with Todd, but was that an act? Todd looked at Gary. There were tears in his eyes. Todd looked at Stacy. She smiled sweetly at him.

Stacy wasn't sweet.

"You're lying," Todd said. He tugged his hand away from Stacy.

"Yes!" Gary said, flinching away from Stacy's glare.

"Todd? I know it's hard to trust me." Crocodile tears poured down Stacy's face. "But this is our baby." She rubbed her tummy.

"Drop it, Stacy," Todd said. "I'm not buying it."

She cried a bit longer, but then the tears seized up and her face turned a deep red. She was like an engine overheating.

"Do you know what it's like for me to come in here and lie in front of your friends? Do you? All because I love you so much and would do anything to keep you. This is all about my love, Todd. No, I'm not pregnant. But maybe I should be? What do you think? Pull the goalie tonight and roll the dice? Come on, baby," she said, wrapping her arms around him. "Don't let this one night ruin us."

"Thank God for this one night," Todd said. He gently picked her up and carried her to the door.

"Todd?" Stacy said, confused.

He set her down, opened the door, and prodded her outside.

"Todd!" Stacy screamed, slapping at his hands.

"Goodbye," Todd said. "I think it's time I called a lawyer." He forced the door closed and put his back to it while she pounded against it.

Stacy cursed each of Todd's body parts and threw her body against the door for a full minute before she finally went away.

"I owe you an apology," Rory said. "I accused you of cracking. I thought you told Stacy the truth about prom."

"Yup, you did," Todd said.

"You not only didn't crack, but held out under extreme pressure. You know what? Time for a man hug."

Todd laughed and hugged his friend. When Rory released him, there were wet spots around Todd's eyes.

"And you," Todd said, turning to Gary. "You fought for me. You, Gary Bean, are the fourth amigo. Yeehaw!" Todd twirled an imaginary lasso above his head. Gary smiled despite the obvious lingering pain in his crotch.

A knock on the door squelched the fun. Todd sighed. He prepared to face his soon-to-be-ex-wife one more time.

Chapter 41

Rory
Don't Stop Believin'

Alice strutted inside. Rory immediately stood up straight. They all did. She walked to a bathroom stall, peered inside, and glared at Rory.

"You keeping a souvenir?"

She's looking for her panties, Rory realized. What happened to them? Out of the corner of his eye, he caught Gary shoving something white with green polka dots deeper into his pocket.

"Just hand them over," she ordered.

"Don't got them."

Rory would pry them from Gary's horny virgin fingers later, but for now, he didn't have them, so it wasn't a lie.

"Fine. Jerk off with them tonight. *If* you can, limp dick." Alice stalked to the door.

That was a low blow. Brent hissed in sympathy.

"It was nice seeing you again," Rory said. "If I find your panties I'll be sure to run them up the flag pole."

"At least that pole is hard."

His friends snickered. C'mon, guys, Rory thought, laugh at his jokes, not hers.

As Alice reached the door, a desperate need to keep her there seized Rory. "Wait!"

She paused and turned. "Nervous?" she said, without a hint of compassion.

Rory could feel the sweat she saw.

He knew this was his last chance speech. If he didn't get the words right now, those panties would be all he had to show his therapist the story was true.

"I ruined your big night, I get that," Rory said.

"My life, you mean. Stop apologizing. It's worthless. The past is the past." Alice opened the door. The sounds of "The Safety Dance" boomed outside.

Rory grabbed her. "You went through a lot of trouble for me tonight. That means something."

"Nothing good."

"I'm not convinced."

"Neither am I." Alice pushed him. "You want to prove your sincerity? March out there, grab the mic, and tell everyone you lied about your penis."

Of all the things she could pick, Rory thought. Public speaking - fuck! "Can I write a note? Have the bartender pass it around like Todd's picture?"

Alice rolled her eyes. "Or I can just bite your dick. Take a big chunk off the tip—make it official. I thought about that, but since I'm not psycho, I took a more symbolic approach."

"Thank you." Pathetic response, Rory knew, but what else can you say to that?

"I could make an announcement," Gary said. "Rory can stand beside me."

"And just nod like a dumbass?" Alice said. "Sure, okay, I'd accept that."

"No, I can do it," Rory said. Or Ace Plutonium can, he thought. "But thanks for offering, Gary. And then what – all is forgiven and we try again?"

Alice laughed. "Are you thinking we're getting back together? Are you delusional?"

Delusional? Rory thought, although coherent thought was difficult while his brain doused his dreams with gasoline and lit a match.

"Rory?" Brent's voice. "Let her go."

Rory recomposed himself. No, there's something here still. He could feel it. This is just an act. "Why not?" he asked.

Her face turned serious. "Because I won't get burned again. I won't."

"Did you know Todd and Stacy are getting divorced? That happened tonight. Big decision. Gutsy, but the right call."

"Congratulations, Todd," Alice said, waving past Rory.

"Brent discovered Gary got him suspended. Serious baggage. Lots of resentment. Now look. They're friends."

"Bravo. I'm inspired. Not."

"Why are you hanging onto to your bad mojo? You know I didn't mean to break up with you."

"No, I don't know that because you never tried to get me back. You didn't even call to explain."

Shit, thought Rory. He knew he should have called from the hospital. "It was hard to pick up the phone and call."

"Why? Do you dial with your penis?"

Laughter from behind him. "Sorry, sorry," they all said because they all laughed.

Alice smiled. She ruled the stage and knew it. Rory needed ammunition.

"Jamaican Bob? Hello?" She can't defend that, Rory thought.

"My stupidity with Jamaican Bob hurt me more than it hurt you. You couldn't get past yourself to see it. You're selfish. You've always been selfish. And I never spoke to that creep after prom. You didn't get any clues from that?"

"You never spoke to him before prom, so what did I know?"

"Not a whole lot, apparently."

Rory had no comeback. How did he lose on the Jamaican Bob issue? There was one sympathy card left to play. If this didn't work, Rory was done.

"PTSD," Rory said. "I had trouble reaching out."

"Post-Traumatic-Stress-Disorder?" Alice said.

"Yup, that's what my therapist told me. Blue death cream. Unless it's happened to you, you don't know."

"Oh, please," she said. "You didn't have to hide that from me; you chose to."

"That was maximum humiliation!" Rory said. "You have to understand the male brain. Everything runs through your penis. When it fails, you fail."

"I have no problem believing that."

"Okay, well . . ." Rory stumbled, unsure what to say next. "You never called me either!" he blurted. "I figured after a month it had to be over."

"Good detective work."

She stared at him, saying nothing. Rory had officially run out of words. The situation became awkward.

"Rory," Todd said. "Divorce. Think about it."

Alice looked away, back down the hallway to the dance. Rory was ready to give up and say 'goodbye,' when he remembered something he learned tonight: Brent's sensitivity theory was bullshit, and if that theory was bullshit, than the opposite was true.

Mr. Nice Guy, holding his nutz out for her to gargle and spit like she was testing wine, with all his speeches, and his tip-toeing, and his lame apologies, would get nowhere. He needed to be brave. Could he be that brave?

Rory focused, and punted Mr. Nice Guy out of his head.

"Listen." He wrapped an arm around her waist and pulled her close.

"What are you doing?" She tensed, arms hanging limp at her sides, but she let him whisper what he had to say. Rory slid his hand down to her ass. He didn't squeeze like she had, but his grip let her know what he was thinking.

He did not whisper in her ear.

He kissed her.

Hard like Ace Plutonium would.

Her arms rose to push him away, but Rory was already on his way out, pulling back.

Alice stood motionless, in shock.

Rory said his last lines, cocky and cool. "I'm not your past anymore. I'm right here."

After staring blankly for a few seconds, Alice turned and left. The bathroom door closed behind her and Rory faced his friends.

"Did you see what I did?"

"A last kiss?" Brent said.

"Maybe."

"Did she kiss you back?" Todd said.

"Not really."

"Why are you happy?" Brent said.

Rory knew it didn't make sense to them. Why was he happy about a one-sided kiss? Didn't she just about give him a hand-job hours ago? Sure, but she'd been acting, reading off a script, in control of every fake moment. But she wasn't in control of what just happened. He put real emotion behind that kiss, the right stuff, unscripted, romantic—and the move was all Rory's.

In Rory's life women are a paradox. They could scare him into a bathroom stall, make him blow chunks, and freeze him with fears of rejection, failure, and limp dick. But nothing inspired him more than the woman of his dreams. She is a vaccine. To get the benefits she provides he had to take some shots. Rory knew it wasn't going to be easy. Todd's example was a warning. You can marry someone you love, or you can marry someone who loves you, but only the luckiest achieve both.

"Brent, you still have that condom?" Rory said.

"Wow," Brent said. He fished out the condom and handed it over. "For Alice?"

Rory shrugged. "Can you believe tonight? I mean can you believe it! We were done, broken, finished. All three of us, four of us." Rory included Gary, who nodded back. "Now look. Anybody feel different?"

Everyone smiled and shook their heads, each probably thinking back to a few hours ago when their lives were vastly different.

"I was planning to sneak out and lie to my therapist tomorrow," Rory said. "Now I'm planning my next move with the girl who owns these. Gary? Panties, please?"

Sheepishly, Gary pulled out Alice's panties. "I was keeping them for you."

Todd roared with laughter. "Like hell you perv! You and I might just have some fun out there!"

"Three new friends and almost a pair of panties," Rory said. "Not bad for one night's work, Gary. Todd, you're single again, major game changer. It won't be easy, but it won't be boring either. And Brent. New job, new school, and a new outlook on life?"

Brent smiled. "Could happen."

"Can you feel it?" Rory said. "The universe aligned for us tonight. Let's do this decade right and celebrate our 20th reunion like rock stars."

Todd thumped the counter, caught up in Rory's enthusiasm. "We're at a party. There's a gym full of ladies out there."

"For decorum purposes, I recommend you don't hit on anything at the reunion," Brent said. "That's too Rory/Alice at the prom."

"How about the bartender?"

Brent laughed. "You found a loophole."

The sound of a note sliding under the door halted the conversation. Everyone stared at it, but nobody moved.

"Allow me," Brent said. He stuffed Mickey in his pocket, and then picked up the note. He paused as he held it, a surprised look on his face. "Says 'Brent.'"

Everyone peered over Brent's shoulders as he unraveled the note.

Dear Brent,
You looked through the crack but did not see,
You paid the price but came up empty.
To set things to rights and make amends,
Meet me outside, but don't bring a friend.
You won't have to squint, I promise that,
You'll get a good look after the fact.

Patricia M

"Patricia Mendelson?" Brent said.

"Holy shit," Todd said. "I better get one of these fucking notes too. Hey, what was the name of that girl I dated with the pink panties? The one from my 'Frame a Friend' picture?"

Brent pocketed the note. "Well, amigos, are we getting out of this bathroom, or not?"

Brent, Todd, and Gary filed outside, whispering excitedly. Rory lingered, just long enough to pull a lone green pill from his pocket. He tossed the pill in the garbage. Probably a placebo anyway, he thought. He heard the opening of "St. Elmo's Fire" rise behind him as the bathroom door opened.

"I'm coming!" Rory walked halfway to the door before looking up.

Alice stood there, arms crossed and nostrils flaring. She looked like a hungry badger debating which morsel to bite first.

Rory stood quietly and waited. Her return meant his kiss had the desired effect; he was still in the game.

"Did you trip?" she said. "Did your face hit my face by accident? What's going on in your head?"

Play it cool and confident, keep it light and funny, and no more begging or apologies—that's what was going on in Rory's head.

"You're serious? Poof!" Alice threw her arms in the air. "Everything's fine, forgiven, and forgotten."

"Which leads us to another F-word," Rory said.

"Of course. We're supposed to jump in the sack like we never broke up."

"I meant 'friends.'" Good one, thought Rory. "But we can do your word first. Works both ways."

Alice made a face. "When does the joke end, Rory? When do you disappear? Before prom, at prom, for ten years, tomorrow—that's what you do."

Alice bowed her head and rubbed it like it hurt. Rory put his hand on her arm. The seconds ticked by as he stroked her skin . . .

"What, Rory?" Alice looked up. "What do you want?" She seemed tired all of a sudden, pale.

Did he know the answer? One-night stand? Long-distance relationship? House with white picket fence? Kids? No fuckin' idea. *Her.* That was the answer. He wanted Alice, someway, somehow, for some time.

"Are you wearing strawberry or cherry lip gloss? I haven't been able to figure it out."

"Stop joking." Alice grabbed him, almost yanking him off-balance. "This is serious. I hate you. I do."

Yet she clung to his jacket and leaned her head onto his chest.

Rory lifted her chin. Alice's guard was down. He saw past the tough act and glimpsed the cracks, the damage that rumor had done.

He went in for a kiss.

Alice pushed him away. She dashed into a stall and shut the door.

Rory didn't move. He checked his breath. Boozy, but fine. What just happened?

He opened Alice's stall. "Are you—?"

"Get out!" Alice was on her knees, head over the toilet. She kicked the stall door like a horse, slamming it into his face.

Rory stumbled back. "Are you okay?"

"I don't want you to hear me throw up! Go!"

Rory was suddenly in an alternate reality. It should be him in that stall, but it wasn't. He'd had a dream like this once, where he helped the nauseous people of the world, curing them all. Nobody empathized with the fear and humiliation of public puking better than him. He wanted to rush into her stall and comfort her, tell her that it's okay, that he didn't care. Just hurl, baby.

Rory tried the door again. Locked.

"I said go! And don't let anyone inside, please!"

He wanted to be her hero. Rory Chase, not Ace Plutonium, could save the day this time. But she told him to go. Rory made his way to the door, walking slowly.

"Rory!"

He was two steps towards her before the "y" on Rory.

He pulled on the door. "It's still locked!"

Rory heard Alice fumble with the latch. The door popped open.

"My hair!" Alice bent over the bowl, holding her hair with one hand, strands falling into her face.

Rory bunched her hair into a ponytail and held it through the first purge.

"Stupid tequila," Alice said, crying. "I hate throwing up. It hurts."

"It's okay," Rory said. "Don't hold it in. Just get it out." He was an expert, after all.

A second purge. Alice was bawling now.

Rory stuffed her hair into one hand and passed her his hanky. "Here ya go."

"Thanks," she croaked, wiping her chin. "Rory?"

"Yeah?"

"Are these my panties?"

Whhhhaaattt?

Son of a bitch! He'd reached into the wrong pocket! "I just found them. I swear. Here." Rory shoved his hanky at her.

"Ugggghhhh!" Hot puke splashed over his hand. He dropped his hanky.

"Rory!" she screamed.

"It's okay, it's okay." Still holding her hair, Rory shook his hand clean.

"You need to borrow my panties?" Alice said. She fell onto her side, laughing.

"You better?" Rory said, not knowing if he should laugh or not.

She waved her panties at him. Tears of laughter poured down her face.

Rory put the seat down and flushed.

"Can you hear that?" Alice said, between bursts of laughter.

"What?" The flush was loud, so Rory stuck his head outside the stall.

Chants of "Ror-y, Ror-y, Ror-y" rose beyond the bathroom door.

"Your idiot friends think we're screwing." Alice threw her panties at him, and crumpled into another fit of laughter.

"I got one," Rory said, showing off his shiny red condom package. He laughed with her. It only took ten years, and he didn't know how it would all end, but he knew that from now on he'd never be nervous about puking in front of Alice again.

"This," Alice climbed onto the toilet seat, laughing uncontrollably. "Is the start." She could barely get the words out. "Of something beautiful."

Outside the stall, the bathroom's leaky faucet went drip, drip; drip, drip . . . drip . . . drip . . . . . . drip . . . and dripped no more.

Epilogue

Mitchell
Condition Critical

A half hour later.

Finally, those assholes left! Holding his guts in pain, Mitchell peeked under the first stall. Empty!

He slammed the door and whipped down his pants. He'd held it too long. His mother always told him, "Don't hold that in, young man, that's poison inside of you."

It was an all-out assault. First a tsunami, then a meteor shower, and finally a leisurely lava flow. It burned as it moved, but it moved. The pain was gone and the world was light and fluffy and full of promise once more.

But there had been splashes. Most high enough to coat his ass like an oil slick.

Mitchell reached for the toilet paper.

Empty. Shit.

The sound of the bathroom door opening solved his problem. "Hey," he called out. "Little help? I'm out of toilet paper."

There was a pause before the person responded.

"Matthews?"

"Yeah, who's that?"

Another pause.

"You need help?" The person asked, ignoring his question.

"Yeah, big load, out of paper," Mitchell laughed. "Can you pass me a roll from the next stall."

"Sure." The mystery person approached the stall. His shoes sounded like metal hitting the floor.

"Maybe you can guess my name?" asked the mystery person.

"Why? Who is that?"

"Does this jog your memory?"

BAM! Something whacked the stall door.

BAM! BAM!

"Heeellppp! Heeellppp! I'm drowning!"

Mitchell recoiled as the cane (he knew what it was now) slammed his stall door repeatedly. That, plus the shouting had the desired effect. His memory was jogged.

It was Rufus Pendergast, the man whose foot he mangled and whose girlfriend he stole.

"Use your hand, ass-wipe." Rufus laughed as he rummaged through the stalls, removing all paper and all hope of cleanliness for Mitchell.

"Come on, Rufus! It was an accident. Let me buy you a beer."

"Fuck you, Matthews."

Rufus was out the door, still laughing.

Did he take all the paper? Mitchell wondered. He'd have to walk around to check, and since pulling up his pants meant brown stains, and not pulling up his pants was too risky, Mitchell stayed glued to the seat.

His ass itched, and not the kind he could endure or that eventually goes away.

Mitchell looked at his hand and sighed. This was going to take some time.

Thank you

I hope you enjoyed reading *Stalled*. If you have a moment and would like to share your thoughts on the book, I'd appreciate the feedback. You can add your review on Amazon.com or Amazon.ca.

As always, check for updates and news on my official author website crbrucewrites.com

Thanks again!
C.R. Bruce

Acknowledgments

We don't stop playing because we grow old; we grow old because we stop playing.

George Bernard Shaw

Special thanks to those helpful individuals who gave their time and energy to making me a better writer or helping this book see the light of day: Gina Reed, Tony Larder, Tony Sekulich, John Heinstein, Warren P. Sonoda, Bill Gaston, Barry Cameron, and Giles Walker.

And to my family, the biggest thanks of all. Dad, Mom, Craig—I couldn't have done any of it without you.

- Chris

SMILELYNN BOOKS
Stalled
Christopher R. Bruce
Copyright © 2015 by Christopher R. Bruce
All Rights Reserved

This is a work of fiction. All the characters, places, and events portrayed in this book are fictitious. Any resemblance to actual events, locales or real people, living or dead, is entirely coincidental.

Copyeditor: Arlene Miller. The Grammar Diva™ bigwords101.com
Cover Design: damonza.com
Interior Design: damonza.com
Author Portrait: TheMeeDes artcorgi.com

All rights reserved. This book was published by the author Christopher R. Bruce under Smilelynn Books. No part of this book may be reproduced in any form by any means without the express written permission of the author. This includes reprints, excerpts, photocopying, recording, or any future means of reproducing text.

Published in Canada by Smilelynn Books
ISBN: 978-0-9939694-1-6
eBook ISBN: 978-0-9939694-0-9

Version 1.0

www.ingramcontent.com/pod-product-compliance
Lightning Source LLC
LaVergne TN
LVHW041247080426
835510LV00009B/632